KU-174-337

Religious Pluralism and Unbelief

Religious Pluralism and Unbelief

Studies Critical and Comparative

Edited by Ian Hamnett

Routledge

London and New York

First published 1990
by Routledge
11 New Fetter Lane, London EC4P 4EE

Simultaneously published in the USA and Canada
by Routledge
a division of Routledge, Chapman and Hall, Inc.
29 West 35th Street, New York, NY 10001

© 1990 The Colston Research Society

Printed in Great Britain by
T. J. Press (Padstow) Ltd, Padstow, Cornwall

All rights reserved. No part of this book may be reprinted or reproduced
or utilized in any form or by any electronic, mechanical, or other
means, now known or hereafter invented, including photocopying and
recording, or in any information storage or retrieval system, without
permission in writing from the publishers.

British Library Cataloguing in Publication Data
Religious pluralism and unbelief: studies critical and comparative
1. Religion. Pluralism
I. Hamnett, Ian
291

ISBN 0–415–04192–9

Library of Congress Cataloging in Publication Data
Religious pluralism and unbelief: studies critical and comparative/
edited by Ian Hamnett.
p.   cm.
Bibliography: p.
Includes index.
1. Religious pluralism–Congresses.
BL85.R388 1990
291.1′7–dc20   89–10323

Contents

Contents

Notes on contributors

Antony Allott is Professor of African and Comparative Law at the University of Buckingham. His many publications include *The Limits of Law* (1980) and *People's Law and State Law* (jointly with G. Woodman, 1985).

Eileen Barker lectures at the London School of Economics and is active in the field of the sociology of religion. *The Making of a Moonie* was published in 1984.

Gavin D'Costa teaches at the West London Institute of Higher Education and has published *Theology and Religious Pluralism* (1986) and *John Hick's Theory of Religion* (1987).

Kieran Flanagan is a lecturer in sociology at Bristol University. He has published extensively in the field of liturgy. His monograph, *Sociology and Liturgy*, is forthcoming.

Richard Gombrich is Boden Professor of Sanskrit at Oxford University and a Fellow of Balliol. Publications include *Precept and Practice* (1971) and (jointly with H. Bechert) *The World of Buddhism* (1984).

Ian Hamnett is Reader in Anthropology at Bristol University and has written extensively on the sociology of religion.

Adrian Hastings is Professor of Theology at the University of Leeds and a Catholic priest. He has published major monographs on African Christianity and on twentieth-century British Christianity. His *African Catholicism* is forthcoming.

Mary Hesse was formerly Professor of the Philosophy of Science at Cambridge University. *Revolution and Reconstruction in the Philosophy of Science* was published in 1980, and (jointly with M. A. Arbib) *The Construction of Reality* in 1987.

Ioan Lewis is Professor of Anthropology at the London School of Economics. His edited volume *Symbols and Sentiments* was published in 1977, and *Nationalism and Self Determination in the Horn of Africa* in 1983.

Peter McCaffery lectures in sociology at Aberdeen University and has specialized in the comparative study of Dutch Catholicism.

Paul Morris is a lecturer in the Department of Religious Studies at the University of Lancaster and works in the field of Judaism.

Christopher Sugden is ordained into the Church of England and is attached to the Oxford Centre for Mission Studies.

Kenneth Surin is a Professor of Theology at Duke University, North Carolina, and the editor of *Modern Theology*. His *Theodicy and the Problem of Evil* was published in 1987.

Keith Ward is Professor of the History and Philosophy of Religion at King's College, London. His numerous publications include *Battle for the Soul* (1985) and *Images of Eternity* (1987).

Thomas Wiedemann is Lecturer in Roman History in the Department of Classics, Bristol University. His *Greek and Roman Slavery* was published in 1981, and *Adults and Children in the Roman Empire* in 1989.

I

Introduction

1

Religious pluralism

Ian Hamnett

I

Religious pluralism suggested itself as a suitable topic for a symposium under the auspices of the Colston Research Society on several grounds. First, it is an aspect of the cultural and ethnic pluralism that characterizes many areas of British life today, and forms the subject of much political and sociological debate. As a conference theme, therefore, religious pluralism had the merit of relevance to some major contemporary concerns. This very fact, however, carried with it some dangers. It opened the door to the possibility that the symposium would be diverted into overtly political debate about matters of public and social policy, which (however deserving of attention in another forum) were not intended to be the focus of this meeting. Hence it was that the decision was taken to exclude contributions from local religious and ethnic groups. This decision was arrived at reluctantly, since in other contexts Bristol itself would be an ideal city in which to study a whole range of religious variation – indeed, a whole range of pluralisms. On rather similar grounds, no contributions were invited that would deal specifically with Irish issues. The present volume, consequently, contains little or nothing of direct or immediate relevance to social policy. As with all that can be styled 'fundamental research', however, it is to be hoped that most of the papers that follow will at another level be of interest and profit to those engaged in practical 'hands-on' work in the field of religious and ethnic community relations.

In the months that elapsed between the holding of the symposium and the publication of its proceedings, one issue that seemed dormant has sprung into renewed prominence in direct and concrete form: the teaching of religion in schools. The liberal consensus is well illustrated by works such as David Simmonds's aptly titled classroom handbook, *Believers All* (Simmonds 1984),

3

a pleasant and sympathetic survey of six 'world religions'. Some problems, however, remain intractable. Virtually all analysts in the social-science tradition regard a religion as a cultural system. This does not, of course imply that religions are to be regarded *only* as cultural systems, and provided this is kept in mind it might seem that committed believers have little cause for complaint. However, the matter is less simple. Objectors can argue that it is asking too much of schoolchildren to expect them to draw an analytical distinction between culture and belief, with the result that in practice the effect of religiously neutral teaching would be to reduce faith to a purely cultural level. Satisfactory though such an outcome would be to agnostics, and to some religious liberals, it would be as unwelcome to most Moslems (for example) as it would be to many committed Christians. Moreover, some strongly committed believers go further and deny the propriety of all cultural considerations in Christian belief and practice. Such a denial marked Karl Barth's neo-orthodox theology and is the basis of Gollwitzer's response to Marxism (Gollwitzer 1970). Religion, on this view, is a man-made cultural artefact. Christianity, by contrast, is not a 'religion' at all, but rather the revealed truth of God. *Mutatis mutandis*, somewhat similar arguments can be found in the adherents of other faiths.

With the benefit of hindsight, it is clear that a formal paper in this general area would have added to the interest of the collection. Professor Hastings's admirable discussion of university teaching, none the less, deals with contiguous topics, raising questions about the relationship of a multi-religious culture to the practice of education which extend beyond the sphere of higher education as such. These matters are also discussed, often quite contentiously, by other contributors (see especially Flanagan, Surin, and Ward).

A second and more strictly academic recommendation for religious pluralism as a conference topic was its openness to inter-disciplinary treatment – which is also, as it happens, the approach favoured by the Colston Research Society in its symposia. Religious studies and sociology perhaps lead the field in this collection (a point that is amplified below), but ample room has been found for contributions from classical studies, history, law, philosophy, social anthropology, and theology; and of course many of these categories overlap. It was our general experience that dialogue across these disciplinary boundaries proved not merely possible but largely unproblematic. Some of the fruits of this interchange are to be found in the revised versions of many of the papers submitted by authors after they had had the benefit of general discussion. Needless to say, these exchanges of ideas were (happily) quite as likely to lead to a sharper perception of difference as to a relaxed consensus of view. Several papers, indeed, are marked by a degree of combativeness that we found to be welcome and invigorating: those by Flanagan, Morris, Sugden, Surin, and Ward might be particularly mentioned in this regard.

An associated attraction in the study of religious pluralism is the ease with which it lends itself to the comparative approach, in both historical and geographical terms. Different forms of pluralism, and different problems arising from it, have existed in the past and exist now. Social anthropologists have an obvious role to play here, but historians, sociologists, and lawyers had major contributions to make. To varying degrees, the papers by Allott, Barker, Gombrich, Lewis, McCaffery, Ward and Wiedemann all share this comparative approach.

A word is called for to account for the relative numerical strength of the social science contributions. In a recent article, Robert Morgan has observed that 'the social sciences have begun to supplant history as the natural partner for theology' (Morgan 1988: 280). And not only a partner, but a sparring-partner too: Peter Berger has remarked that sociology (and one would want to add social anthropology as well) is the 'fiery brook', the Feuerbach, of our time (Berger 1969: 44). It offers the strongest contemporary challenge to belief, taking the place successively occupied in the past by higher criticism, by scientific historiography, and by psychoanalytic theory, confronting theology as a challenge with which the believer cannot fail to engage. At the same time, the sociological approach in a broad sense has reshaped disciplines such as history, philosophy, and religious studies so profoundly that it would be hard to imagine them existing today in forms innocent of social science attitudes and methodology. Allott as a lawyer, Hastings as a theologian, Surin as a philosopher, Wiedemann as a classicist all display a sensitive sociological awareness that largely makes nonsense of any notion that sociology can be isolated as an empirical discipline standing apart from the rest of the arts and sciences. In a real sense, we are all sociologists now.

II

The formal topic of the symposium, in spite of its attractiveness as a subject for general discussion, poses certain threshold problems of definition. Indeed, the imprecision of the central terms of the debate furnished talking-points which few of the contributors have been able to ignore.

There are indeed two senses in which the term 'religious pluralism' is imprecise. One kind of imprecision arises from the uncertain definition of the empirical situation to which it refers. If it is taken to mean simply a state of affairs in which more than one religious system exists within a given territory, it could well be objected that this is far too broad a sense to be useful. In the modern world at least, religious pluralism would emerge as a more or less universal feature of political society, only such states as Iran (possibly) or (in a negative version of the same thing) Albania constituting plausible exceptions. But if this definition of pluralism is unhelpfully broad, there appears to be no sound theoretical basis for deciding, in advance of particular cases, how the scope of the term can be convincingly narrowed. Probably the best solution to this difficulty is a practical one: we can accept, as a working rule, that religious pluralism becomes a rewarding field of study at the point where it presents itself to the observer as some kind of problem. In the extreme case, the problem can express itself as conflict. Northern Ireland (though not, as I have noted, a topic formally discussed in this collection) may be taken as such a case, for although it would be naïve to define its troubles in wholly religious terms, it would be perverse to deny that there is a religious dimension to them, or that they are consistently articulated through the language of religious difference. Some of the papers in this volume (notably that of Wiedemann) reflect a concern with problems arising from or reflecting political differences of 'cohabitation' between religious groups.

From this starting-point, inquiry can move into the study of pluralisms where the question of 'problems' becomes less acute. Paradoxically, it is then the very absence of religious conflict that creates surprise and thus stimulates sociological and historical curiosity. The common reader can easily forget, or even never have known, that for much of the Middle Ages – till the Crusades, in fact – relations between Christians, Moslems, and Jews in what is now the Middle East were generally pacific and relaxed. But this state of affairs would not arouse interest were it not that contemporary observers tend to assume, on the basis of their own modern experience, that pluralism breeds conflict. Thus both the presence and the absence of conflict can form, in contrasting ways, apt objects of study.

A subtler kind of imprecision (or perhaps 'ambiguity' would be a better word) in the notion of religious pluralism arises from the fact that the term can refer either to a state of affairs as we have just seen (namely, the coexistence of two or more major religious systems within one society or culture), or to an ideological posture, commonly associated with a 'liberal', syncretistic, and relativist approach to religious belief as such. In the first sense, only a society or a culture or a state can be described as 'plural'. In the ideological sense, however, it is possible to describe an individual, or a school, or a theology, or a tradition of thought and practice, as manifesting 'religious pluralism'. This is usually intended to mean a posture or perspective where differences of religious belief and practice are treated as legitimate, and where as a rule 'exclusivist' (cf. D'Costa) claims are not advanced on behalf of one particular system at the expense of others. Several of the papers in this volume refer to or focus on pluralism in this ideological sense, for the most part in a sharply critical tone (Flanagan, Surin). (One very searching paper reminds us that science too is open to a pluralist reading: see Hesse, below.) Although pluralism as a state of affairs is compatible with committed religious belief (and can, as we shall see, actually contribute to it), it is a question whether ideological pluralism has the same compatibility, or whether it is not essentially parasitic upon an inherited tradition which it then proceeds to erode.

Although pluralism as a state of affairs and pluralism as an ideology are logically and analytically distinct concepts, they find a point of convergence where Berger has located it (1969, 1970, 1980). In given historical circumstances, *de facto* pluralism can modify the internal character of religious belief-systems for the believers themselves. Where this occurs, pluralism cannot be understood simply as a political 'state of affairs' involving only the external relations *between* groups. Stout fences make good neighbours; and it may often be observed that where religious groups or associations are self-contained, where conversions are rare or even prohibited, and where close contact between members of such groups is kept within strict limits even in non-religious fields, the internal features of each belief-system tend to remain intact. Again, the earlier medieval history of the Middle East furnishes an example. This is radically different from the 'market place' pluralism encountered today (Barker). Here, we are not so much free to choose as compelled to choose. Heresy (*haeresis*), as Berger (1980) stresses, becomes an imperative. For better or worse, this alters the structure of belief in profound ways. When the fences are crumbling, or have quite collapsed, the believer (and the unbeliever too, for that matter) finds himself exiled into an unorganized and anomic world of choice where, whether he likes it or not, he is 'forced to be free'. Belief loses something, or much, or all, of that quality of givenness which well-patrolled boundaries formerly secured for those held safe within the camp.

7

Nietzsche somewhere remarked that 'we have made eunuchs of ourselves so that we can come and go as we please in the great harem of world culture' (cf. 1983: 84). Pluralism as an ideology he saw not so much in sociological as in historical terms, but in his own way he engaged with the same debate about relativism that is taken up, though in very different language, in several of the papers here (D'Costa, Flanagan, Hesse, Morris, Surin, Ward). Where 'the historical sense reigns without restraint', Nietzsche writes (1983: 95), the effect is to emasculate honest and free commitment to truthfulness – much the same threat that modern observers are inclined to see in the unrestrained exercise of the sociological sense. 'Sociology', in fact, could for us replace the first word in Nietzsche's assertion that 'history can be borne only by strong personalities, weak ones are utterly extinguished by it' (1983: 86).

A contrasting view, on the other hand, welcomes the necessity of choice – and precisely in committed religious terms (cf. Sugden). Choice is to be welcomed, not feared, since it is precisely through it that one's eternal destiny is decided. 'I call heaven and earth to witness against you this day, that I have set before you life and death, blessing and curse. Therefore choose life' (Deut. 30: 19). This seems a more appropriate attitude for a proselytizing faith to adopt. An existential choice, rather than a more-or-less passive aquiescence in tradition, is the mark of the believer – where, in other words, *every* believer is a 'convert'. Though Christian traditionalists mock the notion of being 'born again', it is a concept firmly embedded in the foundation texts, and insisted upon by Jesus (John 3: 3–7 – and is directly translated into such common Christian names as René, Renato, etc.). Conservative critics of such religious elitism, favouring an ecclesial over a sectarian model of religious associations (Niebuhr 1929), argue in reply that it offers a plausible programme for faith only in epochs and societies where believers are in a minority. For such critics, 'habits' (in the Aristotelian sense) of belief and practice are not to be so lightly depreciated. The institutions of infant baptism and (in Judaism and Islam) infant circumcision imply a communal or ascribed, rather than a bleakly individualistic or achieved, view of what religious membership means (and cf. von Balthasar 1982: 579 f.: 'the decision for infant-baptism was perhaps the most portentous decision in the entire history of the Church').

One contributor (Morris), writing from a Jewish perspective but moving well beyond it, joins forces with some conservative critics in assailing what he identifies as the *coerciveness* of liberal pluralism, seeing in it not so much an engine for compelling authentic choices as a device for making them impossible. Inasmuch as certain kinds (at least) of religious commitment imply an extensive programme of life and practice as their context, to that extent the 'privatizing' thrust of pluralism as an ideology renders difficult or impossible the effective embracement of any religious system that falls outside the permitted limits of the liberal consensus. The author gave as an example the difficulty of living the full life of a Hasidic Jew in modern London. Oral comments maintained, in sharp retort to this, that Morris was assuming that strong religious commitment 'ought' to be made easy, whereas an opposite assumption might well be held to be theologically and morally more convincing. The debate, at the very least, served to remind liberals of what they often perhaps prefer to forget, that the ideology of pluralism is itself a substantive 'position' and cannot be permitted *a priori* claims to privilege on its own behalf, as though the very fact of its openness allowed it to judge others and not be judged itself.

In *A Rumour of Angels*, and elsewhere, Peter Berger puts liberal pluralism under the same open judgment that hangs over all systems of belief, arguing wittily and compellingly for the possibility (and he, unlike some of his followers, is careful to put it no higher) that by 'relativizing the relativizers', what the Feuerbachian sceptic reads as 'projections' can equally be regarded as 'reflections'. In other words, an echo of the divine can perhaps be heard in the very aptitude of human cultures to project our aspirations and fantasies (if such they are) on to the cosmological order itself. In a recent book, John Bowker has advanced a convergent thesis (Bowker 1987). As several contributors might be cited to show, the *fact* of pluralism as a state of affairs neither in logic nor in practice leads inevitably to either syncretism or unbelief (Barker, Morris, Sugden, Surin). Indeed, fundamentalism may often be a likely response (see especially Barker). I have argued elsewhere (Hamnett 1986) that strongly committed and dogmatically uncompromising religious beliefs can and do flourish in environments where sceptics used blithely to assume they would wither and die. Confronted with market-place pluralism and its *embarras de choix*, the believer may react not by asking himself 'which of these should I choose?' but by seeking an alternative to choice itself. In this way, he may seek to escape the subjectivity of 'choosing', believing himself to be simply acknowledging the authority of an objective truth 'out there'. This is probably one aspect of most committed religious positions, though a difference in kind becomes apparent when this claim to objectivity is made the basis for a purported right to impose the truth on others. If I say no more than 'I am right and you are wrong', I can mount no plausible claim to bend you to my will; but if this becomes 'God is right and you are wrong' (or 'Nature is right and you are wrong'), the inhibition flies off.

III

Conferences are conceived in an ideal world but come to birth in the real one. The coincidence, in the week in question, of both the Christian Holy Week and the Jewish Passover, made it difficult and in some cases impossible for some hoped-for contributors to accept. Necessary limitations on numbers and time also meant that, in any case, only a small selection could be made from the large range of possibilities that religious pluralism presents to the modern student. The precise constituents of the symposium cannot therefore be given complete logical coherence – indeed, perhaps it was not altogether inappropriate that a conference on the subject of pluralism should itself display something of the contingency of its theme . . .

Some omissions call for further comment. A paper on modern Islam was read to the conference but was not made available for publication. The collection that follows unfortunately also lacks the valuable paper read by Dr Vieda Skultans, entitled 'Pluralism from within: A Case Study of a Hindu Trancing Temple'. This is for reasons of copyright, but her research-based article can be read in *Man* (Skultans 1987). I have already discussed the decision to exclude topics that might have diverted the symposium into a series of heated debates on immediate political issues; as we have seen, this meant that neither Bristol nor Ireland, for example, were directly discussed. Allott's absorbing discussion of the legal aspects of pluralism, however, furnished an opportunity to consider broadly political issues in their concrete application to modern Britain, and elsewhere.

This volume opens, as did the symposium, with Keith Ward's panoptic *mise-en-scène*, laying open the theoretical questions which pluralism raises for religious studies. This is followed by a group of papers under the heading 'Ethnographic and Historical Perspectives', comprising contributions from Eileen Barker (on new religious movements), Ioan Lewis (principally East and West Africa), Peter McCaffery (Netherlands Catholicism), and Thomas Wiedemann (late Roman Empire). The following section, on 'Theoretical Perspectives', includes contributions by Kieran Flanagan and Kenneth Surin, each in his own way mounting a sustained critique of ideological pluralism in general and John

Hick (and followers) in particular; by Gavin D'Costa, who explores different approaches to the 'Extra Ecclesiam Nulla Salus' watchword – again with reference to Hick; by Christopher Sugden, writing (uniquely in the symposium) from an explicitly conservative Evangelical position; and by Mary Hesse and Paul Morris, whose papers have been referred to in this introduction. Antony Allott on law, and Adrian Hastings on university departments of Theology and Religious Studies, whose papers have also been mentioned earlier, share a shorter section on 'Institutional Aspects of Pluralism'.

A special word must be said about the paper that concludes the volume. Professor Richard Gombrich kindly agreed to attend the symposium as a special guest, and – as a principal part of his role – to deliver a public lecture at the annual dinner of the Colston Research Society. His address has been only slightly modified from its original presentation, and invites reading as a relatively informal and personal contribution to the proceedings.

As convener of the conference and editor of this volume, I should like to express my thanks to all the contributors for the efficiency with which they produced – and, in many cases, revised and produced again – the papers they had agreed to give. My special gratitude is due to the Colston Research Society for its generous sponsorship, and to its officers for their help and advice: especially to Professor R. G. Chambers, Professor Richard Gregory, and Dr James Franklin. Dr Kieran Flanagan and Dr Vieda Skultans gave much-needed practical help at the conference itself. To Kieran Flanagan, above all, I am happy to acknowledge a vast debt; his advice, encouragement, and friendship have contributed more than I like to admit to whatever success the symposium, and this publication, may have achieved.

References

Berger, P. L. (1969) *The Social Reality of Religion*, London: Faber & Faber (published in US under the title *The Sacred Canopy*, 1967).
—(1970) *A Rumour of Angels*, London: Allen Lane, The Penguin Press.
—(1980) *The Heretical Imperative: Contemporary Possibilities of Religious Affirmation*, London: Collins.
Bowker, J. (1987) *Licensed Insanities: Religions and Belief in God in the Contemporary World*, London: Darton Longman and Todd.
Gollwitzer, H. (1970) *The Christian Faith and the Marxist Criticism of Religion*, Edinburgh: St Andrew's Press.

Hamnett, I. (1986) 'A mistake about error', *New Blackfriars* vol. 67, no. 788: 69–78.

Morgan, R. (1988) 'A decade of theology', *Theology* vol. 91, no. 742: 274–83.

Niebuhr, H. R. (1929) *The Social Sources of Denominationalism*, New York: Henry Holt.

Nietzsche, F. (1983) *Untimely Meditations*, trans. R. J. Hollingdale, Cambridge University Press (German original *Unzeitgemässe Betrachtungen*, 1873–6).

Simmonds, D. (1984) *Believers All*, Glasgow: Blackie.

Skultans, V. (1987) 'The management of mental illness among Maharashtrian families', *Man* 22: 661–79.

Von Balthasar, Hans-Urs (1982) *The Glory of the Lord*, 1. *Seeing the Form*, trans. E. Leiva-Merikakis, Edinburgh: T. and T. Clark (German original *Herrlichkeit: Eine theologische Ästhetik*, I. *Schau der Gestalt*, 2nd edn 1967).

2

Imperialism and co-existence in religious ideology

Keith Ward

As he reached the end of his monumental work, *The Golden Bough*, Sir James Frazer recorded that his study of the religious life of mankind had uncovered a 'melancholy record of human error and folly' (abridged edn, p. 711).[1] And he makes it fairly clear that he was speaking not only of what he termed 'savage religion', but also of such things as the Christian Eucharist, which was, after all, a bowdlerized version of primitive sacrificial rites of corn and vegetation-spirits to procure fertility. Frazer is not much in fashion at present among anthropologists; yet it is salutary to recall that error and folly, if not omnipresent, are at least frequent in religion; that much blood has been shed in its name; and that there is still some sting in Frazer's remark that 'the history of religion is a long attempt . . . to find a sound theory for an absurd practice' (p. 477).

If this is so, even in some measure, it is clearly impossible to desire the coexistence of all possible religious practices and beliefs. It is impossible to wish for the flourishing of folly and error. One could not even tolerate it if it actively caused harm and spread ignorance needlessly among people ill-prepared to resist its onslaughts. But what is harm, in religion, and what is knowledge? And who decides the answers to those questions?

It is tempting to give up in despair. Looking at the millions of religions in the world, and at the utter disparity in their practices and beliefs – from scientologists to shamanistic animists – it might seem that there can be no common standards of assessment, that decisions about good and harm, reasonableness and folly, truth and error are all subjective and relative. If we look at sciences like physics or chemistry, then there are publicly available checking-procedures for the truth of any assertions made. All those expert enough to understand the relevant material can come to a very broad measure of agreement, by commonly accepted rational procedures of argument. There is an established, universally accepted body of expertise; and definite progress is made in the amount of knowledge we possess, as each generation supplements or corrects the work of its predecessors. In religion, however, none of these things is so. We have, instead, a large number of competing claims to authority, all of which appear to ignore the others. There is no way of checking the truth of even the most basic assertions that are made, and there seems to be no way of procuring agreement even among equally informed and intelligent scholars. There is no progress in religious knowledge. The same old questions revolve around and around, and theologians are even proud to proclaim their adherence to ancient doctrines, despite all changes in knowledge in every other field. The problem of pluralism in religion presents itself as the problem of how there can be, not only a lack of progress in one accepted, developing field of knowledge, but a plethora of mutually conflicting claims to final truth, which there is no agreed method for resolving. Does it make sense to claim knowledge of truth, when there is no agreed method of deciding truth-values in this area, even among fully informed disputants? And does the apparent conflict of religious doctrines not throw doubt on the claims of any one of them to possess a truth which cannot even be rendered probable to those of a different religious persuasion?

These problems can be seen as particular cases of more general problems about truth, verifiability, and rationality. But they also occur as theological problems for adherents of particular faiths, who have a problem about why the truth of the view they hold is not perceived by others; or what account can be given of the diversity of religious beliefs from one theological point of view.

One solution to these problems, widely canvassed among philosophers, is to propose a non-cognitivist account of religious language, where knowledge and truth are no longer claimed. Then religions become ways of life or poetic, but false, pictures by which we may regulate our lives, if they happen to attract us.[2] I will ignore these suggestions, since they entail that most reflective religious believers are mistaken when they think they are making truth-claims. I am concerned with religions as they actually are, not as some philosophers think they should be. And it is quite clear that many religions arise precisely by contradicting the truth-claims of other religions. So Buddhism denies the Vedantic view that there is an eternal Self; Islam denies that Jesus is the Son of God; and Judaism denies that there is any other god than Yahweh.

It is, of course, true that the truth-claims made by sophisticated religious believers are extremely difficult to render specific; that the interpretation given to them can change markedly; and that they can be very hard to understand at all. Yet it is necessarily the case that every truth-claim must exclude something; and such claims are often made, in religion as elsewhere, precisely to exclude something. Quite simply '$p \rightarrow - (-p)$'. Where it seems that this is not so, p must in fact be qualified. To give a well-known example, 'It is raining and it is not raining' may make sense, if there exists a Scotch mist. But then one can say, 'It is damp and large raindrops are not falling', and all is clear. Similarly, if one says, 'Light is waves and particles', that must be expanded to say, 'In conditions x, light produces wave-patterns; in conditions y, it produces quantum-effects'. Again, the appearance of contradiction gives way to a more detailed specification of what one is saying.

In a religious case, one might say, 'God is personal and impersonal', and thereby claim to resolve the apparent contradiction produced by some religious claims to have a personal relation with God, and other religious claims that the ultimate reality is not personal at all. Or, in John Hick's more subtle formulation, 'God is an unknowable reality which manifests in both personal and impersonal forms'.[3] When such a proposition is expanded in the way required to avoid contradiction, one has something like: 'God has some personal properties, apparent in some conditions; and some impersonal properties, apparent in other conditions'. Now all persons seem to have some impersonal properties – being 8 stones in weight could be called an impersonal property of me. It is not therefore very surprising if God has some impersonal properties. Perhaps, then, all apparently conflicting truth-claims in religion may be easily resolved by viewing them as partial insights into a very complex reality.

Such a proposal, however, does not remove disagreement at all. Some Christians may insist that God is primarily a person with impersonal properties; whereas some Vedantins may say that God is primarily an unrelated objectless Intelligence, though it may appear in personal form. Professor Hick is not, in fact, agreeing with these two views or reconciling them. He is rejecting both, and proposing a third alternative of his own. His is a revisionary proposal. Is it an attractive one? Or is it yet another, rather thinly disguised, version of the oft-repeated cry, 'If only everyone agreed with me, there would be no arguments'?

If we compare the God of the later Hebrew prophets – a dynamic, active, and responsive will, demanding justice in a particular community and having particular purposes in history – with the Brahman of Badarayana – unlimited consciousness and bliss, which creatures come to perceive by denying activity and

15

individuality – these notions turn out to be very different both in detail and in the central determining images of the active Will and the unmoving Self, respectively. There is, in the end, a great practical difference between one who accepts devotion as a device to help beginners, but places ascetic renunciation as the true and highest goal; and one who enjoins prayer and fasting as a means to a closer obedience to God, but regards God's gracious gift of personal love as the pinnacle of religious life. It is the difference between the solitary forest-dweller and the devotee who dances for joy before the Lord.

But can we not have both? We can; and, in a sense, there is an orthodox teaching in each main religious tradition which allows us to do so. Thus the classical Thomist idea of God is of an infinite, passionless, immutable being, although it is undeniably Christian. And Sankara, the arch-Advaitan, agrees that Brahman manifests as a glorious Lord for the sake of his devotees, and that the reality of this personal Lord (Isvara) is as real as the reality of the things of the world around us, and not to be denied by 'would-be philosophers'.[4] One can see here and in other traditions, too – in Maimonides, al-Ghazali – the idea of an unlimited ocean of being which manifests as a Lord of innumerable excellences. Such a concept is even to be found in what is often called that atheistic religion, Buddhism, where it takes the form of the Void being manifested under the forms of space and time as the glorified Buddha-nature, omniscient and inexhaustible in excellent qualities.[5] Here, then, is a way of seeing God, or the supreme reality, as both personal and impersonal – personal in his possession of innumerable excellences, knowledge, and will; yet impersonal in being far different in kind from any finite thing, unlimited and ineffable.

Of course, there will still be Christian Personalists, who reject Thomism as unbiblical, and Vedantins who insist that devotion is for lower orders only, and solitary contemplation is the true goal of the religious life. It cannot be the case, as Professor Hick sometimes seems to suggest, that all religions, whatever they say, are equally paths to the same goal or are all equally partial versions of a greater truth. Indeed, the spelling-out of the theistic paradox of personal and impersonal, active and transcendent, and unchanging and immanent in the way just canvassed is itself a claim to advance to a more adequate view of God, which excludes both a literal personalism and an unqualified monism. It is certainly significant that this is not simply a newly invented view, but is deeply embedded in the works of centrally orthodox thinkers in different traditions of faith. Nevertheless, it is only one strand of thought in these traditions. It is not by any means accepted by all orthodox believers. Nor is it the only strand of thinking present in those orthodox theologians who do accept it. On more particular topics, such as the nature of immortality and of revelation, vast disagreements remain.

However, it is worth dwelling on the fact that there is a deep ultimate agnosticism present in the orthodox scriptural faiths about the nature of God. Thomas Aquinas begins his great *Summa Theologiae* by saying that we do not know what God is, but only what he is not, and how the world is related to him. God, being simple, eternal, and infinite, cannot be grasped by human concepts. Even if we may truly say of him that he is good and wise, these terms cannot mean what we understand them to mean.[6] Likewise, Maimonides remarks that if anyone believes that there is a substance with the qualities of omniscience, omnipotence, and so on, he is not a theist; for God has no attributes.[7] Al-Ghazali writes that God is hidden behind ten thousand veils, and when the veils fall away there is nothing that can any longer be said.[8]: 'we find an existent who transcends all that is comprehensible'. And Sankara holds that *nirguna Brahman*, Brahman without qualities, is the highest reality we can point towards though never grasp.[9]

If such an agnosticism is an authentic religious insight, it is bound to qualify any of the truths any tradition affirms of God. So, if Christians say that God is a morally judging and gracious saviour, the Buddhist, who has no God, can say that the universe is morally ordered by the law of karma so that our good and evil acts issue in their due rewards and punishment, and that the compassionate Bodhisattvas help us towards our ultimate goal. And if Buddhists say that the self is to be extinguished in nirvana, the Christian, who believes in an endless continuance of the human personality, can say that we must be so transfigured by the indwelling presence of Christ that all those self-centred desires which form our present personalities must fall away and we shall be sharers in the beatitude of eternity. Taken strictly, the ideas contradict. But qualified by an ultimate agnosticism about the fundamental character of reality and our relation to it, they can be seen as partial insights into a common goal which is unlike any of our presently available concepts. This is not an agnosticism which leaves us with a total blank; rather, it functions to qualify all our present, restricted concepts in the direction of a goal which we cannot fully comprehend.

Within particular traditions, this qualification is effected by paradoxical uses of concepts which force a qualification of any literal interpretation. Whereas Christians say that Christ is Pantocrator, Judge of the world, they also say that Christ is within 'me', and 'my' true life. So a dialectical movement of difference and unity works to evoke and sustain an ever-expanding vision of the final goal of human life. It by no means follows that all models are equally good or lead to the same goal. How, then, is one to discern the most adequate models? To answer this question, one needs some conception of the distinctiveness and value of a religious scheme; and perhaps one that is different from Frazer's definition of religion as 'a propitiation or conciliation of powers superior to man which are believed to direct and control the course of nature and of human life' (p. 50). If one can get some idea of the function and goal of religious practice (that is, of the function which is thought to be worth preserving and encouraging), one may have some way of beginning to assess the concepts which are meant to serve that goal.

Despite the earnest entreaties of the Charity Commissioners, it has not been possible to establish an agreed definition of what a religion is. This is scarcely surprising, since J. H. Leuba, in *A Psychological Study of Religion*,[10] lists 48 putative definitions, all of which merely furnish yet more material for lecturers in religious studies to expound and discard. However, without attempting such a definition, it is possible to discern a certain structure in the major scriptural traditions at least. Various religions doubtless have many diverse functions and goals; yet basic to the major scriptural faiths is the exposition of a way of self-discipline and mental training which is claimed to liberate or release one from certain basic limiting conditions of human life. The semitic faiths of Judaism, Christianity, and Islam offer a way of deliverance from divine judgement and its consequent suffering, by penitence and obedience to a divinely revealed pattern of life, leading to a state of eternal bliss. The Indian traditions of Vedanta and Buddhism offer a way of deliverance from ignorance and the chain of temporal ills, by asceticism and meditation, to a realm Unborn and Undying, of unconditioned knowledge and bliss. In all these traditions, there is a general agreement that the limiting conditions from which liberation is to be sought are suffering, ignorance, and bondage. Thus the released state is spoken of as one of bliss, knowledge, and freedom.

This agreement is entirely unsurprising. For no one would choose sadness; it is clear that ignorance leads to unprofitable actions; and also that the bondage of passion and of selfish desire is inherently unsatisfying and destructive, if left to itself. If one examines the means which are offered to overcome these limitations, differences at once begin to appear. Some stress an active engagement in social concerns; others discipline and strict obedience to a set of written or traditional laws. Some seek to extinguish all passion and craving completely; and others recommend a simple and emotional submission to a personal saviour. These are not differences which exist only between religions. They exist between adherents of the same faith. Mahayana Buddhists have been known to regard Theravadin calm and serenity as the pursuit of a negative emptiness. Strict and particular Baptists regard with horror the creative seeking for unconditional love which liberal Christians tend to favour. It seems that each tradition contains a complex overlapping of many strands; and perhaps no strand is totally lacking in any tradition. The apparent legalism of the Torah requires passionate love for God. The romantic surrender to the love of Jesus involves obedience to his commands. And the heroic conquest of desire can be helped by the grace of compassionate Bodhisattvas. So although there are clear differences, it does not seem to be a matter of sheer contradiction. There is a basic agreement on what one needs deliverance from; on the range of ways in which deliverance might be found; and on the general attributes of bliss, knowledge, and freedom which would characterize salvation or release. The basic fiduciary structure is of self-transcendence in relation to transcending and manifesting Mind.

I would argue that this structure is central to the great scriptural traditions, and that the concept of God, where it is used, functions to specify the way of life which leads to the goal of liberation or release. Yet it is characteristic of scriptural traditions that they define themselves by reference to a definite authority. There is a community of accepted interpreters of some scriptural canon, and their views are taken to be finally authoritative, even infallible. It is clear that, while that is so, a commitment to many very specific doctrines will be considered essential to being a believer; and the scriptural traditions accordingly find themselves in confrontation with each other at many specific points. They might each accept a common structure between their traditions; the presence of a similar doctrine of the final goal, elaborated by orthodox theologians; and the possibility of a number of diverse paths which individuals may take to that goal. Yet a dividing line will come on the question of authority, which renders each tradition imperialistic with regard to the others.

It is precisely such doctrines of scriptural authority, however, which have been placed in an entirely new light by the revolution in human thinking which began in Europe in the sixteenth century. This revolution consists of three main strands: the rise of science;

the rise of historical method; and the acceptance of critical methods in human thought, which insist on questioning traditional attitudes and the accumulated wisdom of the past and applying the cold light of reason to all areas of human knowledge.

The great scriptural traditions which now exist began with a claim to direct, perhaps verbal, revelation from God or at least from a uniquely infallible insight into the nature of things. Anyone who claims such a thing today is liable to be regarded as an anachronism. It is inevitable that scientific and critical modes of thought must modify almost all existing religious views, which were framed in a world of very different beliefs and social practices. In the first place, the discovery of the great laws of nature, which are mathematically expressible and which explain physical changes very accurately, has very much modified the extent to which spirit, or demonic or divine activity, can be detected in nature. The theory of evolution has modified the extent to which God can be seen as deciding each new change in the world, and the degree to which divine providence reaches to every part of life, for life develops by random mutation, with many accidents and mistakes even if it is set on the path towards some general evolutionary goal. And the view that human life has evolved by a long, slow process from more primitive forms has rendered most traditional scriptural stories of origin obsolete. The biblical view that the earth is the centre of the universe, with the stars set on an arch over the surface and the great deep beneath, is wholly set aside, just as are the Upanishadic myths about souls going to the moon and the development of the physical universe by a series of strange etymological processions. This is all bound to change one's attitudes to the authoritativeness of scripture; exactly how the amendment will be made is unclear.

Second, the rise of the historical method which is well expressed with Troeltsch's three principles has transformed our attitude to religious traditions in general.[11] The principle of criticism is that you should never believe what you are told, but always check your sources and have a generally sceptical attitude to reports of events, especially where bias may be present. The principle of analogy states that the past must be presumed to be like the present in its general features. And the principle of correlation calls one to correlate historical reports with similar reports from the same sort of time and context, and to treat them in a similar way. When these principles are applied, it becomes impossible to accept one scripture with reverence and total belief while subjecting others, of a similar sort, to critical scrutiny. In general, a sceptical attitude to historical reports will lead one to treat past writers as products of their age and culture, with all the partialities and defects that implies. There is a new stress on the culturally conditioned nature of documents, on the personal background of beliefs, and on human tendency to exaggerate and embroider. All this has profound implications for our attitude to scripture. And even if Troeltsch must himself be regarded as a child of his (Enlightenment) age, we can never go back beyond it, as though it had never happened.

Third, and closely related to this, is the rise of a generally critical consciousness. Scriptural documents must be subjected to the closest critical scrutiny, and we must ask by whom they may have been written, for what purposes, and with what biases and presuppositions. In the Christian case, biblical scholars have become much less certain about exactly what Jesus taught, as opposed to the interpretations of many diverse groups of disciples. One is less certain about how binding his teaching is, in detail, anyway, about such things as the imminent end of the world. And one is less certain about the authority of particular moral regulations, if they no longer have the force of guaranteed infallibility. The same will be true of other scriptures, too. So, in the post-critical age, one has to be prepared to live with many more doubts and many more open questions about the details of revealed truth. Many old certainties about the details of the divine purpose or about human destiny were based solely on the assumed infallibility of scripture. When that goes, much else will change, too. This all marks a huge divide between traditional attitudes to a religious tradition, as definitively and unchangeably revealed by authority, and a view which accepts tradition as part of a continuing, developing way of life, which must be constantly subjected to review and reassessment.

As a matter of fact, it is within Christianity and Judaism that this process has really taken place. Most theologians accept that whatever view we take of the physical universe has to be consistent with evolutionary science; that historical methods must be applied to the Bible, and show it to be not literally true in some of its seemingly historical accounts; and that revered traditional ways of talking about God and Jesus, framed largely in terms of Platonic philosophy, need to be thoroughly reformulated in terms of our post-Cartesian world-view. Opinions vary as to how far these processes will take us; but it is clear that if the old religious traditions face squarely up to the findings of the sciences and to critical investigation of documents and received traditions, many changes must come to them.

One result, within Christianity, has been the recognition that one's own tradition does embody many historical layers, the views of which can be seen to be partial or inadequate, relative to later strata of the tradition (though I am not suggesting that traditions always progress). By parity of reasoning, this is liable to be true of other traditions. Thus it becomes reasonable to regard many traditions as partial and tentative responses to a suprahuman reality, the alleged knowledge of which is always clothed with the possibility of human error. If, in addition, one takes a broadly evolutionary or developmental view of the history of religions – the view that, generally speaking, human knowledge grows and experience brings refinements of theory and practice – one will look for developing insights into truth as we look more widely and critically. We will not be disposed to think that the whole truth has been decisively given, once for all. This is not some sort of claim to new revelation; it will apply similar methods to all religious claims to revelation. It is thus likely that it will bring all those traditions closer together, as their detailed differences become less binding and less important. Nevertheless, no gulf could be greater than that between those who assert that all traditions, as they stand, are ways to the same God, and those who assert that virtually all traditions need to be transformed by exposure to critical scientific thought.

Professor Hick provides a good example of the way in which this process might work out. First of all, commitment to particular doctrines of judgement, heaven and hell is undermined by a criti-cal study of the Gospels, and by recognition that the biblical world-picture has been radically changed by new knowledge in the sciences. Then the way is open to speculate on what a good God who wanted creatures to love him would be likely to do. Hick's view is that such a God is bound to offer salvation to people in many faiths; the old exclusivist view that only people of one faith can be saved is incompatible with the idea of a God of universal love. The positive alternative he proposes turns out (unsurprisingly, given his own background) to be the apotheosis of the liberal way of life – humanism projected on to the figure of a tolerant, kindly president of the democratic republic of heaven. There is no judgement, no hell, no objective atonement, no Incarnation – all these myths have gone, leaving the hope of endless self-realization, the ultimate Californian dream, available on no particular terms except good intentions. Naturally, all religions equally provide the possibility of salvation; for one can be equally well-intentioned in all of them or none.

These can seem very plausible thoughts, to western liberals; but where does the idea that God loves all creatures come from? For

Hick, it is a belief founded upon something that purports to be a disclosure of the divine nature in history. What has happened is not a rejection of revelation altogether; but a reinterpretation of some traditional views of it. It is no longer seen as a written record, infallible in every respect. It is embodied in a series of human responses to divine initiatives, not wholly free of error, but reliable in those things necessary for salvation. And this re-interpretation is not wilfully adopted. It seems compelled by close investigation of the original documents themselves, disclosing many strands of moral and factual belief which stand in need of correction in the light of further well-established knowledge.

It can seem that liberal theologians pick and choose what appeals to them and discard the rest; but that would be an unfair way of representing the case. There is no question of standing outside the stream of time and claiming to adjudicate between differing views with total impartiality. One of the problems of the intellectual study of religions is that it can seem to open up to us an infinity of choices, with little to choose between them. The more alternatives we face, the less free we are to choose any one of them: in the end, all threaten to become equally fantastic, riddled with folly and error. A unity of existing religions can be achieved only when all become equally absurd. So we need to remember that each structure of beliefs has a place and context in history. If we have any sense of what may be called the iconic vision of which the great orthodox theologians speak – the sense of unconditioned indescribable reality mediated through finite images – and if we feel the attraction of following a way of self-transcendence, then we will inevitably find ourselves standing within one tradition, at a particular place and time. What is required is the reassessment of this tradition in the light of new moral and intellectual insights which may come from many places. In particular, the critical method of thinking forces us to reassess the nature of revelation and authority, and the pre-scientific and culturally limited aspects which are characteristic of all the great scriptural traditions.

We are thereby committed to the view that all religious traditions are revisable, in the light of new and probably unpredictable advances in knowledge. Such revisions cannot be made in advance of knowing the factors which will, in time, seem to compel them. It would be absurd to hold that one's own beliefs were false and continue to hold them. What one can say, however, is that although certain beliefs seem to be true, the form in which we express them may not be, or in some cases is probably not, fully adequate to the reality we are trying to have beliefs about.

23

It is, nevertheless, incoherent to believe that all religious truth-claims are only partial truths, and therefore all partial truths are equally acceptable, perhaps under special conditions, depending on one's place of birth. Anyone who holds coherent views on the subject must hold a core of beliefs which are asserted to be true without qualification, even if not unrevisably or incorrigibly. Any proposition which contradicts such claims must be false, even if belief in it is excusable or explicable by lack of knowledge, relevant experience, and so on. Anyone who says that all religions are equally valid presumably thinks that we should all have retained human sacrifice and the reading of sheep's entrails as the core of our faith. The extreme liberal view, that the more religions there are, the better, is therefore intellectually untenable. Yet a given set of attitudes may be restricting or over-partial, and require completion or even opposition to its repressive possibilities. All of us must be aware that religious claims are essentially contestable – they cannot be established to the satisfaction of all rational people. It is therefore reasonable to think that each perspective takes the known facts and arranges them from its own point of view. Each pattern has its strong points and its weak ones. Few can be decisively overthrown, though particular beliefs may be discarded or reformulated to meet objections from other viewpoints. As Nietzsche said, 'the spiritualisation of enmity . . . consists in profoundly grasping the value of having enemies'.[12] That is, in the intellectual realm, oppositions of doctrine perform a salutary function if they point up the weaknesses in one's own way of putting things, and stress ranges of values that we neglect at our peril, even if we must transform them within our own preferred system of concepts.

What the fact of pluralism makes clear is that there are deeply differing perspectives on human life, none of them universally establishable. None of us is neutral. And this strongly suggests the partial nature of human knowing and interacting with the world. That cannot in itself lead us to give up our own perspective; we cannot be free of all perspectives. But it leads us to believe that our view is one among many which have an equal epistemic right to exist and even a function to perform in reminding us of aspects we may have overlooked or ways in which we restrict rather than extend our vision of things. It also suggests that any view which regards itself as final and complete, without considering other views and seeking to understand them fully, is to that extent irrational. It is unacceptable, from a rational point of view, to assert one religious view as certainly true, on exactly the same grounds as some other view alleges (for example, the self-evident appeal of scripture).

I will conclude by suggesting some answer to the questions posed at the beginning of this paper, in the light of this discussion, brief as it is. First, it does make sense to make truth-claims even when there is no agreed method of resolving disagreements. It is part of the epistemic position of human beings that many beliefs are essentially contestable – simple examples would be whether lower animals can feel, whether embryos are persons, or whether the brain-mind identity theory is true. This cannot stop us making truth-claims in such essentially contested areas. But it should lead us to try to be very careful about just what those areas are, and to be alert to the insights that other perspectives can bring. Claims to possess certain and absolutely unrevisable truth should be met with scepticism; and an agnostic qualification must be placed against many of the claims our own religious traditions make. If one asks why the truth one perceives is not perceived by others, I think a positive account needs to be given of this; and the most obvious suggestion is that each view is partial in many respects; that each has developed within one historical tradition of practice, theory, and origin; and that growing understanding and knowledge may lead these traditions to be revised in unpredictable ways. The view which gives the most reasonable account of the diversity of religious beliefs seems to be one which envisages a development of moral and factual knowledge, as tribal traditions are overtaken by scriptural faiths, and they in turn begin to engage in a new set of transformations by mutual contact.

What this suggests is that imperialism – the view that my faith alone is true, and all others are false, just as such, and to be eliminated – is due to a myopia which has no rational account to offer of how other faiths have come to exist and succeed. Moreover, it encourages intolerance and hatred, as one eventually has to put down the failure of others to be converted to some form of demonic bad faith. But co-existence – the view that all religious faiths are to be encouraged and left to develop alone – is due to a lack of serious concern for truth, which in the end trivializes religion, and regards it simply as a minority preference. And it can encourage the existence of ideological ghettos and fragmentation, in a world which needs unity more than ever before. Perhaps one could look for an acceptance of a process of historical development by the mutual interaction of traditions, as each attempts an ever-wider integration of other knowledge and moral and spiritual experience into itself.

I am aware, of course, that perhaps the majority of major

religious faiths would not accept the way I have put things in this chapter – especially in regard to the necessity fully to assimilate post-critical attitudes. My view, too, is contestable – as it should be, if the view is right.

I have tried, from the viewpoint of a sympathetic philosopher, to wrestle with the basic problem of discovering what it is reasonable to believe, in a world of conflicting views which are not decidable by any practically available method. I suggested that a study of some central religious traditions reveals factors which may help to explain the phenomenon of religious pluralism, at the level of belief. Most traditions contain strands which emphasize the incomprehensibility of God or the supreme reality. They consequently stress the partiality of all human concepts and images of God. Such images tend to be qualified, within traditions, by paradoxical affirmations which negate any exclusive or literal force they have. Moreover, it is common for different sorts of emphasis to be accepted within a broad religious tradition – on ways of obedience and love, or of active and quietist devotion, for example. And one can find structural parallels between various faiths quite easily, which stress the necessity for self-renunciation in pursuit of bliss, knowledge, and freedom. All these factors suggest that varying ways of faith are not simply in conflict with one another. They rather seem to be partial attempts to approach an incomprehensible perfection, in pursuit of human good; and a certain plurality of approach is usually accepted and even required in recognition of the infinity of God and the finitude of human understanding.

To say that all are partial and many-stranded, however, is not to say that all are equally valid. Some criteria of rational belief need to be developed. In the classical scriptural traditions, written revelation functioned as an unquestioned authority for faith. But I argued that the rise of the scientific enterprise, of historical method, and of critical thinking has irrevocably changed rational human attitudes to authority. With reference to revealed belief, it leads to acceptance that errors exist in revelation, and that there are many uncertainties. It emphasizes the cultural milieu in which religious writings originate, and exposes the limitations of such a milieu. And, by parity of reasoning, it demands taking the scriptures of other faiths much more seriously than has been done in the past. The overall effect of these changes has been to make possible a view of revelation as a fallible and developing human response to divine initiative. The criteria of rational belief will not be purely internal to a religious scheme, but will involve consideration of wider patterns of knowledge and evaluation, especially from traditions which may have perceived what we have missed.

One cannot escape the fact that one belongs to a particular tradition and to a place in history; one cannot aspire to an archangel's view of the world. One can, however, seek to be clear about what is involved in one's own belief-structure – the lineaments of its historical development and the possibilities it presents for further understanding. My suggestion has been that it is possible to discern some features of religious views which point to the possibility of a development and convergence of religious traditions in a post-critical age. The suggestion is, I think, rather far removed from the position of Mr Sugden's chapter; but I hope that it is consistent with at least the main thrust of what Professor Hastings and Dr D'Costa have to say. Perhaps I am just a little more agnostic than they are about where such convergence may lead. And I suppose that I may fairly be taken as a defender of 'religious pluralism' in at least one sense that John Hick has argued for, though on grounds far removed from those excoriated by Dr Surin.

Notes

1 J. G. Fraser *The Golden Bough*, London: Macmillan (1924; abridged edn, 1980).
2 Cf. R. B. Braithwaite, 'An empiricist's view of the nature of religious belief', in B. Mitchell (ed.) *Philosophy of Religion*, Oxford University Press (1971).
3 J. Hick, *God Has Many Names*, Philadelphia: Westminster Press (1982).
4 Sankara, The Vedanta-Sutras, trans. G. Thibaut, in M. Müller (ed.), *Sacred Books of the East*, 50 vols, Oxford University Press (1879–1910), volumes 34 & 38.
5 Asvagosha [Ashvagosha], *The Awakening of Faith*, trans. Y. S. Hakeda, Columbia University Press (1967).
6 Aquinas, *Summa Theologiae*, Blackfriars edn, 60 vols, London: Eyre & Spottiswoode (1964–81), Ia, q. 3, intro.
7 Maimonides, *Guide for the Perplexed*, trans. Shlomo Pines, University of Chicago Press (1963).
8 Al-Gazali [al-Ghazali], *The Niche for Lights*, trans. W. H. T. Gairdner, London: Royal Asiatic Society, monograph 19 (1924, repr. 1952).
9 Sankara, The Vedanta-Sutras, p. 80.
10 J. H. Leuba, *A Psychological Study of Religion*, London: Constable (1912).
11 Ernst Troeltsch, 'Über historische und dogmatische methode in der

Theologie', *Gesammelte Schriften* II, Tübingen (1956), pp. 236 ff. (No English translation).
12 F. Nietzsche, *Twilight of the Idols*, trans. R. J. Hollingdale, Harmondsworth: Penguin (1969), 5. 3.

II
Ethnographic and historical perspectives

New lines in the supra-market
How much can we buy?[1]

Eileen Barker

If by pluralism we are referring to a society in which members of minority groups maintain independent traditions of one sort or another,[2] then it is clear that, despite its having two Churches 'by Law Established', Britain has had a fairly respectable history of religious pluralism (and a slightly less respectable history of religious toleration) for several hundred years. In the second half of the twentieth century, however, the variety to be found in the religious supra-market has not only increased quantitatively, it has also assumed a completely new quality. This is partly due to the immigration of peoples who have brought their own religions with them to this country, but it is also due to the growth of a number of new religious movements, a few of which are indigenous to the United Kingdom or continental Europe, but most of which originated in either North America (frequently California) or the East (frequently India).

While an earlier generation of new religions might have espoused various unorthodox versions of Christianity, they could usually be recognized as, at worst, a heresy within the Christian tradition. Jehovah's Witnesses, Christadelphians, Christian Scientists, members of the Church of Jesus Christ of Latter-Day Saints (the Mormons), and even Theosophists can be found classified as non-Trinitarian churches, while Seventh Day Adventists and the Salvation Army now seem to fit, without dispute, into an 'Other Protestant' bracket.[3] Furthermore, although a satisfying degree of taxonomic order has been bestowed by Bryan Wilson on the variety that exists between such movements,[4] this is a feat that neither he nor anyone else has been able to accomplish with a similar success in the case of the current wave of new religions.[5]

Today, when we talk about religious pluralism in Britain, are not talking merely about splits or schisms within a single tradition such as Christianity – or even of eastern influences on

Christianity. We are talking about movements that come from a variety of traditions, many of them quite alien to most of the West until fairly recently. We are also referring to movements that seem to have no religious tradition at all:[6] although it is sometimes possible to trace some sort of religious precursor, this is often so smothered by contemporary packaging that it is difficult to decide whether or not the traditional aspects have an ontological status that is of a genuinely greater significance than the wrapping.[7]

In other words, when wandering around the contemporary supra-market of religions, it is extremely difficult to know how this unprecedented range of goods on offer might be arranged. One system of display could be helpful for some purposes but useless for other purposes. We might, for example, take the origins or traditions from which a movement comes as the primary criterion for order. To do so would place together the International Society for Krishna Consciousness (ISKCON), the followers of Bhagwan Rajneesh, Sai Baba, Meher Baba, the Brahma Kumaris, and the Ananda Marga on the shelf marked 'Religions of Indian origin'. On another shelf, marked 'Japanese Exports' we might find Nichiren Shoshu (Soka Gakkai), Rissho Kosei Kai, P. L. Kyodan, Sekai Kyusei Kyo, and various Zen groups (and there would, of course, be other Zen groups on, for example, the Chinese, Tibetan, and Korean shelves).

A shelf marked 'Christian Variations' would boast the Children of God (later known as the 'Family of Love', and now selling its literature under the name of 'Heavenly Magic'), the Bugbrooke Jesus Fellowship, The Way International, the ill-fated People's Temple, and the Unification Church – unless, of course, it was geographical rather than religious tradition that was being emphasized, in which case the Unification Church would be on the 'Korean' shelf. The Rastafarian movement could be on a Judaic or a West Indian or, possibly, an Ethiopian shelf. There might be a shelf marked 'Human Potential Movement', the goods on this shelf having a strongly Californian flavour and bearing such names as *est* (Erhard Seminars Training, now The Centres Network or The Forum), Primal Therapy, Rebirthing, and, possibly, the Church of Scientology. In a dark corner there would be a shelf devoted to new varieties of Voodoo, Occultism, Paganism, Witchcraft, and Magic; and, perhaps not too far away, there would be the 'Satanism' shelf (which appears to be serving an expanding market not only in the West but also in parts of Eastern Europe). If the store were sufficiently international, there would be further shelves housing the African Independent Churches. And if the store were to define novelty sufficiently widely it might expand its 'Christian Variations' shelf to make room for the Charismatic Renewal, Neo-Pentecostalism and the House Church (or Restorationist) movement – and, perhaps, from within the Roman Catholic Church, for Opus Dei.

Such a display system does, however, produce some very strange bed-fellows. Take, for example, the Rajneeshee sannyasins and the ISKCON devotees: both would undoubtedly shudder at the thought of such proximity to the other. More popularly known as the Hare Krishna (on account of their chant 'Hare Krishna Hare Krishna, Krishna Krishna, Hare Hare, Hare Rama Hare Rama, Rama Rama, Hare Hare'), ISKCON devotees are enjoined to lead extremely ascetic lives. From the time of initiation they are expected not to take any kinds of drugs or alcohol, not to eat meat, and not to indulge in sexual intercourse, except for the specific purpose of procreation within marriage. The Rajneeshees, on the other hand, have been encouraged by their Bhagwan to indulge in multifarious sexual extravaganzas – although the spread of sexually transmitted diseases and the threat of AIDS has led to a decidedly more circumspect path to enlightenment in recent years.

If, to consider another taxonomic possibility, we were to arrange the movements according to their political stance, we would find the People's Temple and the Children of God embracing a militantly left-wing position; the Unification Church is militantly anti-communist; the Ananda Marga advocates a kind of socialist anarchy; the Soka Gakkai is closely connected with the fifth largest party in Japan, the *laissez-faire* Komeito (Clean Government Party); and movements such as the Divine Light Mission, ISKCON, and the Rajneeshees disclaim any interest in politics.[8]

So far as finances are concerned, some, like the Unification Church and ISKCON rely largely on their members to collect money, either by 'fund-raising' in the streets or by working for minimum remuneration in businesses owned by the movement; others tithe their members; and yet others gain their income through charging (often exorbitant) fees for courses of various kinds that offer enlightenment, self-development, or freedom from the slings and arrows of outrageous modern capitalism.

Some movements are authoritarian bureaucracies, others consist of loosely knit networks. The degree to which a movement will make itself responsible for the lives of its members introduces a further area of diversity: while some movements claim the right to control every aspect of their members' lives – their work, where they live, whom they shall marry, and when they can sleep with their partner – other movements expect little more than the occasional visit or perhaps merely a commitment to attend the occasional refresher course. While there might be promiscuous 'shopping around' among the seekers investigating the techniques on display in the Human Potential shelves of the supra-market, with clients purchasing several wares at one time, the more obviously religious movements are likely to expect an exclusive loyalty and commitment to their brand from their members.

Even *within* the movements there is considerable diversity in beliefs and practices according to time and geographical area. Involvement within any particular movement can vary. There will be those who are the main core-members (the priests), then the committed congregation-members, the affiliated, and, on a somewhat different level, the sympathisers who may actually be members of a more conventional religion.[9]

No one knows exactly how many new religions there are, nor does anyone know how many members are in each movement. Depending on how 'new religious movement' is defined, it is possible to claim that there are hundreds, thousands, or tens of thousands, but many of these movements will have well under a hundred members.[10] What is rarely admitted by either the movements or their detractors is that there is a very high turnover rate, with far more people leaving the movements than staying in them for more than a limited period. In other words, many people have 'gone through' the movements, but only a few have stayed. There are, for example, only about 250 full-time Moonies in Britain at the present time, with roughly the same number of British Moonies overseas, mainly in North America; the number of Krishna devotees is comparable. Such statistics obviously question the so-called 'brainwashing thesis', which claims that once such a movement has got a victim into its clutches, he or she will never be able to escape.[11]

Given the variety to be found within and between the movements, it is not altogether surprising that variety is to be found in the characteristics of those who join them. It is certainly not the case that all those who become members of one of the new religious movements are necessarily oppressed and/or inadequate. In fact, although some movements (the Rastafarians and the People's Temple are examples) have appealed to poor blacks, it is quite clear that the majority of the new religions attract their members from the privileged middle classes, and a growing body of research has indicated that those who join the movements are no more likely to be psychologically disturbed than are the majority of their peers.[12] Those who enter into a life of total commitment are likely to be in their twenties; those who enter upon expensive courses are more likely to be in their thirties or forties.

It is possible to argue that one of the reasons for the variety of the new religions and the attraction that they hold for some people is related directly to the more general, secular pluralism of modern society. At a fairly obvious level, one can point to the ever-increasing division of labour, with sons and daughters less and less commonly following in their fathers' or mothers' footsteps, frequent social and geographical mobility, and greatly enhanced opportunities to travel, to learn about alternative world-views and life-styles through the diverse channels of the media and the continuous waves of immigration from the East (and, indeed, previously unfamiliar parts of the West).

All this means that people have different experiences, different (often heightened) expectations, and different opportunities to shop around in the various markets of a pluralist society. To switch the metaphor: rather than producing a melting-pot in which differences disappear, the increased input has resulted in an ever-expanding smorgasbord. It can, indeed, be argued that each new potential for experiencing a variety of cultural, political, and/or economic aspects of a society results in a further potential for novel schisms and syntheses; pluralism can reinforce itself as it leads to the creation of further divisions, distinctions, distortions, and discoveries. But pluralism can also foster a potential threat to pluralism from within itself.

While *societal* pluralism allows for, and can even encourage, the existence of a wide range of permissible attitudes, beliefs, life-styles, and values, it is also the case that the very permission which allows the supra- (and other) markets to offer such variety will encompass organizations that can restrict rather than enhance the options available at the *individual level* – sometimes, but by no means always, as a consequence of the individual's own volition.

Not all values and not all ways of life are compatible – many of those celebrated by contemporary western society are in direct conflict with each other. We find, for example, value placed on both individualism *and* community; on both freedom and security. This can lead not only to tensions but also to some curious contradictions. For example, it is not difficult to recognize instances of conforming individualism, organized spontaneity, determined freedom – and so on.[13]

There are various ways of dealing with the contradictory options that arise within society. One is to allow the contradictions to appear side by side; another is to try to eliminate any inconsistency by adhering to a single truth that excludes all competition. The first (the pluralist) solution has both the strengths and the weaknesses of ambiguity and uncertainty. While it enables there to be constant checks, balancing, and flexibility in dealing with problems as they arise, many people find the lack of absolute certainties psychologically uncomfortable. It is possible that these people will seek an ideology that espouses unambiguous truths and a community of like-minded believers. This is, indeed, what many of the new religions offer their members – a haven of certainty within the shifting sands of modern pluralism.[14] At the same time, there are new religions that offer their members release from those constraints which exist in a complex, impersonal society, and which extend the promise of enriched relationships, self-development, heightened spirituality, and unbridled explorations into the true, inner being of consciousness (or whatever). Neither of these types of new religious movements is likely to permit much in the way of 'internal pluralism'.

Not all sects are new religious movements, but many of the new religions exhibit the sectarian characteristic of proclaiming an exclusive truth, and even those that claim that they do not do so may, in practice, turn out to be far less internally tolerant of diversity than might at first appear. It could be claimed that the same was true of many of the 'old religions', but religions tend to change in many ways as they become more established;[15] second and subsequent generations are less likely to be as fervent as the convert in their beliefs; the mere fact of growth in numbers means that believers in a differentiated modern society will have different experiences, and it will become increasingly unlikely that each member will have the same perception and understanding of the faith. This is not to say that large, well-organized, and long-established religions may not be monolithic – history clearly shows us that they can be, but it is to suggest that the more established a religion is in a pluralistic society, the more 'internal pluralism' it is likely to display.[16]

Even those who have argued that established, traditional religions present a major hegemonic force can recognize their potential for developing an 'internal pluralism':

> Every religion, even the Catholic (in fact, especially the Catholic, precisely because of its efforts to remain united superficially, and not to split up into national churches and into various social strata) is in reality a multiplicity of distinct and often contradictory religions: there is the Catholicism of the

petite bourgeoisie and city workers, a women's Catholicism, an intellectual's Catholicism equally varied and disconnected.[17]

The coexistence of variety in and around the Church of England has been cogently illuminated by Robert Towler's analysis of the letters received by the then Bishop of Woolwich, John Robinson, after the publication of what has been described as the best-known religious book of the twentieth century, *Honest to God*.[18] Some 4,000 people (most of whom had heard about, but not actually read the book) wrote to Dr Robinson, telling him of their own faith, beliefs, convictions, feelings, or special knowledge concerning matters religious. These letters provided the data that Towler used to construct a set of 'Ideal Types' which would describe a range of ways in which the British population is 'conventionally religious'.[19]

Five distinct types emerged from the analysis. The first type, 'exemplarism' is a Christian form of humanism; the idea of God is seen as unnecessary and unreal; 'Jesus appears as the pinnacle of human aspiration, not as the link between the human and the divine.' The second type, 'conversionism', is based on the conviction that the only hope for salvation is to have been 'born again'. Two boundaries define the conversionist's life: for the individual, there is the wretched period before, and the completely transformed period after, rebirth; within society, there are those who have not accepted the Lord Jesus, and there is the fellowship of true believers who have. The third type, 'theism', is a religious attitude that is grounded in a sense of wonder and awe, and which focuses on God as a benevolent creator. Jesus is not seen as especially divine, for such a vision would detract from the greatness and majesty of God. Theists tend not to 'believe that' so much as to 'believe in'. 'Gnostics', however, 'know that', and concentrate on knowledge of the spiritual world; God is perceived as a principle rather than a person or a being. A strongly defined dualism distinguishes between the (everlasting) divine soul within each one of us, and the (transitory) material body which clothes it. Finally, there is the 'traditionalist', who believes in and will 'cherish and hold dear' everything that is conventionally a part of the Christian religion. Not altogether surprisingly, traditionalists tended to be exceedingly upset by the publication of *Honest to God*.

Towler does not claim that his typology was exhaustive – he might, for example, have added mysticism or millenarianism – but he convincingly demonstrates that assumptions that only one type of religiousness represents 'real' Christianity or even 'real'

Anglicanism are unwarranted. The conclusion is that orthodox, conventional religion is composed of a number of distortions that exaggerate different, but legitimate, strands, which 'taken together, and held together . . . keep one another in check, and the result is "normal" Christianity'.[20]

So long as these different, but legitimate strands are taken together and held together within the institutional boundaries of the Church of England and, to a lesser or greater extent, other traditional churches, they can keep each other in check. But, as has already been suggested, the pluralism of modern society also embraces options that are internally monolithic in belief and/or practice. In other words, within the pluralist society, one is free to choose to be unconfronted by choice; one may find oneself choosing *from* the variety to have *no* variety.

It has already been suggested that not only might one make such a choice at a relatively conscious level in the case of those movements that clearly demand an unquestioning commitment to an uncompromising, absolute truth, but also that the denial of one's freedom can, just as surely, be the unintended consequence of becoming embroiled in one of the movements that actually promise their members freedom from the constraints of modern society. Within such a movement the pursuit of freedom can be a genuine source of individual freedom, but it can also result in surrender to the well-nigh unconditional control of others.

There are numerous variables that can contribute towards an increasing totalitarianism within a new religious movement: one fairly obvious one is physical isolation. This was, of course, evident in the tragic case of Jonestown, Guyana, where over 900 of the followers of Jim Jones committed suicide or were murdered in 1978. While not in a remote part of the jungle of an alien country, relatively isolated communities such as Bhagwan's Oregon ranch, Rajneeshpuram, and the ISKCON Temple complex, New Vrindaban, West Virginia, have been recent examples of authoritarian control being wielded by a charismatic individual and/or a small elite group. In such situations, criminal acts have been performed by those who find themselves falling victim to some of the very evils from which they had hoped to escape by joining the movement.[21]

I hope that enough has already been said about the differences between the movements to make it clear that no single scenario could possibly describe the range of their potential development, but one scenario that is by no means confined to a single movement can be briefly sketched. Movements that demand surrender from their members tend to erect a strong social barrier that will cut them off from the rest of society, even when there is little in the way of a geographical barrier.[22] In such cases, it is likely that the movement will regard non-members with a suspicion that leads them (the non-members) to react in a way that seems to confirm to the insiders that they are fully justified in their distrust. Suspicion of outsiders is quite likely to develop into a suspicion that there are insiders who may not be sufficiently committed to the Truth. Anyone who questions the beliefs or actions of the leaders becomes defined first as disruptive, then as disloyal. Members become more and more constrained – less and less free to explore ideas. The Truth that is conceived in absolute, unidimensional terms is so unquestionably Right that methods which go against even the stated values of the Truth are thought to be justified by reference to the Ultimate goal of establishing the Truth at a higher and/or more complete level. Eventually there is no permissible way of redressing the balance when things go too far in one direction. It is expected that those who are suggesting alternative ideas or means of achieving the common goal will be reported to the leaders, and then, when the potential reporters are suspected of not reporting, a 1984-type system of spying (possibly incorporating the use of electronic surveillance) is established. So too is Big Brother (or, in the case of Ma Prem Sheela, Big Sister) and his/her every whim.[23]

Let me stress, I am not suggesting that this is by any means an inevitable process – or even a very common one. In fact, most new movements will eventually accommodate to society and allow for a wider range of truths within their midst, or they will keep themselves very much to themselves and cease trying to proselytize once they recognize that there is only a limited number of people who are capable of accepting such radical and complete truths – or, perhaps most commonly of all, they will fade away.

What I am suggesting is that progressive totalitarianism is a process that can occur – and has occurred too often for comfort – within some of the new religions to be found within western pluralism. Usually those who suffer are the members and their close relatives or friends, but there is always the possibility that if such movements were to gain a position of power in society then the outsiders would find themselves as constrained as the believers.[24] In other words, a religiously plural society is quite likely to be nurturing movements that aspire to deny to others the freedoms within which they themselves have been allowed to flourish. The chances of their total success may be minimal, but the chances of their enjoying a totalitarian success within the confines of their own boundaries are very real.

Those who celebrate religious pluralism and deplore the idea of rigid brand-control over the shelves of the supra-market are unlikely to want to ban any of the diverse products on display – however shoddy or wrong they may feel some of these packages to be. If, however, they wish to preserve the possibility of variety, they will have to keep a sharp eye on new products and on new developments in old products. The price of pluralism is eternal vigilance.

Notes

1 I would like to thank the Nuffield Foundation for a grant that enabled me to carry out the research referred to in this paper.

2 *Concise Oxford Dictionary*, seventh edn (1982).

3 I take these classifications from Peter Brierley (ed.), *UK Christian Handbook 1987/88 Edition*, London: Marc Europe, the Evangelical Alliance and the Bible Society (1986), 145–7.

4 It must, however, be admitted that Wilson, in his book *Religious Sects: A Sociological Study*, London: Weidenfeld & Nicholson (1970), does have a chapter entitled 'Some exceptional cases', but chief among these he numbers the followers of Father Divine, the Catholic Apostolic Church, and the Mormons. He also has a chapter devoted to sects in Africa and Japan, but these are described in order to show what might occur in developing countries, not what might be expected were such movements to be transferred to the West.

5 Although I consider that they have only limited applicability, I do not wish to dismiss completely all attempts that have been made to give the new religious movements some order from a sociological perspective. Among the more useful suggestions see, for example, R. Wallis, *The Elementary Forms of the New Religious Life*, London: Routledge & Kegan Paul (1984), who classifies the movements according to orientations towards the world; James A. Beckford, *Cult Controversies: The Societal Response to the New Religious Movements*, London: Tavistock (1985), is concerned to distinguish styles of 'insertion' in the host society; Dick Anthony and Thomas Robbins 'Contemporary religious ferment and moral ambiguity', in Eileen Barker (ed.), *New Religious Movements: A Perspective for Understanding Society*, New York: Edwin Mellen Press (1982), distinguish, as their title might suggest, between responses to the moral ambiguities to be found in American society.

6 There is not much point in asking the movements themselves whether or not they are 'really' a religion, for there are often secular advantages or disadvantages to their being defined one way rather than the other. For example, the Church of Scientology has fought (and won) a battle in the Australian courts to be recognized as a religion so that it could gain a tax-exempt status, while the Science of Creative Intelligence (Transcendental Meditation) fought (and lost) a battle in the New Jersey courts in which it was claiming that it was *not* a

religion and could, therefore, be taught in a state school (the First Amendment of the United States' Constitution forbids religion to be taught in the states' public schools).

7 It is a further symptom of religious conpetition in a pluralist society that, whatever the content, the wrapping is almost certain to have a scientific seal of approval stamped upon it. See Eileen Barker, 'Thus Spake the Scientist: a comparative account of the new priesthood and its organizational bases', *The Annual Review of the Social Sciences of Religion*, 3 (1979).

8 See Eileen Barker, *New Religious Movements and Political Orders*, Canterbury: University of Kent, Centre for the Study of Religion and Society, Pamphlet Library 15 (1987).

9 For statistics relating to the various types of membership of new religious movements in the UK, see Eileen Barker, *New Religious Movements: A Practical Introduction*, Norwich: HMSO (1980), App. II. For a useful summary of available statistics for the United States and Canada see Robert Wuthnow, 'Religious movements in North America', in James A. Beckford (ed.) *New Religious Movements and Rapid Social Change*, London: Sage, and Paris: UNESCO (1986).

10 For a discussion of the comparative proportion of sects and cults per population in North America and Western Europe, see Rodney Stark and William S. Bainbridge, *Future of Religion: Secularization, Revival and Cult Formation*, University of California Press (1985). See also Gordon Melton, *The Encyclopedia of American Religions*, second edn, Detroit: Gale Research Company (1987).

11 Eileen Barker, *The Making of a Moonie: Brainwashing or Choice?* Oxford: Blackwell (1984).

12 See, for example, Burke Rochford, *Hare Krishna!*, New Brunswick, NJ: Rutgers University Press (1985); Larry D. Shinn, 'The many faces of Krishna', in J. Fichter (ed.), *Alternatives to Mainline Churches*, New York: Rose of Sharon Press (1983); and Eileen Barker, *The Making of a Moonie*.

13 An example of conforming individualism was recently provided for me by my daughter when I noticed that she was wearing only one ear-ring. 'You've lost an ear-ring', I informed her. 'No, I haven't,' she replied patiently. 'I'm asserting my individuality. Not to be outdone, I took off one of my ear-rings. 'Look!' I boasted, 'I'm an individual too!' 'Oh, Mummy,' came the exasperated reply, 'It has to be the *left* one.'

14 I am not suggesting that this is the only, or even the main, reason why people join such movements.

15 See Bryan Wilson, *Religion in Sociological Perspective*, Oxford University Press (1982), for a discussion of the ways in which religions institutionalize with the passage of time.

16 There are some very important qualifications (concerning the general state of the society) that need to be made to this statement, but there is no space to elaborate these in the present paper. Good discussions can be found in, for example, Robert S. Michaelsen and Wade Clark Roof (eds), *Liberal Protestantism: Realities and Possibilities*, New

York: Pilgrim Press (1986); and Jeffrey K. Hadden and Anson Shupe (eds) *Prophetic Religions and Politics: Religion and the Political Order*, New York: Paragon House (1986). Furthermore, the opportunities for an attack on pluralism are clearly greater under some circumstances than under others – when, for example, a large number of members of a society feel the need for a strong leader, absolute truths, and clear direction. To recognize that there are plenty of old contenders for the loyalties of those who feel uncomfortable in a liberal and/or pluralistic society one has only to look at the aspirations and, indeed, achievements of certain fundamentalist Islamic sects in the Middle East or the rise of the Moral Majority and the mushrooming of fundamentalist Christians schools in the United States at the present time. For an excellent account of the socialization of young fundamentalists in the United States, see Alan Peshkin, *God's Choice: The Total World of a Fundamentalist Christian School*, University of Chicago Press (1986).

17 Antonio Gramsci, *Quaderni del Carcere*, critical edn of the Instituto Gramsci, ed. V. Gerratana, Turin: Einaudi (1975) 1396–7; trans. by John Fulton and quoted in his unpublished Ph.D. thesis 'The Historical and Social Ground of Religion and Conflict in Modern Ireland: A Critical, Holistic Approach', London school of Economics (1987).

18 John Robinson, *Honest to God*, London: SCM Press (1963).

19 Robert Towler, *The Need for Certainty: A Sociological Study of Conventional Religion*, London: Routledge & Kegan Paul (1984).

20 ibid., 98.

21 For graphic descriptions of life in Rajneeshpuram see (for a disillusioned insider's perspective) Hugh Milne, *Bhagwan: The God that Failed*, London: Caliban (1986), and (for an outsider's report) Frances FitzGerald, *Cities on a Hill: A Journey through Contemporary American Cultures*, New York and London: Simon & Schuster (1987). The story of the troubles at New Vrindaban has yet to be told, but an introduction to the sorts of 'goings-on' that have been occurring can be found in an undoubtedly over-dramatized account by John Hubner and Lindsey Gruson: 'Dial Om for murder', *Rolling Stone*, 9 Apr. 1987.

22 The surrender may be in either the 'in whose service is perfect freedom' sense, or in the sense that surrender is a central ingredient of a technique by which release from current constraints can be obtained, the individual being freed in order to be the better able to pursue his or her particular form of transcendence. For analysis of these two types see Eileen Barker, *Armageddon and Aquarius: New Religious Movements in Contemporary Christendom*, Manchester University Press (forthcoming).

23 For a discussion of this issue, see Eileen Barker, 'Freedom to surrender with Bhagwan', *Self and Society*, vol. 15, no. 5 (Sept./Oct. 1987), 209–16.

24 See my *New Religious Movements and Political Orders* for an elaboration of details concerning this potential.

4

Gender and religious pluralism
Exorcism and inspiration in the family

I. M. Lewis

I

Religiosity, in most religious traditions, seems to vary according to age and sex. Such variations are usually discussed within a single religious tradition. Even age-related differences may, however, assume a wider pluralist pattern in which different stages in the human life-cycle are associated not merely with varying degrees of religious devotion but actually with distinct religions. I am not referring here to eclectic individuals, but rather to recurrent patterns, characteristic of a whole culture or society. Thus, the religious career of lay-people in Japan has stereotypically a dual format in which, in one's most active competitive years, religious devotion centres on Shinto shrines where miraculous aids to success are sought. In later years, and especially towards the end of life, the emphasis switches from this-worldly Shinto to transcendent Buddhism as the key to eternity. Although Shinto and Buddhism interpenetrate in many complex, syncretic patterns (Smith 1974; Davis 1980), they perhaps assume their most discrete identities in everyday life in this life-cycle pattern of religious pluralism.

Gender can also be systematically linked with differences not merely in religiosity but, again, in religion itself. If, as has been asserted (Holden 1983: 4), 'religion is invariably male-dominated', within a particular masculine religious tradition, women may espouse an alternative religion – although this may be disguised and represented in the official male universe as treatment for illness. Focusing on the role of religion in alleviating illness and distress, this chapter explores the significance of contrasting interpretations of, and responses to, affliction affecting women in a variety of cultures. It traces the contrasting implications of treating spirit-attributed complaints by exorcism, utilizing the apparatus of official male religion, or by absorption or accommodation of the pathogenic agencies involved. The latter procedure leads to the formation of a 'cult of affliction', the patient's illness serving retrospectively as an initiation into a cult of women devotees whose shared religious experience is officially presented, in the male religious context, as merely a form of therapy. For men there is only their officially dominant religion; women are simply engaged in securing medical treatment. But, when these female therapeutic rites are seen in a less male-biased perspective, it becomes evident that we have in fact here religious pluralism – with complementary male and female religious beliefs and practices. The official male cosmology may overshadow its female counterpart which, in turn, may serve as a valuable foil or mirror, facilitating the definition of male ideology and orthodoxy. From this point of view, I suggest that the religious significance of such 'cults of affliction' is highlighted when the therapy of initiation is contrasted with that of exorcism. Exorcism is, as it were, aborted initiation; spirit-possession is not allowed to be formalized as inspiration – but the germ of an alternative religious movement is nevertheless there, suggesting a potential for religious pluralism.

II

The logically opposed alternative modes of therapeutic response – exorcism or accommodation – are sometimes both present in the same cultural setting as options for treatment. Sometimes only *one* of these two styles of therapy is apparently available – if so, it usually seems to be exorcism. I want to start this discussion, therefore, by examining cases where exorcism is reported to be alone in the field.

I begin with the well-documented and analytically impressive account of exorcism in Muslim Malaysia provided by Clive Kessler (1977; cf. Firth 1967). Here the majority of patients with spirit-caused afflictions treated in this way are women who, according to Kessler, fall into three categories. These are, first, young brides forced against their will to marry husbands of their parents' choosing; second, middle-aged wives caught in the toils of polygyny; and, third, widows and divorcees. Various presenting symptoms (sometimes associated with organic illnesses ranging from malaria to tuberculosis, in other cases psychosomatic) are diagnosed by specialist male exorcists (called *bomoh* in Malay).

Treatment takes the form of a highly dramatic exorcistic ritual conducted by the *bomoh*. In the course of this seance, with the aid of his spirit familiar who comes to possess him, the exorcist first identifies the pathogenic spirit involved, and then summons an appropriate healing spirit to possess him and drive out the

malignant agent. The final, successful expulsion of the spirit causing the sickness is signalled by the patient dancing in a trance-
state with the *bomoh* exorcist at the climax of the healing rite.
This dramatic healing seance, known literally as 'Princess play'
(*main peteri*) is strongly charged with regal symbolism. In the
course of the ritual, the patient dances and trances to tunes from
the puppet shadow-play, evoking the heroic battles of *Ramayana*,
or courtly scenes from the *mak yong* royalty folk-operas. Explicit
analogies are drawn between the patient's disordered condition
and a disordered body politic, a 'disarticulated realm' to which
regal authority, invoked here by the *bomoh*, restores order and
well-being.

In some cases, this royal metaphor is pursued even more literally. A model palace (*balai*), in the form of an elaborate ritual
boat, is constructed to attract and capture the patient's pathogenic
spirits, and this is then set adrift on a stream, or cast into the sea,
to carry away the sources of disorder. If, in the seance, female
patients thus perform classic heroic macho-roles, the drama ends
with the *bomoh* casting out anarchic spirit-forces and restoring
order in the 'palace' of the patient's body. Appropriately, the
bomoh exorcists describe themselves as playing a political role,
referring to their familiar helping spirits as spiritual 'district head-
men' or 'state assembly men'. Although the role may ultimately
hark back to pre-Islamic beliefs, in the contemporary Muslim
Malay context the male *bomoh* exorcist presents himself as a local
agent of the cosmic hierarchy, presided over by Allah, sovereign
of the universe. Thus, however aggressively female patients may
appropriate male roles in the seance dramas, in the end the subversive spirits involved (a somewhat pluralist assemblage of Arab
jinns, Hindu and Indonesian gods, and local spirits) are tri-
umphantly expelled, and the male-dominated Islamic order is
restored by the healing statecraft of the male exorcist.

While the afflicted women patients may benefit psychologically
from their trance-experiences, and more tangibly from the attentions they receive in these expensive rituals (as Kessler 1977
argues), they do so subject ultimately to surrendering their pos-
sessing spirits to the superior power of Islam. From the male point
of view, whatever the material costs to the patient's kin, the spirit
of subversion is held in check by extracting and exorcising it from
the patient's body which is a microcosm of the body politic. It is
nipped in the bud and not allowed to flower into a separate,
gender-specific cult.

A similar presentation of exorcism as the only available spiritual
therapy is contained in Kapferer's recent account (1983) of the

treatment of demon-obsessed women in Buddhist Sri Lanka. The prevalence of largely working-class and peasant female victims here is explained culturologically by Kapferer as a 'function' of the 'cultural typification' which places women 'in a special and significant relation to the demonic'. As in Malaysia, the pathogenic spirits plaguing these women are regarded as signs of disorder, and the exorcistic rituals, again conducted by men, thus seek to restore the cosmic Buddhist order. Such exorcism would seem to underline and strengthen Buddhist ideology and power, as the nationalist, revitalized Buddhist middle classes seek to distance themselves from practices which, in their discourse, represent 'primitive survivals', opposed to Buddhism.

III

Exorcism is believed to restore and promote health by expelling pathogenic spirit-agencies which cause disorder. Where those afflicted are women and the exorcists are men, men are obviously demonstrating the superiority of their religion and using it to control women. I turn now to consider the alternative treatment which, instead of externalizing and driving away the invading spirit-force, seeks a cure through developing a harmonious relationship between it and the patient. Luc de Heusch (1962) calls this process of coming to terms with a spirit by internalizing it 'adorcism' – a term I see no need to quarrel with here. To highlight the contrasting implications of this therapeutic technique I will consider briefly three examples in which both treatments are available – each in the setting of a different 'world religion'.

First, Buddhist Burma, as described by Spiro 1967. Here illnesses affecting women may be diagnosed as malevolent intervention by subversive local spirits called *nats*. One line of treatment involves male Buddhist exorcists, known as 'masters of the Upper Path' who belong to a messianic Buddhist association and are empowered by their superior Buddhist gods (*devas*) to overcome and cast out these troublesome demons. Alternatively, recourse may be had to the expertise of a *nat*-inspired shaman. Such specialists, most of whom are women, are typically ex-patients recruited through initiatory episodes which are interpreted as having a love-affair with a *nat* spirit. This, in turn, leads to a formal – and expensive – *nat* wedding – the shaman being known literally as a '*nat*-wife', whose lusty spiritual sex-life contrasts sharply with the asexual asceticism of the contemplative Buddhist monk.

The shaman's relations with her *nat* spirit empower her to

diagnose and treat *nat* afflictions in other women. In cases of persistent disorders ascribed to *nat* intervention, the patient may in turn seek a cure through therapeutic shamanic initiation. Thus, in contrast to Buddhism, the healing cult of *nats* is monopolized by women who appear to have, in effect, appropriated the local pre-Buddhist religion formerly controlled by men. This Burmese religion – relegated by Buddhism to the status of magic and witch-craft – has become a primarily feminine counter-culture which, in uneasy syncretic tension with male-dominated Buddhism, serves additionally to emphasize the supremacy of this world religion in its Burmese context. Although, from the orthodox Buddhist point of view, we have here only religion (Buddhism) and superstition (*nats*) – from a more objective point of view this constitutes, at one level at least, a gender-specific religious pluralism.

Here, obviously, the two available treatments for women's afflictions have significantly different outcomes and implications. Exorcism provides a cure which demonstrates the superior religious power of Buddhism and of men. The shamanic treat-ment, on the other hand, points towards an alternative religion for women – transforming illness into religious blessing. These divergent conclusions may, of course, proceed from the same symptoms since although the *nats* are in general represented as capricious and evil, they may be tamed and turned into powerful protective forces. Nevertheless, the shaman has much lower status than the Buddhist exorcist. Their respective treatments are ranked correspondingly, although detailed information on the relative costs of their treatments seems to be lacking in our sources.

The second example which I want to consider here, of sexual religious pluralism and the dialectic between exorcism and accom-modation, concerns the Muslim Hausa-speaking peoples of West Africa. Although Islam has for several centuries been the domi-nant faith of the Hausa and has found militant expression in many holy wars, there still exist pockets of non-Muslim Hausa adhering to the traditional pre-Islamic religion. In the dominant Muslim society, these beliefs have been marginalized and feminized in the form of the well-known *bori* spirit-possession cult, a true 'cult of affliction' in which spirit-possessed patients may become initiated devotees – 'mares of the gods'. This subversive cult, whose leaders are divorced women and prostitutes, is perceived as an affront to official male Muslim respectability, which endeavours to control it in two contradictory ways. On the one hand, men attempt to control wives with spirit-afflictions by engaging the services of Islamic exorcists. On the other, the male establishment of the hierarchical Hausa states has co-opted the *bori* cult by assigning official titles to cult-leaders. Thus, for the orthodox Hausa men, diagnosis and treatment by *bori* specialists represents a 'therapy of last resort' for their wives (Nicolas 1975: 211). For women, especially the secluded wives of bourgeois husbands, the cult has a strong appeal, as the circumstances of contemporary Islamic conversion among residual pagan groups indicate. In the wider setting here a Muslim is defined as one who 'prays' in contrast to a non-Muslim who 'drinks beer'. In the same idiom, competing for consumer attention with advertisements for proprietary brands of beer and whisky, Islam is advertised as 'the wise man's choice'. In this vein, when a non-Muslim Hausa determines to embrace Islam, his wife is likely to join the alternative *bori* cult. For a man, the cost of conversion is considerable, for with the domestic seclusion of his wife he loses most of her labour-services as well as having to pay for *bori* episodes. These costs, and those of joining a trading network, which is usually part of the conversion process, are not covered by the savings on beer-party expenditure (Last 1979). Recourse to Islamic exorcism to control or counter the *bori* outbursts of a rebellious wife entails further costs.

The attractions of exorcism for husbands and of 'adorcism' (accommodation) for wives as rival responses to the spirit-afflictions to which women are prone have been particularly clearly analysed in a discussion of the famous *Zar* cult among the dominant ethnic group of Christian Ethiopia (Young 1975). In contrast to the previous cases, the *Zar* cult is not the marginalized pre-Christian religion of this dominant ethnic group. Here a variety of common symptoms of illness affecting women – such as malaise, listlessness, chronic stomach pains, and headache – may be interpreted as spirit-caused afflictions. Four different types of diagnosis or therapy are traditionally available. The cheapest and least complicated procedure is to seek the help of a herbalist (often not a full-time specialist). If this fails, the patient is likely to be referred to one or more of three types of specialist spirit-healer. Two of these specialists draw upon the power of the Ethiopian Orthodox Church to exorcise pathogenic spirits. At a number of famous churches, leading figures in the Orthodox Church have acquired national reputations as healers utilizing the baptism ritual to expel evil spirits from the bodies of the possessed. These priests, however, are generally regarded as providing a cure for a limited range of afflictions and tend to be approached as a last resort.

More widely available are the services of itinerant clerics (*dabtara*) who perform Christian exorcisms to cast out pathogenic spirits. This treatment, which the laity sees as involving the priest's spirit familiars, is expensive in contrast to that offered by

Zar-cult shamans, many of whom are women. The former treatment, forbidden to non-Christians, mobilizes the awesome might of the church to expel demonic forces which are officially anathematized. The latter, shamanic, treatment, invoking precisely these heretical spirits, conducted by women shamans, typically requires the patient to join the *Zar*-cult coterie, an organization which, with pagan and Muslim associations and close links with prostitution, is extremely threatening to respectable members of the orthodox church.

In Ethiopia, as elsewhere, the best treatments are the most expensive. Hence, despite its high cost, a status-conscious farmer in the central Ethiopian highlands will prefer his sick wife to be treated by Christian exorcism and will endeavour to steer her in this direction rather than surrender her to the attentions of a *Zar* shaman. Whatever the psycho-social origins of the possession affliction, conflict between husband and wife is likely to arise over treatment by these conflicting agencies. Constrained by the preferred male treatment, wives in economically viable Christian households are reported to be likely to experience occasional bouts of sickness attributed to the *Zar* spirits, but with treatment limited to occasional shamanic intervention and stopping short of actual initiation into the *Zar* cult. In such socio-economic circumstances, the latter course would signal marital breakdown, helping to maintain the cult's image as a haven for abandoned wives, divorcees, and prostitutes – especially in towns. Clearly, here, exorcism, which costs more, preserves formal male control and dignity in the name of Christian orthodoxy, while the cheaper shamanic treatment appeals to women who, for one reason or another, seek fulfilment in the subversive *Zar* cult which embraces a syncretic cosmology of Christian, Muslim, and pagan spirits – itself a replica of the real world of contemporary religious pluralism in Ethiopia. Here, as elsewhere, women may exact a high price for male pride.

IV

In the male-dominated Great Tradition settings in which they flourish, these female 'cults of affliction' which recruit devotees from patients institute a family-centred, religious pluralism, tailored to the relations between the sexes. The acceptance by men of these subversive women's cults as therapy indicates a limited male tolerance. Where such accommodating treatment is not available and male exorcism is the rule, these feminist religious tendencies are more firmly held in check. And yet, even if male representatives of the dominant (male) religion are able thus to hold the line against pluralist feminine infiltration, exorcism itself both confirms the reality of the spiritual forces involved and makes their management an expensive male prerogative. Where male-managed exorcism reigns supreme it nevertheless enables women, possessed by spirits, to require men to demonstrate their concern at considerable cost.

It is also true (as Gomm 1975 has forcefully demonstrated) that in such circumstances *husbands* as well as *wives* may also gain prestige and attention by the presentation of a domestic problem in spiritual terms which transcend the direct responsibility of *either* partner. Nevertheless, at whatever cost, the exorcistic option ultimately asserts the superiority of male dominance, whereas accommodation or adorcism represents a more challenging treatment, even if cauterized by its male representation as therapy rather than religion. This seems consistent with the obvious logical antithesis between casting out and accommodating a spirit, and raises the question whether exorcism can ever be fail-safe and not contain a seditious undercurrent of potential cultic accommodation. This, in fact, is what scrutiny of the data reviewed here actually suggests.

I conclude by suggesting audaciously that gender-specific pluralism, however disguised and mystified, is the earliest and most pervasive form of religious pluralism.

References

Davis, W. (1980) *Dojo: Magic and Exorcism in Modern Japan*, Stanford University Press.

Firth, R. (1967) 'Ritual and drama in Malay spirit mediumship', *Comparative Studies in Society and History*, 9: 190–207.

Gomm, R. (1975) 'Bargaining form weakness: spirit, possession on the South Kenya coast', *Man* 10: 530–43.

Heusch, L. de (1962) 'Cultes de possession et religions initiatiques de salut en Afrique', *Annales du Centre d'Etudes des Religions*.

Holden, P. (1983) *Women's Religious Experience*, London: Croom Helm.

Kapferer, B. (1983) *A Celebration of Demons*, Indiana University Press.

Kessler, C. (1977) 'Conflict and sovereignty in Kelantanese Malay spirit seances', in V. Carapanzano and V. Garrison (eds), *Case Studies in Spirit Possession*, London: John Wiley.

Last, M. (1979), 'Some economic aspects of conversion in Hausaland (Nigeria)', in N. Levtzion (ed), *Conversion to Islam*, New York: Holmes and Meier.

Lewis, I. M. (1971) *Ecstatic Religion*, Harmondsworth: Penguin Books.
—(1986)*Religion in Context: Cults and Charisma*, Cambridge University Press.

Nicolas, G. (1975) *Dynamique sociale et apprehension du monde au sein d'une societe Hausa*, Paris: Institut d'Ethnologie.

Smith, R. J. (1974) *Ancestor Worship in Contemporary Japan*, Stanford University Press.

M. Spiro, (1967) *Burmese Supernaturalism*, New York: Prentice-Hall.

Young, A. (1975) 'Why Amhara get *Kureynya*: sickness and possession in an Ethiopian *Zar* Cult', *American Ethnologist* 2: 567–84.

5

The transition from unitary to pluralist Catholicism in the Netherlands 1920–1970

Peter McCaffery

What is to count as an explanation for the profound changes that occurred in Dutch Catholicism during the half-century after 1920? I argue in this chapter that in order to account for these changes, we need to analyse what was happening at three levels. The growth of religious pluralism in this instance is more than a matter of gradual evolution in close institutional structures towards a more accommodating relationship with the social environment; more, too, than a process whereby new concepts of legitimate diversity came to be forged. The pluralism which gained ground in these years was linked to an altered understanding of how human beings arrive at valid conclusions from reasoned argument.

Thus the three levels at which the changes of Dutch Catholicism should be analysed are:

1. events and processes relating to institutional functioning;
2. the meanings attached to diversity among Catholics;
3. views of how reasoning is best conducted.

Needless to say, there is an element of convenient fiction involved in my claim that is is possible to attend to any single one of these three levels of analysis independently of the other two.

The main point I want to make is that the fiction that one can do this is indeed a convenient one. That is to say, there are advantages to isolating Level 3 instead of tacitly taking it for granted in what one says about Levels 1 and 2.

All this is rather abstract. So let us first devote our attention to Level 1, and consider some of the events, processes, and institutions involved in this transition within the Roman Catholic Church in the Netherlands.

The starting-point of 1920 is a suitable one because it was during the decade of the 1920s that two institutions were founded which symbolized the kind of unitary Dutch Catholicism which preceded the changes. These are the Catholic University of Nijmegen, founded in 1923, and the Catholic Broadcasting Organization, the KRO, founded in 1926.[1] These both continue to exist today, even though the structuring of Dutch society in parallel columns or pillars is now a far less pervasive feature of life in the Netherlands than it was before the Second World War. The metaphor of columns is that which the Dutch themselves use: they refer to the structure as 'verzuiling', and to its gradual dismantling as 'ontzuiling', and they call each of the parallel components a 'zuil', a pillar.[2]

The Catholic University and the Catholic Broadcasting Organization may be regarded as the culmination of a process by which the Catholic authorities had striven to insulate their people, so far as possible, from cultural contact with the rest of the Dutch population. This strategy was a twentieth-century continuation of nineteenth-century developments which can be summarized by saying that both the strict Calvinists and the Catholics sought to minimize the influences of liberalism by creating their own institutions. These included political parties, employers' organizations, trade unions, schools, professional associations, and leisure facilities. Thanks to this system of social insulation, a Catholic need never have had social contact in any depth with a non-Catholic throughout a whole lifetime, even in the case of someone living in a predominantly non-Catholic district.

This, then, was the institutional framework of unitary Dutch Catholicism to which the finishing touches were provided during the decade my account begins with. While remaining at Level 1 of my analysis, I have three points to make about the subsequent changes. First, the system contained the seeds of its own eventual dissolution, because in a country wherein Catholics were a minority it was rendered vulnerable by its dependence on financial support from the State. Second, the system was becoming slightly more open even before the Second World War, though it was the war and the post-war era which saw it radically undermined. Third, the advent of what Pope John XXIII called 'aggiornamento' in the 1960s appeared to one section of the Dutch Catholic population as a fulfilment of trends which they had already welcomed, but many of these trends were seen by another section as fundamentally incompatible with their whole conception of the Catholic faith.

Catholics were and are a minority in the Netherlands, taken as a whole. However, within the national boundaries there are large areas in the south where they constitute an overwhelming majority. There are also substantial Catholic populations in some of the major centres of population such as Amsterdam – for reasons similar to those which account for the presence of many Roman Catholics in London or Birmingham. The overall proportion of Catholics in the Dutch population was rather more than one-third throughout the decades we are considering.[3] Partly as a result of this demographic pattern, Catholic politicians were able to strike a series of compromises with politicians representing other voting blocs in order to secure some of the resources needed for the maintenance of separate Catholic institutions. But this meant that they were, in a sense, playing a double game. They had to concern themselves both with the perceptions of their Catholic constituents and with the perceptions of non-Catholic politicians. What they emphasized when addressing themselves to Catholic perceptions was the uniqueness of the Catholic heritage. But when addressing non-Catholics, they needed to present themselves as advocates of solutions to national problems rather than merely sectional ones. Already by the 1920s, discussion of strategic issues had tended to polarize along these lines. One faction, strong in the largely Catholic areas of the south, was more interested in building upon the sense of Catholic communal identity. The rival faction, well represented in the west (in the stretch between Amsterdam and The Hague, and among Catholic intellectuals in Leiden), had a greater interest in demonstrating that Catholic social doctrines were superior to those of liberals or socialists, and thus that Catholics as fellow-citizens could point the way towards the construction of a just and harmonious society in the Netherlands.[4]

One consequence of this pressure on Catholic politicians to argue as convincingly as possible for Catholic social doctrines on their merits, rather than by appeal to authority, was that they became marginally less antagonistic, in the course of the 1930s, towards their socialist counterparts. By 1939 it had become possible for socialist Cabinet ministers to be accepted as members of a coalition government alongside Catholic ministers. Catholic social philosophy had certain affinities with the socialist vision of state planning for collective welfare. Moreover, the class composition of the Catholic population rendered it inadvisable in the long run for Catholic politicians to neglect working-class interests.[5] The German occupation of the Netherlands had a major impact on the ideological balance within the Catholic community, in the direction of enhancing the appeal of national rather than sectional perspectives. The bishops themselves decreed that the separate Catholic organizations should suspend their operations in order to avoid being used for Nazi purposes. Underground resistance brought together individuals who had previously belonged to insulated blocs and had thus been strangers to each other. However, the pre-war divisions were re-erected in 1945. This was facilitated by the fact that the Catholic parts of the Netherlands were liberated many months before the rest of the country. In post-war Dutch politics, the tendency towards accommodation between Catholic and socialist politicians came to the fore. One consequence was the formation in 1950 of the Social and Economic Council.[6] This corporatist body, created partly as a result of Catholic advocacy dating back to the pre-war period, has an advisory function similar to that of a Royal Commission in Britain; but it exists on a permanent rather than an *ad hoc* basis, and its advice is sought on a wide range of topics for legislation. Its significance in the present context is that it symbolizes the involvement of Dutch Catholic elites in the formation of national policies on major social issues. In this sense, the system of segregation can be said to have shown a tendency to become more open quite independently of the effects of the wartime occupation.

The strength of this tendency was revealed in 1954 when the bishops tried to reaffirm the desirability of Catholic separateness. They issued a pronouncement which had two aims. It was primarily a condemnation of a small group of Catholic politicians who had chosen to belong to the Labour Party instead of the Catholic Party. But the bishops also condemned other ways in which Catholics might try to diminish their cultural insulation from the wider social environment, such as membership of the Sexual Reform Society, or regular listening to broadcasts from the Socialist radio station.[7]

In the short run, this warning against internal pluralism had its intended effect. But within five years, a far more open climate of opinion had come about. To ascribe this to the advent of several new bishops in the interval is to give only a partial explanation, though this change of personnel was indeed an important factor. There was also a strongly adverse reaction to the 1954 pronouncement from many Catholic intellectuals, including some theologians at the Catholic University of Nijmegen. A study-commission was set up by the bishops in 1958 to examine how Dutch Catholic organizations should implement the principles which that pronouncement had appealed to. By the time this commission reported in 1965, there could be no question of anything but a public reversal of the 1954 policy. In the years during which the study-commission deliberated, the change which had been on the way had become thoroughly manifest. The Catholic faith was by now being expressed in new ways designed to appeal to people of a more questioning mentality than before.

Hierarchical relationships between clergy and laity were being widely criticized. Contraception was being described by a Dutch bishop on television as a practical matter for married couples to decide about for themselves rather than a moral issue where they needed guidance from the clergy. The culmination of these changes came about in the late 1960s, when a Pastoral Council was held, at which lay Catholics were given every encouragement to think of themselves as contributing to the creation of church policies.

This mention of the Pastoral Council of 1966–70 brings me to the final point in my Level 1 account of the transition in Dutch Catholicism. There has, needless to say, been a lot of opposition to the process. Those opposing the changes have refused to accept some of the pluralist features of the new Dutch Catholicism as legitimate manifestations of the Catholic faith. The year 1970 provides two instances of the clash between a more unitary and a more pluralist conception of Catholicism. One of these instances centres on the rule of clerical celibacy. In its final session, the Pastoral Council voted in favour of abolishing this rule in the Netherlands. The bishops were not willing to do more in response to the Council's vote than discuss the matter with the Pope, who predictably refused to authorize any such change. This episode emphasized that while church doctrines might be given a wide variety of interpretations, organizational practice would in certain important respects continue to follow a standardized, unitary pattern. The other instance again concerns organizational practice. The Bishop of Rotterdam retired at the beginning of 1970. The customary consultative procedures were followed as a prelude to his successor's appointment. Given the context, these procedures took on the flavour of an attempt to find which potential successor might be most widely acceptable to majority opinion among both clergy and laity in the diocese. None of the names commanding widespread local support was taken up. Instead, a conservative curate was appointed by the personal intervention of the Pope.[8] In both of these episodes, something of the older, unitary conception of Catholicism as a hierarchical structure was reaffirmed. The limits thus set to Catholic pluralism in 1970 were vigorously welcomed by the various groups of conservative Catholics who had by now begun to organize themselves. The events of 1970, taken together with the divided reaction to them, revealed the limited applicability of the term 'pluralism' to the Dutch Catholic Church since the Second Vatican Council. There is indeed a plurality of interpretations of what the Catholic faith means. But among these interpretations is a persisting assertion that no other version of Catholicism than a unitary one is legitimate.

The remainder of this paper is concerned with the distinction I began by making between explanations at three levels.

To start with, the reader will recall the purpose for which I outlined that distinction, namely as a preliminary to arguing that we can scarcely regard an account which remains at the local institutional level (Level 1) as an adequate explanation. What I have given so far is one such account. It is more than a straightforward narrative – if, indeed, one can meaningfully envisage any summary narrative of such complex processes as straightforward, in the sense of being neutral between competing explanations. It incorporates an explanatory element; but the types of explanatory factor invoked are strictly limited. The most important characteristic, for my present purposes, of this Level 1 type of account, is that it is mainly couched in terms of institutions in this one country. A richly detailed attempt to explain the transition, while remaining at Level 1, is provided by the Dutch sociologist Thurlings. He quite explicitly argues in the concluding chapter of his book that the most suitable methodological approach to the task of explaining the rapid transition that took place in Dutch Catholicism is largely to prescind from what he calls 'external factors', in favour of an explanation in terms of the internal dynamic arising from the historic confrontation of this minority group with its environment.[9] His analysis is a sophisticated one, but at the risk of drastic oversimplification it can be summarized as follows. The Dutch Catholics, like their strict Calvinist compatriots, found themselves in a socially disadvantaged position at the time when parliamentary democracy came to the Netherlands in the mid-nineteenth century. During the decades which ensued, they constructed for themselves an array of institutions for the fundamentally defensive purpose of protecting their subcultural heritage from the threat posed to it by the secular environment. By the 1960s, a new situation had arisen: their cultural identity had been so successfully defended that they were encountering a quite different sort of crisis. As Thurlings puts it, they failed to score, although they had before them an open goal; and they failed to score because they were no longer united, now that the external threat had been overcome, in the sense that the Catholic community had achieved cultural emancipation.

Against this, a Level 2 explanation would require that we invoke the changes in the world-wide Roman Catholic Church and that we also pay attention to changes in the rest of Dutch society. Broadly speaking, the explanatory power which is gained by invoking these other factors – which from the perspective of an institutional analysis like that of Thurlings are liable to appear 'external' – derives from the fact that in a cultural sense they are by no means 'external'. That is to say, even though one cannot locate these factors within the institutions of Dutch Catholicism, they nevertheless supplied crucial cultural resources which enabled diversity of beliefs and behaviour within the Dutch Catholic community to be perceived as intelligible and manageable. Admittedly, not everybody within that community did find the new diversity intelligible, as I have just pointed out: for some, it was only a church of the old style, wherein the clergy possessed paramount authority, that would make sense as a continuation of the Catholic tradition. But all over the western industrial world, the increasingly numerous Catholics with experience of higher education were for the most part interested in more flexible ways of interpreting their faith and of developing the organizational relationships which gave specific shape to it. These changes in global Catholicism were paralleled by a general reduction in public esteem for institutionally based authority among much of the Dutch population. In other words, the cultural ethos of the 1960s was more favourable to pluralist developments in any given institution such as the Catholic Church in the Netherlands. There was a widespread confidence in the viability of institutional changes in the direction of accommodating widely divergent views within one social framework, be that framework a church, a school, or a family. That kind of development may be more difficult to chart than institutional changes themselves, but it furnishes an essential part of any genuine explanation.

Taking these two levels of explanation together, it might seem as if the transition from unitary to pluralist Catholicism is adequately accounted for. Institutional means for insulating ordinary Catholics from their social environment had come to outlive their usefulness; many Catholics had become concerned to a greater extent than previously with the task of interpreting for outsiders the meaning of their own distinctive religious tradition. This switch from a defensive spirit to an open spirit in the way Dutch Catholics sought to make inherited institutions function was accompanied by external changes taking place in the culture of global Catholicism and in the wider Dutch society. Thus an analysis at Level 1, to do with institutional functioning, is complemented by an analysis at the level of cultural resources, which I have called Level 2.

Nevertheless, the idea that combining analyses at these two levels brings one as close as one can come to explaining the transition leaves me dissatisfied. Cultural change as an explanatory factor accounting for institutional change in this particular social institution still requires a mediating role to be played in the explanation, clarifying how it came about that the cultural changes of the 1960s actually altered Catholicism in keeping with the secular trend, instead of provoking a mere backlash. One way of expressing this point is to draw attention to the importance of the role of doctrine in Catholicism – and of doctrine about how doctrinal authority should be socially organized. In other words, we are dealing here with an institution which is in a variety of ways structured for purposes of teaching. True enough, the salvation offered by the Catholic Church in the late 1960s may look rather different from the salvation which it was offering in the 1920s. For instance, there is a great deal less talk now about an afterlife. But the whole shape of Catholic institutions, even after the transition, continues to reflect a rationale rooted in a set of tasks which include that of imparting doctrines, as well as those of building communitarian relationships inside and outside the church. The transition in Dutch Catholicism is, in a sense, encapsulated in the production of the new 'Cathechism for Adults' which caused much controversy by its shift of emphasis from the supernatural to the natural. But a catechism of any sort still remains a teaching device.

Therefore, if as sociologists we are to account for what happened to Dutch Catholicism between 1920 and 1970, we must attend to the alterations in the ways people deployed notions of evidence, proof, and reasoning. Authoritative teaching on the scale it was being undertaken within the Dutch Catholic community required some fairly sophisticated thinking about how to cope with questions about the underpinning of the doctrines being taught. Ultimately, we cannot afford to conduct a sociological analysis of change in Dutch Catholicism in isolation from discussions in the sociology of science and technology, in the sociology of education and of forensic investigation, and indeed in the sociology of social and philosophical analysis itself. Now, major difficulties beset any attempt at identifying common elements in all these various realms wherein people talk about 'proving' conclusions of one kind or another. And although the importance of concepts like reasoning and rationality has been widely acknowledged by sociologists since Weber, there was until 30 years ago a marked absence of detailed analyses of the social organization of systematic reasoning – a lack which has not yet been filled as systematically as it might be by comparative studies across these diverse fields of cognitive enterprise. In view of the as-yet-undeveloped state of such comparative analysis of reasoning and proof, this is not the place to enter into any great detail about what it will involve. A brief outline must suffice. But before I embark on this, I will indicate why I think that insisting on the importance of explanation at the level of organized cognition (Level 3) can help us to face up to a deep-rooted problem in the sociology of Catholicism.

The problem I am referring to is this: we have difficulty in avoiding teleological explanations which (to the extent that they pay attention to socially organized ideas about valid reasoning at all) can be accused of giving a privileged place to the ideas about reasoning that we ourselves employ as sociologists. It is all too tempting to analyse the transition from unitary to pluralist Catholicism in terms that implicitly suggest it was a foregone conclusion in the wake of rationalization, industrialization and 'modernization'. (The concepts of 'modernization' and 'modernity' are, everywhere one meets them, thoroughly vitiated by their teleological implications.) Applying this point to the question of how one explains the changes in Dutch Catholicism, I would suggest that the Catholic Church in the Netherlands appears in the kind of analysis here being criticized as something analogous to fruit on a tree: unripe in the 1920s and 1930s, ripening in the post-war years, and fully ripe for pluralist transformation by the end of the 1960s – when sociological modes of thought had become widely available through changes at the institutional and cultural level (Levels 1 and 2).

I suggest that what attracts us to explanations that have this teleological character is that very fact – that the transition itself amounted to the permeation of the church by sociological ways of thinking about the nature of evidence, proof, and reasoning. It is hard for us as sociologists to come up with explanations of a change like this which avoid teleological thinking – that is to say, which avoid presenting it as an inevitable process of growing sophistication, which any organization having intellectual pretensions on the scale that the Catholic Church has would have been bound to undergo. Yet historical explanation should not, so far as it can be avoided, be couched in terms which presuppose the unique superiority of our own patterns of thinking.

To avoid this is hard but not impossible. One advantage of trying to isolate as a separate level of analysis the task of clarifying social aspects of reasoning itself (analysis at Level 3) is that it helps towards delineating an important element in our role as sociologists: to account for the spread of sociological modes of thought about reasoning itself, without recourse to teleological explanations.

What this will require can be stated a little more specifically in

terms of the following three pairs of contrasted concepts: formalization and unpredictability; continuity and discontinuity; and
accreditation and discounting.

If we apply the first pair of concepts to the religious sphere, we
can assign the type of Catholicism found in the Netherlands in
the 1920s a position near one end of the spectrum, with, say, early
Quakerism near the other end. It is a question of how salient a
part is played by appeal to some standard format for proof in
efforts made to convince people that what they are asked to
believe is adequately supported by the appropriate kind of evidence. This has, of course, been an issue on which Christians
have been divided in ways scarcely paralleled in other religious
traditions – a fact connected with the social context of late
antiquity within which early theologies developed. Clearly, the
Reformation and the Enlightenment each in complex ways affected what was deemed by people within the Catholic tradition to
count as valid proof for the validity of doctrinal conclusions
officially endorsed by the church's authorities. The contention of
this paper is that a diffuse set of social processes occurred during
the 50-year period we are concerned with, having a similarly
complex impact on how Catholic intellectuals envisaged the task
of establishing the rationality of their beliefs. Only by examining
within a comparative framework how people's views of proof were
altering in other spheres of life where proof is seen as both desirable and attainable can such changes in Catholicism be understood
– not by analyses of the general functioning of institutions or of
cultural change in general.

The contrast between formalization and unpredictability in the
area of proof is closely bound up with the second of my three pairs
of contrasts, between continuity and discontinuity. Formalization
facilitates continuity: a well-established yardstick for judging putative proofs permits the social allocation of cognitive authority to
be organized in accordance with relatively unambiguous roles and
precedents. Now, great importance was attached to continuity in
the justification put forward for Catholic belief in the 1920s, but
the importance of appeals to continuity, though considerable,
declined during the last couple of decades in our period. I find it
implausible to suppose that this change can be adequately
accounted for without any reference to the developments in the
history and philosophy of science exemplified by Thomas Kuhn's
introductions of terms like 'paradigm-shift'.[10]

Third, I would argue that historical change of a systematic
nature could be discerned, if the task were undertaken, in the
manner in which people living at different times set about

61

identifying the social correlates of good and bad proofs. This is what I mean by saying we need an empirically based classification of modes of cognitive accreditation and discounting. Informally, we all recognize these phenomena when we see them: people are impressed by or resistant to this or that piece of reasoning on grounds which combine their assessment of its 'internal' logic with their intuitive perception of how its proponent is motivated. But I am not aware of any comparative work by sociologists analysing how these assessments and perceptions are generated and sustained in a variety of relevant contexts, or how this type of process has changed over time.

All three pairs of concepts have a bearing on the study of the changes in the Roman Catholic Church during the half-century we are concerned with. What people take 'proof' to be undoubtedly differs greatly in other spheres where the term is commonly used, by comparison with the meanings given to it in the religious sphere. So far from being a basis for saying that analyses of reasoning as a social activity should be conducted only piecemeal, this diversity can be taken as grounds for anticipating a fruitful outcome to efforts at placing this activity in a comparative context. Thus, in order to explain adequately why Catholicism both in the Netherlands and elsewhere so strikingly moved in the direction of greater pluralism between 1920 and 1970, it will be seen as necessary to go further than simply analyzing what was happening at the institutional and cultural levels, by analysing also the influence of secular trends at the level of reasoning and proof. The identification of this level of analysis as a separate one will help to protect sociologists against any tendency to assume the inevitability of changes favourable to pluralistic modes of thought which are inherent in sociology itself, and may thus contribute to awareness of the perils of teleological explanations of such changes.

Notes

1 Herman Bakvis, *Catholic Power in the Netherlands*, McGill and Queen's University Press (1981), 26. Bakvis gives a useful account of the transition, from the perspective of a political scientist. A better-known but more general book on political aspects of Dutch social structure is Arend Lijphart, *The Politics of Accommodation*, University of California Press (1968; new edn, 1975).

2 Hence the title of a major Dutch-language study of Dutch Catholicism by J. M. G. Thurlings: *De Wankele Zuil*, Nijmegen: Dekker and Van de Vegt (1971), and Deventer: Van Loghum Slaterus (1978).

3 Bakvis, *Catholic Power*, 92 and 116. In both the 1960 and the 1971

census, 40.4 per cent were recorded as Catholics; this may be compared with the 1920 census figure of 35.6 per cent and with the 1947 figure of 38.5 per cent (Centraal Bureau voor de Statistiek, *Statistisch Zakboek 1978*, The Hague: Staatsuitgeverij (1978) 69).

4 John A. Coleman, *The Evolution of Dutch Catholicism 1958–1974*, University of California Press (1978) 41–2; J. P. Windmuller, *Labor Relations in the Netherlands*, Cornell University Press (1968) 37–8; E. H. Kossmann, *The Low Countries 1780–1940*, Oxford University Press (1978) 490–1.

5 Figures on the occupational structure of the pre-war Dutch Catholic population are not available to me. But Bakvis (*Catholic Power* 49–51) cites data on educational attainment which show that the possession of a university degree was far less common among Catholics than in the rest of the population. Lijphart (*Politics of Accommodation* (1975 edn.) 26–9) found that 34 per cent of those favouring the Catholic party in a 1964 sample were blue collar workers. This was the same percentage as the percentage of blue-collar workers in the sample as a whole. Michael Fogarty, *Christian Democracy in Western Europe 1820–1953*, London: Routledge & Kegan Paul (1957), 369, gives 42 per cent as the percentage of Catholic party supporters in 1945 who were manual workers. Kossmann (*The Low Countries* 592–625) gives a useful analysis of the tensions within and between the *zuilen* during the inter-war years. Ivo Schöffer, 'De nederlandse confessionele partijen 1918–1938', in L. W. G. Scholten *et al.*, *De Confessionelen*, Utrecht: Ambo (1968), emphasizes the strongly hierarchical character of Dutch society in these years.

6 Lijphart, *Politics of Accommodation*, (1975 edn) 113–15; Bakvis, *Catholic Power*, 46; Kossman, *The Low Countries*, 596–98 and 616–18.

7 Bakvis, *Catholic Power*, 98 and 84–5; Coleman, *Evolution of Dutch Catholicism*, 55–7. On the subsequent re-thinking see Coleman, ch. 4.

8 On the appointment of Simonis see Coleman, *Evolution of Dutch Catholicism*, 262–72.

9 Thurlings, *De Wankele Zuil* (1978 edn), ch. 9, especially pp. 192–6 and 218–22.

10 Cf. T. Kuhn, *The Structure of Scientific Revolutions*, Chicago University Press (2nd edn. 1970).

6

Polytheism, monotheism, and religious co-existence
Paganism and Christianity in the Roman Empire[1]

Thomas Wiedemann

One of the things that this collection of essays has demonstrated is that the word 'pluralism' can be made to refer to a wide range of different modes of religious coexistence. What I would like to do in this chapter is suggest that those who have been ideologically committed to religious 'pluralism' in the sense in which Western Europeans have inherited it from the French Enlightenment and from English liberalism have erred in assuming that their approval ought automatically to be extended to other kinds of religious 'pluralism'.

I would like to take two late antique texts as my starting-point. The first comes from the third *Relatio* (§§. 8–10) of Symmachus, the second from the series of imperial biographies known as the *Augustan History*.

> (8)   Everyone has his own customs, his own religious practices; the divine mind has assigned to different cities different religions to be their guardians. Each man is given at birth a separate soul; in the same way each community is given its own particular genius to watch over its destiny. To this line of thought must be added the argument derived from 'benefits conferred', for herein rests the most emphatic proof to man of the existence of the gods. Man's reason moves entirely in the dark; his knowledge of divine influences can be drawn from no better source than the recollection and the evidences of good fortune received from them. If long passage of time lends validity to religious observances, we ought to keep faith with so many centuries, we ought to follow our forefathers who followed their forefathers and were blessed in so doing.
>
> (9)   Let us imagine that Rome itself stands in your presence and pleads with you thus, 'Best of emperors, fathers of your country,[2] respect my length of years won for me by the dutiful observance of rite, let me continue to practise my ancient

ceremonies, for I do not regret them. Let me live in my own way, for I am free. This worship of mine brought the whole world under the rule of my laws, these sacred rites drove back Hannibal from my walls and the Senones from the Capitol.[3] Is it true that I have been kept alive solely for the purpose of being reprimanded at my age? (10) I will see what kind of changes I think should be set on foot, but reformation of old age comes rather late and is humiliating.' Accordingly we ask for peace for the gods of our fathers, for the gods of our native land. It is reasonable that whatever everyone worships is really to be considered one and the same. We gaze up at the same stars, the sky covers us all, the same universe encompasses us. What does it matter what practical system we adopt in our search for the truth? Not by one avenue only can we arrive at so tremendous a secret. But this is the kind of case for men to put with time on their hands; at the moment it is prayers that we present to you, not debating arguments.[4]

Quintus Aurelius Symmachus was one of the wealthiest men in the Roman world in the late fourth century AD. From the summer of 384 to early 385, he held the office of Prefect of the City of Rome, *Praefectus Urbi*. This was the highest office in the late Roman Empire that was not directly part of the emperor's administration. While the Prefect was the emperor's representative at Rome (emperors during this period were normally elsewhere, at Milan or Trier in the west and Constantinople or Antioch in the east), he was also the spokesman for the senatorial class – the thousand or so wealthiest families in the empire – *vis-à-vis* the emperor. In this double capacity, Symmachus sent a number of reports, *Relationes*, to the Christian emperor Valentinian, 49 of which survive (approximately one for every four days of his prefecture).

In the third *Relatio*, Symmachus appeals to the emperor on behalf of the still-largely-pagan aristocracy of Rome to allow an altar to the goddess Victory to be set up in the Senate House (the building still exists as the NE end of the Foro Romano, since the seventh century as the Church of S. Adriano). Such an altar had originally been set up in an earlier building by Augustus after he had conquered Egypt, as a symbol – so the third century AD historian and senator Cassius Dio tells us[5] – of the superiority of Rome over any potential enemy. When the emperor Constantius, Constantine's son, visited Rome in 356 AD, he had no wish to attend a Senate whose meeting began with cult-acts honouring a pagan deity. The statue of Victory was removed. Constantius' successor Julian, whom we know as 'the Apostate', was a convinced pagan: he replaced the altar. The next emperors, Valentinian I and Valens, although Christians, left it in position: in 379, Valentinian's son Gratian rejected the title of Chief Priest, *Pontifex Maximus* – soon to be taken over by the Popes; and in 382, he went further, abolishing the privileges of pagan priesthoods, ending all grants of money from the state towards pagan ceremonies, and once again removing the altar of Victory from the Senate House. Symmachus travelled to Trier to appeal to Gratian on behalf of his pagan fellow-senators, but the emperor refused to hear his petition. Two years later, when Symmachus was Prefect of the City, the emperor had no choice but to listen to him. The ensuing appeal contained some of the standard arguments of ancient philosophers against the possibility of certainty in religious matters, as developed by the Sceptics, and in favour of the unity of God, as argued by the Stoics in particular (we may note the reference to 'debating arguments' at the end of §. 10). Most of these arguments had been introduced to Latin literature and applied to a Roman context by Cicero in his philosophical dialogues, especially the *De Natura Deorum* (On the Nature of the Gods). Aequum est, quidquid omnes colunt, unum putari: 'It is reasonable that whatever everyone worships is really to be considered one and the same.' Pagan polytheism and Christian monotheism, Symmachus seems to argue, are equally valid attempts to make sense of the divine. Uno itinere non potest perveniri ad tam grande secretum: 'Not by one avenue only can we arrive at so tremendous a secret.'

> If he had the opportunity – that is, if he was not spending the night with his wife – he would perform the divine office during the morning hours in his household shrine. Here he kept [images of] those emperors who had been deified, as well as all outstanding and holy minds; amongst them Apollonius and, according to a writer of his own times, Christ, Abraham, and Orpheus, and others of the same kind, as well as the images of his ancestors. If he did not have the opportunity, he would go out for a ride or go fishing or go for a walk or go hunting, depending upon the nature of the place where he was staying.[6]

This second passage is taken from the life of the emperor Alexander Severus (reigned 222–35) in the *Scriptores Historiae Augustae* or Augustan History. Fortunately, this is not the place for a discussion of who wrote the *Historia Augusta* and when; that problem has been a major source of activity amongst ancient historians for over a century.[7] What matters for us is that the author, writing at the end of the fourth or beginning of the fifth century AD – when the empire had become formally Christian, and public pagan ceremonies were banned – described Alexander Severus in terms of his ideal of how an emperor should behave. What was his attitude to religion? On the night of his birth, his father dreamt that he was carried up to heaven by the Roman Victory – explicitly, 'quae in senatu,' the one Gratian removed from the Senate House.[8] What about the opposition? 'He upheld Jewish privileges. He allowed Christians to exist.'[9] Most strikingly, there are his personal devotions as described in the passage quoted above. Apollonius of Tyana was a pagan miracle-worker and itinerant philosopher of the late first century AD, whose life was written up by Philostratus in the early third century in such a way as to rival the biographies of Christ in the synoptic Gospels.[10] The pagan author of the *Historia Augusta* implies that for the ideal emperor, the domestic worship of the pagan heroes Apollonius and Orpheus does not exclude respect for Judaism or even for Christianity. In s. 46, he goes still further: Alexander 'Christo templum facere voluit eumque inter deos recipere' – 'He wanted to erect a temple to Christ and enrol him among the gods', as some other deities had been formally enrolled among those gods publicly worshipped by the Roman state.

What is the modern reader to make of statements such as these?

Since the Enlightenment, a commitment to tolerance has been combined in the minds of many European intellectuals with a bitter hatred of organized Christianity as (together with absolutism) the main enemy of tolerance. Through Edward Gibbon's *Decline and Fall of the Roman Empire*, that attitude has permeated academic attitudes towards late antiquity.[11] For most scholars, it was much easier to identify with the great, aristocratic, or at least cultured, pagan writers – Symmachus, the writer of the *Historia Augusta*, others such as Macrobius – than with their Christian contemporaries Ambrose, Augustine, and Jerome, despised as intolerant, vulgar, and puritanical. Christians were perceived as the fanatical enemies of a civilized, rational, and tolerant secular state – a state, it was believed, of the same sort as that to which most western academics owed their loyalty, and their jobs.[12]

It is hardly surprising therefore that students of antiquity should have tended to interpret Symmachus' *Relatio* as one of the noblest pleas for tolerance and religious pluralism to have been written before the European Enlightenment.[13] But we all know how theoretical arguments have a habit of changing their meaning depending on the context in which the speaker uses them. Symmachus does not only argue that the divinity is one, and can be worshipped in different ways: he asks for 'peace for the gods of our fatherland, the gods who dwell amongst us'. Arguments in favour of tolerating a range of different cults *within* the framework of paganism – including pagan cults of Abraham and Jesus Christ – need not imply a readiness to tolerate Christianity as an *alternative* to paganism – pluralism as we might understand it. If the pagans of the fourth century were as tolerant as Gibbon and his successors imagined, then why had their predecessors in the third century so actively persecuted the Christians?

To answer the question in what sense pagan pluralism was able to 'tolerate' Christianity, we have to make some assessment of what polytheism meant to the polytheists. To enter the mind of a Greek or Roman pagan may ultimately be impossible; but some valid, if limited, propositions may be suggested. Most crucially, polytheism was not 'dead'. Over the last two decades or so – to a great extent as a result of the work of Peter Brown, at least as far as the English-speaking world is concerned – we have come to see how naïve it is to ascribe our superior western scepticism to the pagan aristocracy of the ancient world. That approach implied that the actual pagan cults – with their animal sacrifice, libations, oracles, prophecy, and black magic – were only 'believed in' by the benighted masses, while the educated elite had risen above such superstitions to become enlightened philosophers like Cicero or Marcus Aurelius. But we only have to look at accounts of the epiphanies of gods in classical literature[14] to realize that a wealthy and educated pagan could experience the divine as vividly as a poor and ignorant peasant – indeed, in much the same way as men in any other culture, including our own.

Pagan polytheism had not ceased to be real. In recent years more and more inscriptions have come to light, especially from Asia Minor, showing how in the second and the third centuries AD wealthy pagans continued to have direct experience of the divine, and respond to that experience by spending considerable sums of money to honour the pagan gods with shrines and festivals. New deities might appear on the scene, but that did not affect the structure of paganism. That can be seen in the way in which victorious Christianity sometimes had to come to terms with polytheistic elements in popular culture, most obviously in the cult of the saints.

Second, the question of pagan 'syncretism', the tendency to give the divinities worshipped in several different cults the same name (e.g. for Greeks to talk of Jupiter or Yahweh as the Roman or the Jewish 'Zeus'). We should beware of the idea that there was a natural or automatic progression from polytheism via syncretism to monotheism.[15] In the writings of the Neoplatonist philosophers of late antiquity, the Graeco-Roman gods might indeed be interpreted as aspects of one 'real' God; but that was a product of Neoplatonism, and not of the syncretism inherent in ancient polytheism.

The Roman empire was made up of about 1200 city units, plus a considerable number of ethnic groupings which we label 'tribes' and/or 'client kingdoms'. The divine forces worshipped in each of these units might be seen as similar, analogous, or parallel; one obvious example is the Juno, the cohesive force which gives life to any social unit, whether a family or a city-state. The Romans worshipped not only the Juno who had once belonged to their own kings – Juno Regina – but also the Junones of other states whom the Romans had invited to abandon their original communities and settle at Rome (*evocatio*: examples are the Junones of Falerii, Veii, and Carthage).[16] These Junones were parallel, but not identical, in the same way as the many Jupiters and Zeuses worshipped throughout the empire were parallel but not identical. Each cult honoured its own particular god. With our monotheist presuppositions, we may find it difficult to appreciate that divine powers which shared a common name were neither 'the same god worshipped in different ways (or places)', nor 'different aspects of the same god'. When Herodotus, in Book 2 of his *Histories*, described the Egyptian gods Amon-Ra and Osiris, he called them 'Zeus' and 'Dionysus'. He did not mean by that that 'Amon-Ra' was the Egyptian word for 'Zeus', or that the cult of Osiris and the cult of Dionysus were the Egyptian and the Greek ways of worshipping the same divinity. What he meant was that Amon-Ra and Osiris seemed to him to hold the same position in Egyptian mythology and religious practice as Zeus and Dionysus in Greek. Similarly, the allocation of Latin names to non-Roman deities did not mean that the non-Roman god was 'identified with' the Roman god in the sense of being perceived as 'the same'. For a pagan polytheist, the Celtic culture-god Lug (whose worship at the Lugnaisa-festival survived in a rather attenuated form until the beginning of this century in the form of the Irish potato-harvest on the Sunday preceding the first of August) could be perceived as fulfilling the same sorts of functions as the Roman Mercury. When, in the late first century BC, the emperor Augustus imposed a Mediterranean-type city-culture on the Gauls, his divine powers too were perceived as analogous to those of Lug; and it was entirely appropriate that the chieftains of Gaul should have worshipped Augustus as Mercury at Lyon (Lug-dunum) on the first day of August. But there was no question of 'replacing' Lug with Mercury, or treating 'Lug' as just the Celtic name for Mercury or the divine Augustus.

It is perhaps in considering the household cults of the Greeks and Romans that it is easiest for us to recognize that homonymous deities were parallel but not identical. Every one of hundreds of thousands of households might have a Hestia or a Vesta and Penates at its centre, and a Hermes or Lares at the point of contact with the outside world; but in each case these gods were peculiar to that household, parallel to but distinct from those of other households.[17]

Third, I would suggest that, in some way which it is not easy to define, the pluralism of Graeco-Roman paganism reflected that of the city-society of the Greeks and Romans (and also, it would appear, the Punic cities of North Africa). The competition for honour amongst the gods reflected the competition for prestige which was the salient feature of classical culture. Politics and citizenship – concepts which we have inherited from Greece and Rome respectively – were inextricably linked to competition for honour and glory (two words derived from Latin) or, in Greek *timē* and *doxa*. That competition might on occasion spill over into violence: normally it was channelled into peaceful rivalry, of which Greek athletics is the most obvious example (since Jacob Burckhardt's analysis of 'agonal man', it has been clear how characteristic the Olympic games were of the culture of the Greek city-state). The need to win glory by spending your wealth freely ('liberally', as a free citizen would) was central to the functioning of the ancient city. Public buildings such as baths, porticoes, aqueducts, even city walls; religious temples and shrines; the wine, meat, oil, and firewood required for the activities associated with these buildings; chariot races, wild beast shows, and gladiatorial fights; Athenian comedy and tragedy; even the upkeep of the Athenian navy – these were all gifts which wealthy citizens provided in order to win honour. In a tangible, material form that honour was given expression by the award of ceremonial crowns and in the statues and honorific inscriptions which we can still see in such large numbers when we visit any ancient site in the Mediterranean. The Greek word for these semi-voluntary contributions is *leitourgia* (liturgy), the Latin *munus*.

During the course of the second to third centuries AD, the *pax Romana* led to the gradual breakdown of this system. Centuries of peace inevitably had the effect of concentrating wealth in the hands of ever-fewer families; the Romans were not prepared to countenance the civil strife (Greek *stasis*, lit. 'standing apart') which in 'free' Greek cities so often acted as a mechanism for the redistribution of wealth from the very rich to the rest of the citizen body.[18] As members of powerful provincial families, eastern as well as western, were granted Roman citizenship and began to take part in the public life of Rome itself, a single elite society developed throughout the Roman empire. The *Constitutio Antoniniana* of 212 AD, the enactment granting Roman citizenship to all free (in effect, property-owning) persons throughout the empire, was the most spectacular instance of this process, but it is worth bearing in mind that it was a process that had already been taking place for generations. As 'Romans', these landowning families intermarried and ended up owning property throughout the Mediterranean. The effect was that as the loyalty of the rich was transferred from their local community of origin to Rome, so also their wealth was transferred to the city of Rome. Rome was the seat of the Senate, to which the thousand or so wealthiest families in the Mediterranean world belonged, and of the imperial court (later, of course, other cities became imperial residences, and the recipients of imperial expenditure; but only Rome and, after Constantine, Constantinople had senates whose members drew their wealth from throughout their respective halves of the empire).

Is there any reason to assume that this process resulted in the Mediterranean elite – from the third century on, in effect the Roman senatorial class – turning from polytheism to monotheism? The argument would be that syncretism was attractive to those who owned property in many different communities, who travelled around a great deal, who experienced the divine in a range of different temples and cult sites. This argument does not seem to me to be conclusive. Just because a Roman senator of the third century AD experienced, and worshipped, the city gods of dozens, perhaps even hundreds, of communities, that in itself would not necessarily have led him to think that all these gods were really aspects of one God. What it would have led him to think was what Symmachus said to Valentinian – that there were many ways of worshipping the divine world – and what the writer of the *Historia Augusta* believed – that there was room for all the heroes in the ideal emperor's household shrine. That these heroes might include Christ and Abraham was something that did not make sense only to a few pagan intellectuals whose writings happen to have survived. According to the Christian writer Lactantius (early fourth century), the oracle of Apollo at Claros replied to a question on how Christ fitted into the pagan pantheon by asserting his

71

divinity.[19] We should not make too much of such admissions: the oracle also stressed that Christians themselves were entirely ignorant of the real nature of their Christ, and utterly polluted. These oracles, like the words of the *Historia Augusta* and of Symmachus, were the products of a world in which the existence of Christianity could not be ignored by pagans. They do not mean that paganism was turning gradually and naturally into Christianity: they are attempts by pagans, now on the defensive, to come to terms with the existence of Christianity and to give it a place within, not alongside, the polytheist tradition.

Would Christianity have been accorded a place in a pagan world if it had not been the case that the fourth-century emperors were Christians, and Christians now held power? Judaism had been accorded such a place: although monotheistic, it was acceptable to polytheism. The oracle of Apollo of Didyma was quoted as praising the Jews' worship of the 'Creator of All', and their respect for *nomos* (law): Augustine says that the oracle was once asked by someone whether *logos* (reason) or *nomos* was the better guide to life, and the god replied *nomos*, specifically referring to the *nomoi* which Moses had given the Jews.[20] Although many Greeks and Romans despised the Jews for their peculiar superstitions, which prevented them from participating in the normal civic festivals which constituted the core of social life, the jealous Yahweh was the Jews' ancestral god, the Jupiter of Judaea. As Gibbon put it, the difference between the pagan attitude to Judaism and to Christianity was that 'The Jews were a people which followed, the Christians a sect which deserted, the religion of their fathers.'[21] Yahweh as a parallel to Jupiter was perfectly acceptable. As Iao, he was frequently called upon in pagan magical papyri, and by many Roman writers he was identified with Juppiter Sabazios, a deity of central Anatolian origin whose worship was widespread. Pagan Romans might worship Yahweh as one of the gods; they might even convert to Judaism without becoming social outcasts in their own cities. Marcel Simon's *Verus Israel*[22] reminds us that the number of converts to Judaism in the first century AD was considerable, until the sack of the Temple in 70 and the rise of the rabbis made Judaism turn in on itself, and Christianity enabled those so inclined to accept the moral code of Judaism without committing themselves to its more troublesome practices.

Christianity was not acceptable in the same way. Christians failed to participate in the ceremonies of the gods, and failed to provide the material contributions required for sacrifices.[23] But most (though not all) Jews also had reservations about participating fully in civic festivals. What marked out the Christians – and perhaps this was more important as a reason for the anxiety of pagans about Christianity – was that unlike Jews they did not accept the validity of the competition for glory and honour within the context of city-state society in the first place.

Even if very few people in the second and third century were Christians,[24] and consequently Christianity did not yet constitute a substantial material threat to the funding of civic activities, it nevertheless constituted a threat to the entire value-system of the ancient city. The persecutions of the third century AD have, I believe, to be seen in the context of the wider problems affecting the structure of the city, and the imperial government's response to that crisis.[25] The persecutions of the Christians have been discussed in much detail;[26] what is essential is that we should not conceive of an imperial 'religious policy' divorced from other aspects of imperial policy. Emperors felt that they were responsible for ensuring that cities did not 'decline', i.e. that the basic public ceremonies of the city community continued to be performed with due regularity: and those ceremonies were pagan. Decius' edict, issued in December 249, ordered that sacrifices be performed in every city of the empire, supervised by commissioners chosen by local councils. Decius' legislation should not be explained in political terms, as a reaction against supposed Christian support for his predecessor Philip the Arab.[27] Decius cared personally about restoring the cults of the gods: the city of Cosa in Etruria honoured him as *restitutor sacrorum*.[28] A few years later, in 257, Valerian's persecution imposed death and exile as penalties for Christians of the higher classes, recognizing the special role of bishops within the Christian communities. The final persecution was Diocletian's. Several years of personal hostility to Christians culminated in the famous edict of 23 February 303; again, we should not lose sight of the fact that anti-Christian edicts were only one aspect of imperial attempts to regulate in order to preserve all the institutions of the city community.[29]

It has already been mentioned that the *pax Romana* had the inevitable and entirely unintended effect of siphoning wealth away from most of the 1200-odd cities of the Mediterranean world, and concentrating that wealth in the residences of emperors and Senate. (Much of it, of course, went on the army and on wars, civil and defensive.) As fewer and fewer wealthy men were left in local communities, the burdens of political life began to outweigh the benefits of winning glory and honour: by the third century it was beginning to be difficult to find candidates for civic magistracies. This, rather than civil war or barbarian invasion, was what threatened the classical city in the third century AD, and it was that 'crisis' that emperors felt they had an obligation to try to solve through legislation.[30]

Christians had not just abandoned the pagan gods: they had abandoned the Graeco-Roman city in favour of the heavenly Jerusalem. For pagans, life was concerned with the pursuit of glory: for Christians, that was mere vainglory (and we find a number of fourth-century Christian tracts dealing with that particular vice). In the pursuit of glory, pagans provided liturgies for the benefit of their fellow-citizens: for Christians, the divine liturgy was not one particular kind of civic liturgy, but an alternative to the provision of liturgies for the secular city. (We may note that one of the earliest privileges which Constantine granted the Christian Church, in 313 AD, was to release the clergy of the province of Africa from the obligation to provide *munera*.) Tertullian promised his readers a greater spectacle than any magistrate could provide from his bounty, more enjoyable than the circus, the amphitheatre, or any athletic stadium – the coming of the new city of Jerusalem.[31] The Christian simply did not identify with his local community. His substitute for a community – Greek *ekklēsia*, (popular assembly) – was the universal *ekklēsia*, the Church.

It might also be worth noting that Christian church organization denied the two basic principles of office-holding in the classical city: collegiality and the rotation of offices. These only made sense because the ancient city was pluralist: many citizens competed for office and status – so no single individual ought to monopolize such office (that would have made him a tyrant: compare the problems faced by Roman emperors in masking their monarchical position). But the Christian bishops, when they emerged in the early second century AD, were not magistrates, but monarchs within their communities, like the fathers of secular households (including the pagan philosophical 'schools'); or perhaps more correctly, like the bailiffs who managed particular estates on behalf of the heavenly Lord. Each church had only one (leaving aside the irregularities brought about by schism), and he was chosen for life. If some Christians today are uneasy at the fact that episcopacy does not accord with current political or social principles, they might remember that it was just as peculiar in the context of the pluralism and competition for office-holding of the classical city. For Christians, competition shifted to competition for holiness. 'Do you want to watch boxing and wrestling matches? Then behold impurity thrown by chastity, perfidy killed by faith, cruelty crushed by pity, impudence thrown into the shade by modesty: these are our contests, the contests in which we win our crowns.'[32] The very names 'monk' and 'anchorite' show that these holy men stood outside the life of the city: they are derived respectively from Greek *monakhos* (one who lives alone) and *anakhorēsis* (literally 'getting up and going'), originating as words to describe those who left the city in order to avoid having to hold office or provide liturgies.[33] Christian asceticism, particularly in its attitude to sex and procreation, was an integral aspect of the denial of the city of this world, a rejection of the most personal and intimate social bonds between husband and wife, and parent and child.[34]

The evidence suggests that pagan writers only tolerated Christianity by giving it a place within the framework of their own 'pluralist' system when, with the appearance of Christian emperors, they could no longer ignore it. The intolerance of pagan intellectuals before the fourth century did not arise because Christianity was monotheistic; so was Judaism, and monotheistic ideas had long been accepted by pagan philosophers, and became popular amongst intellectuals with the Neoplatonists Porphyry and Plotinus in the late third century.[35] The underlying reason for the pagans' justified suspicion of Christianity arose because it threatened the pluralism of political life in the ancient city. In that respect, it was not alone as an ideological threat: similar challenges were posed by the religion of Mani in late antiquity, but also – in the classical period – by Epicureanism. Because the Epicureans argued that the supreme aim of man was a life free from anxiety (Greek *ataraxia*), it followed that the anxieties of political life, the struggle for status and office, must be avoided at all costs.[36] Like Christianity, Epicureanism aroused strong emotions: Epicureans as well as Christians were falsely accused of hedonism and atheism. What was ultimately unacceptable about both groups was that they denied the validity of a competitive political life. In practice, of course, Christians and Epicureans could be tolerated so long as they desisted from making an issue of their beliefs.

I began this paper by suggesting that there were differences between the pagan religious 'pluralism' of late antiquity and liberal 'pluralism'. Let me end by suggesting a similarity. A liberal society can, up to a point, tolerate even orthodox or traditionalist adherents of Christianity, Judaism, and Islam: it cannot find a place for a Christian, Jewish, or Moslem *society*. The social and political pluralism of Graeco-Roman paganism could accommodate the Christian God Jesus within its pantheon: but it could not contemplate a social order that was based on Christian values.

Notes

1 Recent years have seen a considerable number of studies of the religious and social environment of Christianity during the first four centuries. For the pre-Constantinian period, the reader may be referred to the detailed bibliographies in Robin Lane Fox, *Pagans and Christians*, Harmondsworth: Penguin (1986). English translations of most of the Greek and Latin authors cited can be found in the Penguin classics or the Loeb Classical Library.

2 Symmachus' *Relationes* were formally addressed to both members of the College of Emperors, Theodosius in the East as well as Valentinian in the West (Gratian had been killed in 383).

3 Hannibal invaded Italy during the Second Punic War, 218–202 BC; the Senones, one of the Celtic tribes of northern Italy, attacked (and according to some versions, not surprisingly ignored by Symmachus, captured) Rome in 390 BC (trad. date).

4 Symmachus, *Relatio* 3, 8–10. The translation is (with some alterations) that of R. H. Barrow, *Prefect and Emperor*, Oxford University Press (1973).

5 Dio Cassius, 51. 22.

6 *SHA* 18: Alexander Severus, 29. 2.

7 R. Syme, *Historia Augusta Papers*, Oxford University Press (1983), and many others.

8 *SHA* 18, 14. 2.

9 *SHA* 18, 22. 4: 'Iudaeis privilegia reservavit. Christianos esse passus est.'

10 There is a trans. by C. P. Jones, Hamondsworth: Penguin (1970).

11 Vol. 1 appeared in 1776. In summary, Gibbon believed that the philosophical education of the Roman elite gave them an enlightened and sceptical attitude to pagan religion which enabled them to control the superstitions of the lower classes; the Stoic emperor Marcus Aurelius (reigned 161–80) was Gibbon's hero because he was the nearest thing to an Enlightenment *philosophe*. The decline of ancient civilization represented 'the triumph of barbarism and religion'. Some of the choicest attacks on Christianity are to be found in ch. 15 of *Decline and Fall* ('The progress of the Christian religion . . .').

12 We may note how a basic textbook such as Schanz-Hosius, *Handbuch der römischen Literatur*, arranges late antique writers into the two categories 'Die nationale Litteratur' and 'Die christliche Litteratur'. This division reflects not only the polarity between Rationalism and Christianity, but also between Bismarck's liberal nationalism and Roman Catholicism in the Germany of the *Kulturkampf*. The assumption that Christianity and classical culture were mutually exclusive persists: e.g. C. W. Fornara's view that late-antique culture was confined to a 'group of intellectuals, pagans all' (*The Nature of History in Ancient Greece and Rome*, University of California Press, (1983)).

13 In his highly satirical account of Symmachus' third *Relatio* in ch. 28, Gibbon characteristically pretends to believe that the truth of

Christianity is self-evident, and ascribes weak arguments and even fanaticism to the conservative pagan: 'the dying embers of freedom were, for a moment, revived and inflamed by the breath of fanaticism'. The arguments he ascribes to Symmachus and Ambrose are largely those of orthodox Christians and Deist rationalists respectively in his own time. Twentieth-century scholars have been explicit in their approval of both the Symmachus and the *Historia Augusta* passages: cf. A. H. M. Jones, *The Decline of the Ancient World*, London: Longman (1966), 352: 'His plea for the Altar of Victory is deeply moving'; Jo-Ann Shelton, *As The Romans Did*, Oxford University Press (1988), 393, refers to a 'poignant plea for tolerance'; A. D. Momigliano, 'Pagan and Christian Historiography in the Fourth Century AD', in *The Conflict between Paganism and Christianity in the Fourth Century*, Oxford University Press (1963), 94 f.: 'The pagans were bound to be prudent – and their mood was altogether that of a generous and fair-minded liberalism. The *Historia Augusta* is by no means the big anti-Christian pamphlet which some scholars have seen in it. On the contrary, the ideal emperor Severus Alexander worships Jesus with Abraham in his private chapel.'

14 e.g. in Ovid's *Fasti* or Artemidorus of Daldis' *Dream Book*. Cf. Robin Lane Fox, *Pagans and Christians*, 102 ff., ch. 4, 'Seeing the gods'. Peter Brown's books on fourth-century religion include *Religion and Society in the Age of St. Augustine*, London: Faber & Faber (1972); *The Making of Late Antiquity*, Harvard University Press (1978); *The Cult of the Saints*, London: SCM (1981).

15 For the view that syncretism led naturally to monotheism see (e.g.) R. MacMullen, *Constantine*, Beckenham: Croom Helm (1987), 69.

16 R. E. A. Palmer, *Roman Religion and Roman Empire*, University of Pennsylvania Press (1975), 3–56, ch. 1: 'Juno in Archaic Italy'.

17 On Lug/Mercury, cf. G. Webster, *The British Celts and their Gods under Rome*, London (1986), 33 f. On Hermes, cf. R. Osborne, 'The erection and mutilation of the Hermai', *Proceedings of the Cambridge Philological Society* 211 (1985), 47–73.

18 Plutarch's essay, *Praecepta gerendae reipublicae* (How to be a politician), trans. in the Loeb edn of the *Moralia*, vol. 10, 159 ff., gives us an insight into the constraints on political activity by Greeks under Roman rule.

19 Lactantius, *Divinae institutiones*, 1, 7; cf. Eusebius, *Demonstratio evangelica*, 3, 6, and Augustine, *City of God*, 19, 23. 2.

20 Augustine, *City of God*, 19, 23; cf. Lactantius, *De ira Dei*, 23, 12.

21 Gibbon, *Decline and Fall*, vol. 2, ch. 16.

22 English trans. by H. McKeating, Oxford University Press (1986).

23 Cf. e.g. Tertullian, *De spectaculis*, on the reasons why Christians must not participate at city-festivals (Loeb trans. by T. R. Glover, 1931).

24 Even in the largest communities like Rome only a few thousand: according to Eusebius, *Historia ecclesiastica*, 6, 43. 11, the Roman church looked after just 1500 widows and poor people in 251 AD.

25 R. MacMullen, *The Roman Government's Response to Crisis*, Yale University Press (1976).
26 For a straightforward account, W. H. C. Frend, *Martyrdom and Persecution in the Early Church*, Oxford: Blackwell (1965). G. E. M. de Ste. Croix, 'Why Were the Early Christians Persecuted?', *Past and Present* 26 (1963), 6 ff., remains basic.
27 For the evidence that Philip had Christian associations, cf. Irfan Shahid, *Rome and the Arabs*, Dumbarton Oaks (1984), 65 ff.
28 R. Syme, *Emperors and Biography*, Oxford University Press (1971), 195–8. Decius' wife came from Etruria.
29 The main source of information about imperial legislation aimed at preserving city institutions is the *Theodosian Code* (English trans. by C. Pharr, New York: Greenwood (1952)), promulgated by the western emperor Theodosius II in 438 AD. The Code contains no pre-Constantinian material, and naturally there are no edicts favouring pagan cults. Nevertheless, it gives us an impression of the sheer weight of legislation aiming to support the institutions of the ancient city: cf. (e.g.) Book 12 title 1, containing 192 edicts pertaining to city councillors ('Decurions').
30 The best account of the problems of the ancient city that I know remains that of A. H. M. Jones, *The Greek City from Alexander to Justinian*, Oxford University Press (1940; repr. 1979).
31 Tertullian, *de spectaculis*, 30: 'Quis tibi praetor aut consul aut quaestor aut sacerdos de sua liberalitate praestabit? . . . Credo, circo et utraque cavea et omni stadio gratiora.' 'Qualis civitas nova Hierusalem.' The idea that Christians were merely 'temporary residents' of the cities in which they happened to be living is already to be found in the *First Epistle of Clement* at the end of the first century.
32 Tertullian, *De spectaculis*, 29: 'Vis et pugilatus et luctatus? . . . Aspice impudicitiam deiectam a castitate, perfidiam caesam a fide, saevitiam a misericordia contusam, petulantiam a modestia adumbratam, et tales sund apud nos agones, in quibus ipsi coronamur.'
Cf. H. Chadwick, *The Early Church*, Harmondsworth: Penguin (1968).
33 D. J. Chitty, *The Desert a City*, Oxford: Blackwell (1966).
34 H. Chadwick, 'Enkrateia', *Reallexikon für Antike und Christentum*, (1962), 343–65; Lane Fox, *Pagans and Christians*, ch. 7.
35 The development of monotheistic ideas by Neoplatonist intellectuals is, in my view, a separate issue which need not be discussed here (see p. 75 above). The 'Apostate' Emperor Julian both expressed himself in monotheistic terms, and favoured the God of the Jews.
36 Cf. the beautiful description of the philosopher watching the politician drown in the storm of public life at the beginning of Book 2 of Lucretius' Epicurean epic 'On the Nature of Things' (*De rerum natura*).

III
Theoretical perspectives

7

Theological pluralism
A sociological critique

Kieran Flanagan

> For if the trumpet give an uncertain sound,
> who shall prepare himself to the battle?
>
> (1 Cor. 14: 8)

In contemporary theology the term 'pluralism' has been magnified in a manner some sociologists might find perplexing. A blessing has been conferred on a wide range of cultural and religious practices. Their right to coexist has been endorsed by some theologians, who argue that diversity of affiliation leads to a mutual enrichment in a common quest for life in the divine. In its most radical form, pluralism leads to confessional positions being discounted in the interests of maximizing an openness to the holy, in which all are called and all are chosen. No religion is allowed to claim a privileged form for addressing God. All religious beliefs are deemed to have an equivalence in gaining successful access to the rewards of afterlife. They share a common capacity to generate a religious phenomenon that has the dual advantage of binding all in harmony, but in a way that permits scrutiny by adherents of a new academic discipline – Religious Studies.

Doubt before diversity is given a theological status. A liberating agnosticism is believed to permit entry to an infinite range of paths to the truth. This embodies a certainty that pluralism is a necessary option in a world riven by religious intolerance. Dogmatism and confessional claims are deemed to be illiberal and unenlightened emblems of past ages, relics of a political imperialism when misguided missionaries sought to convert the heathen to the ways of a western form of Christianity.

Pluralism has come to be used in a bewildering variety of theological positions that range from the mildly liberal to the radical. The more radical and recent expressions of pluralism have been associated with theologians such as John Hick and the contributors to *The Myth of God Incarnate*. The exclusive claims of Christianity are denied, and a leap of faith is made into the field of comparative religion. Buddhism seems to have a particular attraction, for it offers an endless basis for search through its scriptures, without the misfortune of arriving at some binding truth. Confessional positions are regarded as unscientific and restrictive. For Hick, religious affiliations represent outdated tribal ties stamped with the badge of pride, which lead to persecution and intolerance, and which impede doctrinal dialogue between different faiths. An arrogance of certainty shapes the unacceptable face of Christianity for theologians, such as Hick and Smart, who found the comprehensiveness of Anglicanism both a limiting and an inadequate expression of the truth. The development of an interest in pluralism, that gave a liberal assent to the diversity of truth conditions of non-Christian religions, coincided with a radical theology that started with notions of the death of God and approached questions regarding the Virgin Birth and the Resurrection in terms of myth. The domestic uncertainties generated within Anglicanism by such theological adventures led to a receptive climate for pluralism, and to the realization that the issue of truth might lie elsewhere, outside the walls of Christianity.[1]

A more explicitly ideological endorsement of pluralism has been made by liberal theologians in Ireland. They have argued that pluralism should be reflected in the constitution of the state, so that no religion is given a privileged or confessional status. Civil liberties of all religious traditions should be enshrined in a secular constitution. In this theological view, pluralism is regarded as an instrument of reconciliation in a society whose divisions represent a scandal in Christianity. This form of theological pluralism came to be regarded as a political necessity.

Another form has emerged in Catholicism, which shares with the other versions a definite goal. Since the Second Vatican Council (Vatican II), the issue of pluralism has become a central concept in pastoral efforts of the church to open out a dialogue with the world and all its cultures and traditions. There is an increasing concern with infusing the cultural with qualities of faith. This theological recognition of the cultural has coincided with a growing awareness of the need to represent a diversity of societies within a church that claims to be Catholic and universal. Pluralism has become part of a pastoral strategy to maintain unity within this cultural diversity in a fine balance of faith. In this theological form, pluralism is regarded as a means of representing the cultural margins of the church in a manner that will amplify its credibility in an increasingly secular world. The issue of pluralism has been raised in the context of a long-standing problem in the church over how to reconcile authentic and traditional forms of worship with their reception in a diversity of alien cultures. Symbols and actions based on the assumptions of western culture might seem incredible and could be a hindrance to grasping the essence of the faith in other contexts. Issues of cultural diversity existed in another form in the history of missionary work in the church. The term 'pluralism' is a secular term appropriated by theologians at the height of its fashion in the social sciences in the 1960s. It is a new means of expressing an age-old problem in the life of the church, how to plant the faith in alien cultures.

A lot of redundant and outdated sociological baggage has become attached to the term, and theologians using it have taken into the issue of religious belief a number of unnecessary ideological complications. Pluralism is very much part of the heritage of the Enlightenment, representing a reasoned demand for tolerance before a diversity of cultural, ethnic, and political forms. The term contains an ideological imperative, a belief that the rationality of its proclamation will lead to a harmonization of difference and an ending of conflict and intolerance. There is an eschatological basis to the term in its theological, sociological and ideological forms of expression. As a sociological term, it was launched in a time of optimism that characterized the late sixties. It was part of the rhetoric of a particular generation, when hope sprang eternal in a utopian period when concept and ideology merged, and terms such as 'pluralism' became catch-phrases of the market. The cultural emphasis on self-emancipation and group solidarity of the late sixties left a mark on theological and liturgical expectations. The issue of pluralism became embedded in the question of the democratic rights of the People of God in Catholicism. It was also attached to American perceptions of how the church ought to grow. Democratic values found expression in this Catholic emphasis on pluralism, for this new theology complemented a peculiarly American stress on freedom of religions that was enshrined in its constitution.[2]

Pluralism was a child of an age, conceived in a climate of ideological optimism, almost 20 years ago, when the present generation of students was born. High hopes surrounding its delivery sank in the seventies into more prosaic issues such as ecology and feminist rights, when an ideology of grab dominated the middle classes who could reach for the better rhetoric and an approved lifestyle. In the more pessimistic eighties, a fundamentalism and a conservative concern with more traditional certainties came into effect, leaving the issue of pluralism as a rather outdated relic of a time when differences were to be tolerated. Many theologians still have an undue nostalgia for the golden olden days of the sixties, when ideologies were less lean and mean than now. They have been reluctant to abandon the term 'pluralism' which sociologists jettisoned rapidly, being more used to coining prophecies in the cultural market and being closer to its ideological movements.

If theologians had simply latched on to an outmoded concept in sociology, one would not be too worried. They have done this frequently. Unfortunately, they have come to use the term 'pluralism' to represent all questions about how the cultural is to be linked to faith. This ideology has become a substitute for a deeper and more critical sociological analysis about how cultural properties are to be geared to realize a social sense of religious belief. To overstress the incarnational properties of a diversity of cultures carries a price of obscuring the need to manage the social in some way that will allow it to listen to the transcendent. At some point, a limit has to be placed on the cultural, if it is not to slide into the meaningless. Both are sides of God, and one is incomplete without reference to the other. By overstressing the incarnational, a cerebral theology has been proclaimed, one that is deeply concerned with communal relations, but neglects those elements which give the cultural a meaningful significance. A misuse of pluralism has flattened the cultural landscape and has left no gaps in which the holy may resonate. The term disguises a necessary ambiguity in the relation between the transcendent and the incarnational. By failing to specify what is plural about the cultural, it has managed to confuse a failure of an analysis with a mystery it seeks to proclaim. There is a mysterious diversity in the cultural, a sense of opening that admits the incarnational; but equally important is the distinctive capacity in a culture selectively to close off some of its aspects, in a formal ritual, to admit access to a felt sense of mystery.

An emphasis on the diversity of cultures obscures the plurality of meanings that emerge when the social is harnessed to proclaim the holy. Paradoxically, when the social is disciplined into a harmonized order that contains all manner of tensions within, and also limits a diversity of ritual practice, it generates a curiosity that invites the actor to listen and to become liberated before a sense of the holy. Far too much attention has been devoted to opening rituals out to their cultural surroundings, and not enough to the selective means through which the social is to be domesticated in order to hear the transcendent. It is what marks liturgical practices off from the cultural that gives them a distinctive theological and sociological significance. The plurality of meanings these rites give off are far more important than the pluralism of their forms in a wide variety of social settings.

In this chapter I wish to argue that the term 'pluralism' obscures more than it reveals about the link between cultural and religious beliefs. Sociological concepts can become overloaded with expectations in a way that blunts their capacity to make subtle analytical distinctions. For instance, the term 'community' has so many definitions in sociology that it can only be used with great caution.[3] Theologians seldom place sociological concepts within their theoretical frame of reference, in order to examine the genesis of a term and the reasons for its qualified use. Too often, theologians transfer subtle sociological terms into simplified instruments of evangelization where the ambiguities of a concept are neglected.

Pluralism poses particular and complex difficulties within sociology. The diversity and comparison which theologians feel the term expresses are also the domain concerns of the discipline. Sociology is concerned with the interpretation and significance of cultural differences, and with their meaningful implications. Diversity of social condition might form the end of a theological question, but for sociology it can only be a beginning. As a discipline, sociology is concerned with resolving significant differences within the social, and not with postponing their resolution. Pluralism as a term serves so many constituencies of use and meaning as to impair its theoretical viability. More importantly, many of these are ambiguous and contradictory. Within contemporary sociology, 'pluralism' is regarded as a product of the ideological shifts in the 1960s, one that expressed the need for harmony in diversity. The term became discredited in sociology because it disguised the 'real' basis of power and more importantly, was incapable of discriminating between the significant and the insignificant in the diversity it was claimed to affirm within the cultural.

The issues pluralism raised have evolved into a philosophical consideration of the incommensurability of meanings within a diversity of belief-systems. The relativism of efforts to translate and to reconcile often contradictory meanings that emerged from a range of cultural conditions generated a concern with the hermeneutic implications of social actions and how they are to be rendered to theoretical account. Pluralism was a primitive term that has now been bypassed, as theoretical debates are increasingly concerned with providing authentic interpretations and understandings of meanings in a diversity of cultures, whose presuppositions are often mutually contradictory.[4]

It is ironical that a term which became so devalued in sociology was appropriated by theologians in the late sixties and has been so misused ever since. There has been a particular failure in debates on theological pluralism to confront the issue of diversity of practice, such as in ritual actions, where agnosticism will not do and where some form of regulation is required to express the authentic basis of a belief-system. The idea of an unfettered opening to the holy, where the social mechanism is left unregulated, violates elementary assumptions in sociology about the nature of religious life. By disguising the basis of choice in ritual enactment, theologians who endorse an uncritical version of pluralism ignore issues of praxis in their belief-systems. Praxis presupposes selection and, without some principle of choice in ritual enactment, it is difficult to understand how a rite might proceed in terms available to sociological understanding.

In this chapter, it is argued that the term 'pluralism' disguises significant problems of diversity and competition in the enactment of rites within Catholicism. There is a reductionist aspect to pluralism that gives a misleading equivalence to elements of meaning that are inherently incompatible. This precludes the very choice that theological pluralism so warmly affirms, a point that especially arises in the case of the performance of liturgy. If pluralism affirms a diversity of rite, one has to assume some basis upon which these different forms can be evaluated. It cannot be argued that ultimately these differences in ritual form do not count, for if this were the case then the justification for a pluralist position would collapse. We have to assume that social differences that are marked within a ritual *do* make a difference. Paradoxically, theologians who use the term to resist the pressures of what they perceive to be a contemporary cultural imperialism often end up perpetuating it in another form. The main victims of a pluralist position have been the weak and the working class in whose name this 'democratic' theology is proclaimed.

Pluralism leads to a demystification of rite, for by continually exercising a choice within a diversity of possible options, a reductionist position emerges. As von Balthasar suggests, the mystery of the church cannot be reduced to a single conceptual formula. Stressing the contradictions of Catholicism rather than its contrasting qualities leads to an unnecessary fragmentation of belief.[5] By comparing the differing forms of use of pluralism within sociology and theology, and centering this discussion around the problem of a diversity of liturgical forms within Catholicism, it will be argued that the term is misleading and that theologians and liturgists should abandon its use.

In sociology, the term 'pluralism' relates to issues of the

distribution of power and its political forms of accountability in democratic society. The term is also used to examine the diversity of ethnic groups and their fair representation in significant social institutions. It is also connected to the question of fragmentation of social forms under the pressures of rationality and modernization. In political sociology, the term is concerned with the problem of the dispersal of state power. It has been argued that competition between elites ensures an openness of accountability for their decision-making in the institutions of the state. But the difficulty with the term is that it has an ambiguous relationship to the issue of political power. It can suggest that elite formations are a necessary characteristic of democracy, and that a pluralist regime ensures a degree of competition that mitigates this natural right to rule. This conservative reading has to be qualified by a radical interpretation which argues that a pluralist ideology disguises the 'real' basis of power. The capacity to conceal 'hidden agendas' of decision-making means that a pluralism geared to maximize a diversity of response and participation can also weaken the basis of informed democratic redress. Thus, in a Marxist sense, pluralism is an ideology of containment that misleads in the information it reveals about how control is exercised. In this sense, pluralism serves to disguise forces of dominance and to perpetuate an inegalitarian state of affairs. Pluralism represents a façade that masks the 'real' basis of power held in the state.[6] As Bourdieu and Passeron note, the capacity to disguise the basis of power gives its exercise a particular symbolic force to effect and maintain its legitimacy.[7]

Kariel has observed that 'political pluralism as an ideology has lost most of its explicit apologists and only lingers quietly as a submerged, inarticulate ingredient of Western liberalism'.[8] This low status to the term is reflected in the brief uses of it made in introductory sociology texts, where its liberal claims to effect a diffusion of power are met with a high degree of critical scepticism.[9] The term 'pluralism' also arises in race relations, but in a very limited way. The growth of a comparative awareness of diversity of custom, religious belief, and ethnic identity generated a brief interest in pluralism as a means of defending and accounting for differences.[10] The need to have a separate but equal form of pluralism for differing ethnic groups in a society has unacceptable implications which even the most conservative of theologians would reject. Proclamation of an equality with diversity is likely to invite a high degree of sociological scepticism as to the ideological functions of such political utterances, a point that also applies to its theological use.

Within Theology and Religious Studies, the term has taken a different career of meaning, being very much the product of a radical rather than a conservative fringe. It is given an unambiguous status. Diversity is believed to be related to a notion of equality before God. There are, however, a number of domestic reasons peculiar to Theology and Religious Studies that account for its popularity. The mushroom-growth of Religious Studies departments in the United Kingdom coincided with an emphasis on theological pluralism in the late sixties. Immigration of a variety of ethnic groups with diverse religious affiliations seemed to demand a pluralist theological approach, one that would provide a non-judgemental comparative account of non-Christian religions. The journey eastwards of many radical students in the late sixties accelerated an interest in Buddhism. These elements combined to give a stress on a non-judgemental approach. A quest for tolerance and an openness to all major forms of belief in God led to an uneasy alliance between liberal theologians and academics in Religious Studies departments, which stressed the objective scientific qualities of the study of religion. Pluralism seemed to operate in the context of a contradiction, between those who believed that diversity reflected the subjective inclinations of the sincere, and those who adopted a comparative approach that rendered belief subject to a scientific scrutiny. In both cases the issue of ultimate truth was problematic. In the former case, a religious fundamentalism came to reject such a liberal approach to truth, and in the latter, the influence of Kuhn and the debate on scientific paradigms seemed to obscure its possibility.

The scientific approach claimed for the objective study of religion is part of a paradigm, a belief-system which contains its own set of cultural and subjective presuppositions. The quest by liberal theologians for a pluralism of belief disguises the ideological reasons why they themselves have come to affirm such a position. An unanswered question is how a sociology of knowledge could be applied to liberal theology itself. Its practitioners might well succeed in defending doubt as an acceptable theological option, but it cannot be deemed a credible sociological position. If Religious Studies is a paradigm, a belief-system in itself, it becomes caught up in issues of choice and cultural biography. The question of error lies at the root of paradigm-changes, and conversion has been the term that characterizes a movement of affiliation. An elementary sociological question would involve grounding liberal theological formulations within their cultural context of manufacture, use, and marketing.

The 'world-view reflection' of Smart's approach to comparative

Religious Studies seems to admit anything in an agnostic blessing of diversity, affirming anything except the more traditional and exclusive claims of Christian theology. He suggests, that the 'theological establishment is therefore, a problem in that it is a kind of conceptual albatross round the neck of religious studies'.[11] It could be said that Religious Studies is a minor parasite in theology departments. The assertion by those involved in religious studies that they can make non-confessional scientific statements about religious belief is unpersuasive, and is a form of wishful thinking that is deceiving, as well as being misleading in sociological terms.

It suggests some transcendent scientific position where objective arbitration can be made of differing claims to truth in a godlike manner. It represents an insecure position, and one difficult to sustain in present academic and cultural circumstances. Wiebe has pointed to a recent 'failure of nerve' in the study of religion, where confessional stances are creeping back.[12] In a companion essay, Neusner makes an odd point that theological and secular enemies of Religious Studies trivialize religion by emphasizing its private nature, and remove it from the realm of the social.[13] But the reverse point could be made that adherence to a pluralist non-confessional approach to the study of religion removes it from the realm of the sociological.

In wider sociological terms, the non-confessional claims of Religious Studies are confessional in that they are ideological. They represent forms of belief geared to effect a certain dominance. They advance a particular claim that no single religious position can be regarded as privileged. But their own scientific approach to religion reflects a belief-system in itself, which cannot be exempt from sociological scrutiny. It invites a 'hermeneutic of suspicion' as to the 'real' reasons for their retreat into a well-disguised position that converts a theological agnosticism into a scientific certainty. By defending an objective rational position, they are ignoring the degree to which inter-subjective transaction characterizes exchange within and between belief-systems, a point that particularly applies to religion. Admitting a subjective aspect to religious belief draws scientific practitioners into a relativist position, one that demands they look at their own pre-suppositions in approaching the question. There is an increased recognition of a hermeneutic consideration in understanding social actions. Increasingly, it is believed that the questioner is bound into the answer being sought. A narrow scientific defence of pluralism disguises this need to have a confessional position. The basis of the theological choice is often obscured.

The idea that a phenomenon can be studied without ideological commitment is difficult to defend in the light of the development of engaged critical forms of sociology such as those produced by Marxists and feminists. Studies that claim to be disengaged and to be above the ideological are regarded as misleading. Many aspects of contemporary critical theory assume an engagement with their subject-matter, where the sociologist is implicated in what he pronounces about matters that are deemed ideological. The same point can be made about the study of religious belief, if an empathetic understanding is to be realized. To study religion without a confessional position is deceiving and precludes an authentic understanding being realized. Many in Religious Studies act as gelded observers, to misuse Gerald Manley Hopkins, eunuchs of the times, unable to adapt a missionary position to convert. They bear an ideological fig-leaf of pluralism that disguises a missing instrument – a capacity to engage in belief.

Adherence to a pluralist position allows those in Religious Studies to postpone the issue of revealing their position, and their agnosticism disguises a hostility to those who occupy confessional positions within Christianity. The danger of this non-confessional position is that it has become embedded in the secondary school curriculum. An array of ritual practices of about five religions are grouped under conceptual areas, such as rites of passage, symbols, and roles. It is difficult to comprehend how such an artificial classification according to analytical types can add up to an understanding of religious belief. Any religion requires a commitment, and a pseudo-scientific approach that disguises and complicates this need for engagement is difficult to comprehend, except in terms of debasing its subject-matter.

An explicitly confessional position is unremarkable in contemporary sociology, and if a sociologist is a Catholic, he is far more likely to be misunderstood by theologians than by his colleagues.[14] One is sympathetic to Nichols's claim that if 'studiousness were not rooted in Christian faith attempts to write theology would be epistemologically defective'.[15] There is an inter-subjective element in the relationship between a believer and his Master that generates a sense of understanding difficult for a non-believer to grasp. Meanings are enhanced, and hidden properties of ritual, symbol, and action are discerned in a way difficult to account for in explicit terms. Quoting from von Balthasar, Nichols suggests correctly that a 'theology on one's knees' facilitates this capacity to connect and to see into the unseen.[16] Without a religious commitment, it is difficult to believe what is said, or to say what it is to believe. In the introduction to the collection of essays on

Religion and America, Robert Bellah notes the marginality of Religious Studies departments in American society, and scepticism over whether it can be treated as a genuine field of study or as a discipline.[17]

Pluralism is corrosive because it postpones the question of authority and certainty and leaves these to market forces. The growth of a fundamentalism in Islam and in American evangelicalism indicates the dangers of leaving the formation of religious beliefs to the market-place. The dramatic changes in religious belief between the 1960s and the 1980s make some of the arguments of theological pluralists remarkably outmoded. Their failures of prophecy about the stability or otherwise of the religious market-place was less due to a lack of good intentions than an inability to pursue the sociological implications of their liberal stance. Remarkably few theological pluralists have confronted the arguments of their most astute sociological critic, Peter Berger.

More than any other sociologist, Berger has shown the degree to which pluralism has unacceptable consequences for religious belief. He argues that pluralism is a distinctive outcome of two forces: modernization and secularization. Thus he suggests that 'secularization fosters the civic arrangements under which pluralism thrives, while the plurality of world views undermines the plausibility of each one and thus contributes to the secularizing tendency'.[18] Pluralism generates a relativism, fractures belief into a bewildering variety of options, and makes it difficult to choose between the diversity opened. Hammond has noted a particular concern of Berger with the corrosive effects of pluralism on certainty, that it generates a 'crisis of credibility'. Pluralism alienates and effects the growth of a distinctive feature of modernity – the rise of the 'homeless mind'.[19]

Berger provides a moral critique of the ideology of pluralism and gives it a specific theological turn. Because pluralism seeks to maximize choice, a particular casualty of this ideology is the sense of the sacred. Churches which have compromised most with the spirit of the age have not only backed an outdated ideology, but also seem to have sown the seeds of their demise. In American society, Evangelical churches and sects flourish to a remarkable degree, whilst those in Anglicanism and Catholicism, who have tried to be relevant, have ended up disunited, demoralized, and in relative decline. Certainly, one would not look for patterns of growth in numbers in the more radical fringes of these two churches. Berger has argued that conservatives had a far more astute grasp of sociology than their radical counterparts, for they could see the limits of the discipline's interventions in theology. This point is very apparent in the writings of von Balthasar.

There is a cynical aspect to Berger's approach to pluralism that theologians often find difficult to handle. He argues that pluralism gives rise to an indefinite number of social bases or plausibility-structures within which religious belief is made 'real' to its adherents. These compete for scarce believers in a market-place that is bureaucratically controlled. Competition expands the options for belief available to be packaged and 'sold' in the market. Socio-religious structures are rationalized to achieve 'results' in a competitive situation that disenchants and that greatly increases secularization. In this context, Berger makes the acid observation that 'Christianity has been its own gravedigger'.[20]

Berger has exposed a peculiar paradox: that in affirming the need for a diversity of options to make religion credible, pluralism inadvertently renders it incredible. The overarching sacred canopy, within which signals of transcendence resonate unexpectedly, collapses in a market-place of secularizing babble. Many are called and many are fooled in this diversity of witness, the limits of which have been so well expressed in Flannery O'Connor's novel *Wise Blood*, where prophets speak in a market-place without grace of authority. Hazel Moses preaches on the street in competition with the utterances of other self-styled prophets. He seeks to make a distinctive mark with his witness to 'a new church – the church of truth without Jesus Christ Crucified'. All is made plausible in this market-place plural in competitive witness, a point Moses comes to see when he blinds himself with quicklime to see better.[21]

Fragmentation of plausibility-structures moves religious meaning from a question of fate to one of choice and this forms a central theme in Berger's *Heretical Imperative*. Belief can be manipulated to make it more credible in social terms, and a theological pluralism facilitates this possibility. The believer becomes a consumer of the ultimate, and shops around with a right to choose within a diversity of options a theological pluralism presents. An anthropomorphic tendency starts to invade what began as an innocuous theological endorsement and imitation of a secular concept – pluralism. Whereas an objection to secular pluralism was that it concealed what ought to be revealed, its religious use leads it to reveal what ought to be concealed. The hidden aspects of religious belief are made more manifest so that choice might be more rationally made. The effort to make religious belief speak to a market-place, to affirm its message in a diversity of utterances renders signals of transcendence more and more of a rumour, largely confined to children and some sociologists. The effort to make religious belief plausible through an emphasis on pluralism has the fatal effect of making it implausible. For Berger, pluralism is the handmaiden of secularization. It moves religion away from being the manifestation of an objective certainty, transcending all, and eliciting deference from some, to a subjective realm of choice that fuels an heretical imperative.[22]

The crucial difficulty with pluralism is that it reduces the necessary tension between the sacred and the profane. Signals of transcendence often emerge from the unexpected, from the slight and the weak, and those oblivious to the need to choose. The problem with pluralism is that it pre-supposes a rational basis of choice where the customer of religious belief can act on what he elects to choose in the market-place. But a religious sense of awe and wonder comes from those who are not bright enough to shop around the market-place of belief. Yet these often speak of what is hidden to the wise. A conspicuous witness to the invisible is the Anglican choirboy. At Christmas, clad in his ruff, cassock, and long white surplice, he delivers an incredible message in an unexpectedly credible manner, one that rises above the market-place and transcends it.

Debates on pluralism centre usually on issues of comparative religion and focus on the issue of diversity of creed viewed from a tolerant agnosticism. But a different image of pluralism emerges when it is considered from within a particular religion. The shortcomings of the term become even more apparent. There has been an uncritical acceptance of pluralism within Catholicism. The term has become attached to an equation between the incarnational and the cultural. This has led to a stress on the need to represent all aspects of the cultural in the life of the church. Failure to so represent all groups, it is argued, leads to an incompleteness in the manifestation of the body of Christ. To emphasize the totality of cultural life within a theological expression involves a distortion of the nature of culture itself. Culture pre-supposes a skill, a capacity to select and therefore to exclude. To be meaningful in human terms, culture bears an elective element. A total equation of culture with the incarnational implies that it is sinful to select and to exclude. Furthermore, it seems to suggest that the more total an expression of culture is, the more it reflects Christ, an argument that has Durkheimian overtones, where it is suggested that religion is a mirror of the social. The more the totality of culture is defended on incarnational grounds in theology, the more sociological interventions are excluded. Such a theology de-humanizes, for it implies that any form of selectivity is presumptuous. If choice is to be accepted, and selectivity involves a degree of exclusion, some principles have to be established for arbitrating on the detail of practice. It is difficult to understand how theologians who advance an argument for the significance of pluralism can feel that they are absolved from confronting the issue of praxis. At some point, detail has to be taken into account. It might be significant or insignificant, but it cannot be ignored. Reflecting on the concern of Thérèse of Lisieux with the minutiae of convent life, where trifles assumed a disproportionate importance, Monica Furlong noted 'it is the details of life which hurt or which give us joy, which are the straws which tell us what is really going on in our hearts and our souls'.[23]

It is important to understand how interest in pluralism evolved in the sixties within Catholicism. In a critical account of Catholicism in the period after Vatican II, which echoes many of the formulations of Berger, McSweeney argues that efforts to grasp the spirit of the times led to· a misplaced concern with relevance. This became an imperative to engage with contemporary cultural life in a theological effort to open out the church to the World. He argues that pluralism became entwined with a demand for a diversity of moral and theological positions. Based on rights affirmed in a secular ideology, pluralism seemed to entitle some theologians to dissent. They argued that as western culture was liberal, tolerant, and plural, the life of the church should be so characterized, if it were to have a credible mission in the world. But doubt became a virtue, leading McSweeney to claim that ' "theological pluralism" seems to be a euphemism adopted by theologians to disguise the extent of doctrinal tolerance as a consequence of the Council's acceptance of the principle of relativity'.[24] He suggests that 'theological pluralists rested their arguments about cultural diversity on the evidence of sociologists and anthropologists; they felt no need to create the sociological conditions which are necessary for consensus and without which any large group must divide and fragment'.[25] This point still applies to Catholicism.

Since Vatican II, the term 'pluralist' has been used in a wide and often contradictory way. Initially it had a limited use. Barberini argues that the Vatican Council used the term 'plurality' to refer to a diversity within a unified system of authority. The term 'pluralism' was never used in relation to the internal life of the church. He claims that in the Council documents the term referred to the educational and family rights of individuals within civic society.[26] The quasi-sociological rhetoric of one of the major Council documents, *Gaudium et spes*, endorsed a somewhat uncritical opening to cultural formations of the modern world. This attempt to sanctify the world could not have occurred at a more exceptional time than the late sixties, when all manner of ideologies were proclaimed. Unfortunately, an odd bundle of ideologies was blended into some peculiar pronouncements of liberal theologians who legitimated their positions by appeal to what became known as the 'Spirit of Vatican II'. An ideologically based dogmatism became buried in a theological certainty that the proclamation of rights of every cultural constituency, bar that of traditional Catholics, was self-evidently correct. A theological panic gripped some who failed to see that what was ideologically credible could be theologically incredible. Many of these theologians failed to perceive how peculiarly tied to the times were these liberal and radical creeds. There are fortunate signs of a movement in Catholicism back to a more critical and discriminating relationship with society under the present Pope. This has led to an affirmation of the spirit of Catholicism that is more in keeping with its traditional nature. As Ratzinger has aptly observed 'it is time to find again the courage of nonconformism, the capacity to oppose many of the trends of the surrounding culture, renouncing a certain euphoric post-conciliar solidarity'.[27] The attempt to give a more sophisticated interpretation of the link between faith and culture arises from a rediscovered need to maintain a creative tension between the sacred and the profane in contemporary societies. It is a position that complements the direction of sociological debate, and its concern with post-modernism.

The need for an authoritative, uniform Catholic Church that preaches an authentic doctrine establishes a tension with the ideals of pluralism. I argue that the issue of cultural diversity should not be appropriated into the claims and justifications for a theological pluralism. The question of the link between the core and the periphery that arises in a church facing remarkable expansions in Africa and Asia generates complex sociological issues that suggest a deeper and more critical analysis is required than the endless diversity pluralism seems to suggest.[28]

There is a recognized danger that a concern to represent a diversity of cultures within Catholicism can become a form of nationalism. Advocates of a theological pluralism argue that younger and more 'local' churches ought to establish their own cultural roots, in a context that fits their own domestic presuppositions and expectations. It is suggested that their approach to Catholicism ought to be detached from the more traditional and conservative demands of European theology. But such a suggestion poses an acute problem of amplifying their marginal status past some theological limit difficult to define and to handle. European cultural considerations might represent alien assumptions, but many facets of indigenous life pose acute problems for the nature of Christianity. Areas such as polygamy and witchcraft are difficult to reconcile with traditional Christian formulations.[29] The difficulty is that demands for the right to indigenous practices, such as a theology of pluralism would endorse, can lead to the implication that a diluted and second-rate form of Catholicism is acceptable for the Third World in a way that would be unacceptable in the European countries. Pluralism carries a price of perpetuating a marginality under the guise of affirming a diversity of representation for all.

Most of the literature on the adaptation of culture to Catholicism deals with efforts to indigenize on the fringe in the Third World. Thus, one writer has noted in a perplexed way that it is 'unfair to restrict the zone of adaptation to the third world, as if Western countries did not experience the urgency to adapt the Roman liturgy to their cultures'.[30] Efforts to link faith with culture have generated an ambiguous term 'inculturation'. It has developed out of a missionary experience in the Third World, where the need to reconcile the cultural properties of faith and rite with those of their context of delivery seems most evident. Some reference to anthropology is required, and this exposes a crucial deficiency in the debate on the link between faith and culture. A pluralist theology that has sought to encourage 'inculturation' has not developed a theory of ritual or an adequate approach to the opacity of symbols, nor has it even begun to formulate some valid criteria for interpreting performative 'success'. Instead, it has concentrated on a theological intention to deliver a religious belief to a particular cultural context in as sensitive a manner as possible. A deeper critical analysis of the implications of praxis is missing.

Many theologians have struggled with the question of the link between faith and culture. This concern has been expressed in philosophy and literature, but less satisfactorily in sociology where the problem more directly lies. Relationships between sociologists and those in Theology and Religious Studies departments have been very uneasy, if not hostile, for reasons that are themselves sociological. The problems raised by a theology of 'inculturation' in European societies, especially where the link has to be established between ritual and belief, are formidable, and are likely to lead to answers more liberal liturgists and theologians might not like. First, to understand these difficulties, we need to examine why the term 'inculturation' is so riddled with problems, and how these relate to the evaluation of ritual praxis in the Third World, where some unintended consequences have flowed from an effort to experiment. Second, we need to examine how some of these problems arise also in western efforts to handle 'liturgical pluralism'. By this term is meant a diversity of ritual practices that operate in competition between forms in a market-place. This might seem like a reductionist and rather cynical effort to misread the search for a diversity of liturgical forms. Efforts to experiment might be sincere, but an emphasis on pluralism disguises the degree to which adherents of a particular form of worship believe that their style of worship is more effective than that of their rivals in binding ties of affiliation to the holy in an increasingly secularized society.

Efforts to link faith with culture have encountered critical problems of monitoring liturgical practice, and of defining what is meant by an authentic rite. A fundamental distortion will arise if those in the First World do not confront the issue of choice within this effort to operate in a cultural market-place. The issue of comparison is even more apparent in a pluralism within the First World. Any effort to redress an imbalance between periphery and centre is doomed to be counter-productive in the present stage of the debate on theological and liturgical pluralism. The issue of pluralism is a product of western culture, and it will not take long for those in the Third World to wonder why those who are defined as marginal are forced to wrestle with the problems those in the First World consider they are absolved from even considering. It would be paradoxical if what started as a quest to liberate those in the Third World from the deadening clutches of alien western-conceived rites managed to entomb those on a margin in a sociological pit, dealing with a misconceived question for which there was no answer or escape. There are good reasons why the link between faith and culture is problematic. Pastoral short-cuts – and liberal efforts to obscure these under the label of 'pluralism' – will mislead their clients.

This leads to the third, and final, point to be explored. There is an admitted vagueness in more recent works on the problem of the link between faith, liturgical form, and the cultural. Problems over the definition of culture are familiar to anthropologists and sociologists, but obviously less so to theologians and liturgists, who are beginning to grapple with its opaque nature.[31] The latter lay much stress on 'listening' to native cultures, and on speaking in terms that avoid ethnocentrism – very much a term of the 1950s in American sociology. Dangers of an uncritical reception of anything in the cultural have been noted often. But if culture is open to so many different and conflicting definitions, it is hard to exclude those which reflect traditions within western societies. It might be said that had theologians and liturgists 'listened' a bit more to their own surrounding cultures in the period after Vatican II, their aims might have been better realized, without the cruelty and insensitivity that characterized that era, when many traditionalists suffered quite unnecessarily.

A sociologically informed account of rites in their English setting might produce some unexpected outcomes. If Chupungco is correct to argue that 'adaptation means conveying these things according to the thought and language pattern of the people' and that their spontaneous reaction is the best measure to gauge success, then this is a wide enough point to admit into consideration a more formal, traditional liturgy such as that of Sarum, which reflects the essence of an English culture marked with a genius for solid ceremonial.[32]

This recent theological interest in the cultural has not been reciprocated by anthropologists. Certainly, the demand for the indigenization of rites did not come from within anthropology; indeed, there has been a notably frigid response to these efforts from those anthropologists who are Catholics. A number of these were very sympathetic to more traditional forms of liturgy. For instance, the anthropologist Victor Turner, whose approach to the liminal aroused much interest amongst American liturgists, wrote a remarkably sympathetic comparison between the principles of regulation of the Tridentine rite and those in Ndembu rituals, and found little logical difference between them in their availability to anthropological scrutiny.[33] Efforts to modernize rites, to simplify their structures, and to make them more representative of their surrounding cultures of use and reception seem to have increased a sociological disinterest in their existence. For instance, a recently published text on anthropology and religion shows a heavy bias towards Buddhist rituals, and the practices of religious cults. Hardly any references are made to studies of Catholic ritual. This does not reflect a bias of the author, but is a fair representation of the discipline's interest in Catholic forms of worship and efforts to indigenize these within a theological pluralism.[34]

One reason why a concern with comparative religion is more likely to have an impact on traditional rather than liberal approaches to liturgy, is the discovery of a wealth of detail in the rites of other faiths. They have complex ceremonial procedures and rich allegorical symbols that invite a curiosity as to their meaning. There is no evidence that a complex form of ritual alienates participants in these so-called primitive societies. Many liberals scoffed at the detail of the Tridentine rite, its fussy concern with the placing of the hands at the altar, the number of bows to a bishop, and apparently dotty concerns with issues such as the length of surplices, and whether lace was an unfortunate innovation of the Counter-Reformation. One of the more ironical effects of encounters with non-Christian beliefs is the degree to which the need for 'thick' symbols and complex ceremonials is being 're-discovered' by liberal theologians who had earlier sought to escape from such restrictive details through liberating and meaningful dialogues with other faiths.

We wish to argue that an initial concern with issues of pluralism in rite requires a sociological intervention, at some stage, to arbitrate on the degree to which a social form of worship is used to effect an opening to the holy. If forms of rite are contextualized, a performative expectation emerges that begs the question as to which type 'works' best. We have argued elsewhere that the social basis of rite is unimportant – indeed, meaningless without reference to the theological content it is supposed to effect. A sacramental aspect should characterize all social aspects of rite, and unless this is the case the issue of the cultural basis of the liturgy is meaningless. It is the transcendent meaningfulness of rite that gives it a purpose, and the more its form is bound into what cannot be reduced to sociological speculation, the more it is likely to 'work'.[35] Rites are effective to the degree to which they quicken the spirit and do not reduce it to the pedestrian and the mundane that seeps in from a surrounding secular culture. It is the authentic relationship between tradition and the present that gives to liturgy a quality of timelessness, and a capacity to speak of what is best understood in silence.

There is considerable dispute about the origins and exact meaning of the term 'inculturation'. Despite its diversity of meanings, it has come to represent a theological problem, of devising a strategy for coping with the mysterious relationship between faith and culture. The term has become a backcloth to debates on pluralism within Catholicism, and to that degree it needs to be scrutinized. The term arises in the context of efforts to construct 'local' churches in a way that mobilizes the distinctive skills, insights, and capacities of a culture. This effort has arisen in India, Africa, and to a lesser degree in South America. It seems to have a loose link to liberation theology. It is argued that where a church becomes indigenous, it will have to be bound into its surrounding culture, which needs to be infused with a faith that arises from within in a particular context. Thus, it is claimed, 'a borrowed rite is an alien rite. There should be no dichotomy between the liturgy and the life of a native Church'.[36]

Chupungco argues correctly that the adaptation of liturgy to a surrounding culture represents the second stage of renewal since Vatican II.[37] The term 'inculturation' refers to 'the incarnation of the Christian life and message in a specific cultural setting'.[38] An intelligent reading of the term sees it as expressing a 'two-way process' in a dialogue, but one that involves judgement. It refers to an unending process, a passage that is not characterized by an agnosticism of the sort that emerges in more liberal formulations of a theological pluralism. A transformation of culture through faith and hope gives this term a definite theological imperative, so that 'in the full sense, inculturation is going the way from Babel to Pentecost'.[39] Diversity has to be located in a unity of assent and identity. There are difficulties with the term that are similar to some of the objections raised about pluralism. Hardawiryana sees dialectical tensions arising over incompatibilities, such as the tension between unity and pluralism; local churches becoming bound up with issues of national pride, and becoming detached from the centre; and the corruption of symbols in cultural use.[40]

Newer approaches to the issue of 'inculturation' stress the need for an evangelization of culture that seems a little more aware of the sociological complexities of the problem. An odd failure in translation seems partly to account for earlier difficulties with the term 'inculturation', when it was used originally to refer to the sociological process of socialization. According to De Napoli the term seems to have evolved into an equation with contextualization – which raises a more significant set of sociological problems.[41]

If the process of 'inculturation' is deemed to relate to issues of context, then a familiar territory has been opened up to sociologists who accept the relativist implications of Winch.[42] A long-standing debate has been generated about the problems of rationality and relativism, which centre on the issue of the location of presuppositions between the enquirer and the subject-matter.[43] The result has been a certain agnosticism as to which is correct: the sociological views of the questioner, or the subject-matter which endeavours to supply an answer to be understood. The agnosticism that affirms the internal relationship between an idea and its context will hardly suffice in the case of a religious ritual that is geared to success, and which seeks to edify and to convince. The implications of a contextualization of liturgy open up an avenue for sociological consideration.

Chupungco has argued that 'signs which no longer convey the

message of the liturgy nor speak to the people are empty, lack efficacy and betray the very purpose of liturgical signs'.[44] If a liturgical form is not to be alien but is to be available for appropriation and understanding, then its delivery must occur in a manner that is plausible. Unfortunately, there is an element of ambiguity involved in this stipulation, for, as Berger notes, 'the *same* human activity that produces society also produces religion', and the link between the two operates in a dialectic manner.[45] For this reason, it is hard to understand the comment of Race, on Berger's writings, that normative injunctions that rise above the comparative in the study of religion belong to the theologian rather than to the sociologist.[46]

There is always a danger that admitting a plausible dimension into liturgical performance pushes the issue of interpretation into an inaccessible subjectivity. If the ritual is geared to a public form of worship, its domain qualities have to be understood by those attending. Intended stipulated behaviour that produces a definite set of meanings gives sociology a basis for interpretation. Some form of authority has to be exercised to produce a credible rite, and this is where difficulties arise over the issue of pluralism within the Third World.

Those who advance a strong belief in 'listening' to local cultures are well aware of the need to be selective in dealing with other forms of religious belief, or rival rituals, if a syncretism is to be avoided. Nevertheless, there is a strong emphasis on a non-judgemental approach in writers such as Schreiter, who are seeking to establish the possibility of a plurality of 'local theologies' within the church. There are three unintended consequences to his position. First, there is the problem, which he admits, but does not resolve, of the possibility of a local professional theologian dominating the agenda of a particular cultural context. Second, there is the growing worry that liberation theology has managed to detach the people from a popular form of religion, one they well understood in its older form, and has left them in a state of anomie and uncertainty as to how to reconcile changes they never sought, and questions they themselves never raised. An ironic effect of liberation theology in South America is that the uncertainty it generates seems to have decanted the masses into the clutches of right-wing North American evangelicals. The need to cope with this theological and liturgical uncertainty increases and widens the role of the priest in a way that exceeds his former position. Instead of being an agent of the universal church with no powers of discretion, he has to act as a theologian and to speak on their behalf. A sacerdotal paternalism has been exchanged for an ideological version, all the more pernicious for its claim to be free of dominance and to be liberating.[47] At some point, a limit to theological pluralism has to be encountered over any pastoral issues that require arbitration. An authority 'above theology' is called for, that allows a plurality but avoids a disintegration into pluralism.[48]

Third, a limit to a non-judgemental approach seems to be reached in the case of traditionalists, who might want to follow a more authentic interpretation of a Roman rite, one that fits in with *their* cultural sentiments as they arise in a particular context. Writers such as Schreiter and Chupungco regard these as constituting an obstacle to the development of a 'local theology' and indigenous forms of rite.[49] An odder point is made by Hardawiryana, that shows a curious insensitivity to the fuller implications of 'inculturation'. He suggests that 'meaningful contextual reflections on the faith' have encountered resistance from clergy (and presumably their flock) 'who tenaciously cling to traditional outdated formulas'. He claims that reformulating the Christian faith in various cultural terms, and celebrating the mystery of salvation in different rituals and symbols, bears on 'real actual problems'. Thus he argues, with a certain unintended irony that, dogmatism alienates.[50] This is to suggest that his principle of certainty is liberating, whereas that of traditionalists is 'dogmatic'. Why should the liberal ideas of a Dutch missionary not grant rights to those traditionalists in Africa and Asia who wish to interpret their faith in the way they felt their immediate ancestors had understood it?

One begins to understand von Balthasar's point that the demand to open the church to the world did not come from the laity who lived in it. Rather, what happened was a clerical revolution, the main victims of which have been the laity in whose name many odd ideas were put forward. They were not responsible for the confusion and chaos that followed.[51] He wonders also whether the church was ever less pluralist than today, when there is so much talk of pluralism, and adds 'the gospel of tolerance is preached with intolerance, the gospel of pluralism with a zeal that betrays its sectarian character by "tolerating" those who do not subscribe to it as old-fashioned and objects of pity'.[52] One result of an over-emphasis on active participation in the reformed liturgy has been a stress on maximizing a diversity of external forms of engagement, but, as Ratzinger suggests, 'it is strange that the postconciliar pluralism has created uniformity in one respect at least; it will not tolerate a high standard of expression'.[53] Such objections to the negative effects of pluralism are by no means the preserve of traditional Catholic theologians. Berger is a Lutheran. An American Methodist theologian noted the degree to which a very real intolerance arises in the name of tolerance of pluralism. He adds that an overstress on pluralism 'inevitably encourages religious privatism and theological illiteracy'.[54]

'Inculturation' encounters a sociological problem it cannot resolve simply through stipulating a theological intention. Some criteria for estimating the 'success' or 'failure' of a strategy for indigenization of rite has to be found. It cannot be said that the sociological means of monitoring the effects of change and adaptation are in any way adequate. To emphasize the 'spontaneous' response of people to efforts to indigenize rites removes the issue from sociological speculation. Apart from being tautological, there is a Pelagian element bound up in such a criterion. It suggests that if the people manage to assemble a cultural form of rite that reflects their wishes, then God is somehow constrained to be present before such a social consensus.[55]

The issue of pluralism within Catholicism in western countries has been no less disruptive to the ordinary laity, and its liberal proclamation conceals an acute crisis few seem to want to recognize. Some theologians have expressed the view – one often reflected in editorials in the *Tablet* – that if structures of the Catholic Church were liberalized, if women were to be admitted to non-ordained ministries, and more permissive attitudes were taken to variations in interpretation of liturgy, morals, and theology, then in some way the laity would be galvanized in their response to the church's message. The laity would be liberated and more representative of how the People of God ought to look to a society, just waiting for such an image to emerge that would convince them to join up in mass-conversions when these repressive structures had been rent asunder. In sociological terms, such a view is peculiarly naïve. The liberal quest to make things easier for the laity in liturgy has increased their burdens.

Since the early seventies, some sociologists had been aware of the degree to which pluralism unsettles the weak and the working class. In America it had been noted that the supportive subcultures that bound the working class and ethnic groups into Catholicism, that insulated them against the cold forces of secularization in a mass advanced industrialized society, had been broken up in the enthusiasms that descended on liberal theologians in the post-conciliar period. As these traditional structures were ruptured, it was also noted that conservative evangelical churches were growing rapidly.[56] Certainly, those radical and liberal theologians of the seventies, who forced through so dogmatically their interpretation of the spirit of the conciliar reforms, did little to listen to the weaker sections of their flock. Sociologists were left to speak for these, the most famous and oft-quoted example being Mary Douglas's analysis of the effects of loosening the Friday fast on the supportive subculture of the 'Bog Irish'.[57] The failure to monitor the effects of change that was so iconoclastic in its effects, so sweeping in its scope, and so enthusiastically implemented, obscured a social process of the detachment of weaker sections of Catholicism from their own church.[58] The egalitarian rhetoric of this liberal theology made the sociological effects of what it pronounced all the more ironical.

In 1986, the thesis that the conciliar reforms had inadvertently damaged working-class subcultures in England appeared in a coherent form in Antony Archer's *Two Catholic Churches*[59]. He argued that the main beneficiaries of the reforms were the middle class, who shaped the reforms to their capacities for joining, proclaiming, and lobbying. Rules that became more discretionary, and theological and liturgical assumptions that were more implicit and more testing, fitted with middle-class notions of negotiation and discretion. Shifts in approaches to liturgical renewal stressed the relational aspects of rite, and participation became increasingly influenced by demands for self-fulfilment. An odd combination of the worst aspects of American approaches to liturgical renewal, combined with some of the assumptions of social work and education, was wrapped in a liberal ideological package. The image so produced seemed to match middle-class expectations of how the church ought to appear credible in an increasingly sceptical culture. But the price of this connection was that a condition of anomie descended on the working class, who did not gain their living from coping with theological uncertainties.

In the rush to make rite lubricate social sensibilities, the sacred and the secular got mixed together, and the only person who seemed obsessed by the question of sacrilege was the sociologist. An uncertainty grew over how this liberal rhetoric that dominated the post-conciliar period was to be expressed in the detail of practice. This embourgeoisement of Catholicism under the guise of an egalitarian rhetoric was the price paid by the working class for liberal theological venturers who tried to see how far they could go. None of the contributors to the special issue of *New Blackfriars* devoted to the book disagreed.[60]

The argument that the working class had paid the price of middle-class reforms has been noted elsewhere. To that degree, there was little surprise that this thesis could be applied to English society. But there was a crucial twist in Archer's approach to the link between class and reform that gave his book a significance for debates on the limits of pluralism as applied to an understanding of liturgy. Archer was suggesting that it was illusory to regard a pluralism of rite as being egalitarian. All such diversity of rite did was facilitate a middle-class capacity to shop around and to act as consumers of the holy. There is no sociological evidence to suggest that the endless permutations of rite in the Alternative Service Book in the Anglican Church have in any way strengthened its weak grip on the working class. What was innovative in Archer's book was the argument that linked egalitarianism to the sacralization of the rite. He argued that the Latin mass with its transcendent qualities of timelessness bound all class-divisions together before what it effected.[61] The inegalitarian nature of its performance as a ritual was egalitarian in effect. All classes were unequal before a form of rite which placed the issue of the plurality of what it effected in the right place – in the diversity of meanings its performance reproduced. By concentrating on the meanings effected, rather than on the relationships within the form of the rite, a diversity of possibilities is opened out to a plurality of participants. Re-sacralizing the form of rite, its shape, its symbols, and its actions to secure an equality of participation for all was a central plank of the liturgical renewal movement, and one that has become obscured. There is a similarity between the solution Archer felt was ignored – of a strong authoritative rite that stood over cultural and class interests – and what was originally conceived in the Benedictine concern with liturgical renewal in mid-nineteenth century France. The forces that gave rise to a concern with the standardization of rite were also those associated with the rise of sociology in the same period. Both were concerned with the corrosive effects of individualism.

In the nineteenth century the price of pluralism for the working class was recognized. In his commentary on the impact of Guéranger on liturgical renewal, Franklin notes that his concern with uniformity and with strong authoritative symbols was intended to bind all classes into a true understanding of what these were believed to signify.[62] A simplistic approach to the issue of culture has failed to distinguish between its general characteristics and its particular expression within a liturgical form. Until recently, liberal theologians rejected the idea that there could or should be anything ritualistic about rite. Without a sociological account of the distinctive ritual basis of liturgy, efforts to relate it to a surrounding culture are doomed to failure.

A theology concerned with decentralization and with the dispersal of rite to 'local' churches has not come to terms with the cultural responses to ritual, how it is defined and used in an anthropological sense. There is a difficulty that anthropological interpretations of ritual follow principles and conclusions completely at odds with the assumptions of practice built into the liturgical reforms after Vatican II. The question as to how liturgy can be considered a form of ritual has barely been asked. Unless the social elements of liturgy are examined in terms of their relationship to sociology, little progress can be made on adapting rites to cultures. It might be well to remember Guardini's assessment of liturgy, which offers an insight compatible with sociological expectations of how to approach ritual. He suggested that

> in liturgy we deal directly not with thoughts, but with actualities. And not with past actualities, but with those now present; with actions ever done on and by us; with human activity in form and performance.[63]

To gain access to the social basis of liturgical performance, reference to pluralism is required, but not in the form liberal theologians would use. Elsewhere, we have argued that a diversity of rite conceals a competition in a market-place, where rival forms within a creed impute to each other liabilities in performance which adherents of a particular liturgical brand would know they ought to deny. Liturgical competition operates on the basis that each form claims that its rival is inherently corrupting by the nature of its style. By recognizing that which they wish to deny, one gains sociological access to what they intend to effect in the performance of the rite. Thus, a solemn high mass can be described as an aesthetic treat for the effete, whose concern with ceremonial niceties drowns holiness in what could be deemed an operatic spectacle intended for a holy gaze. This tendency to liturgical corruption justifies a pared-down form that squashes symbolism and ritual into the confines of a bare ruined choir where claps of the puritanical will summon up God.[64]

Efforts to experiment with the social basis of the rite are doomed to failure, for one can argue that the meaning and purpose of the liturgy does not lie at the level of the form, but within the content it effects. Uncertainty belongs in the effect, not in the apparatus. In so far as play occurs in relation to the purpose of liturgy, there is a pluralist element in rite. It resides in the meanings, paradoxes, and ambiguities it discloses and opens out. These mark a limit to the social, that allows its insignificance to be transcended by a content which the form is incapable of manufacturing. The social resources of rite can merely act as an opening that involves an element of petition, one that carries the risk that a sense of God might not come to those present from that which of its nature abides in the absent.[65] Paradoxically, the 'success' of a rite is more likely to lie in its social failure. This point marks a limit to a strategy of pluralism which claims that if liturgy is contextualized, and if the populace is 'listened' to, then in some way the transcendent will emerge, for this is believed to be implicated in a 'successful' manipulation of what is believed to be incarnational.

Any sociological account of rite has to take into account the degree to which the tangible is mingled with the intangible to produce a distinctive effect, one hallowed by time but which operates above it. The meaningful properties of rite lie in the mysterious diversity of effects that mark a limit which an authentic sociological interpretation of its social basis would wish to defend in order to preserve its distinctive ritual qualities. This bears on a point of von Balthasar, whose approach to liturgy and theology is remarkably congruent with the domain assumptions of contemporary sociology. He argues that

> wherever, in our elucidation of the mystery, some aspect appears really lucidly clear from a rational point of view, causing the mystery quality (which announces the 'greater dissimilarity' of God, his distinctive divinity) to retreat at that point and opening up a wider spiritual landscape – there heresy is to be found, or at least the boundary of permissible theological pluralism has been overstepped.[66]

As the implications of von Balthasar's stress on the limits of rationality and the need for reflection on the beauty of God revealed in form seep into the minds of liberal English and American theologians and liturgists besotted with efforts to sanctify the ideological, a whole new direction of thought is likely to be opened up – one that will admit an authentic sociological interpretation of rite. Increasingly, in a post-modernist era of thought, sociological theory is becoming aware of the meaningful limits of rationality. Recognition of such a constraint within sociology complements von Balthasar's approach to theology. Of all the major theologians writing today, von Balthasar and perhaps Ratzinger are most aware of the limits of sociology in addressing theological issues.[67] If they err, it is in a failure to recognize how a sociological acceptance of limits of meaning facilitates a type of theological speculation they would warmly support. There is a remarkable contrast between their approach to sociology and the perplexity of a liberal Anglican such as Habgood, who tried to hold a sociological mirror to his church, and saw things more darkly.[68]

Weber points to the dangers of a prophecy based on the needs of modern intellectuals who find religion embedded in antiquity and reflecting a truth they do not possess. A comparative question leads to the demand for a substitute, where academics

> play at decorating a sort of domestic chapel with small sacred images from all over the world, or . . . produce surrogates through all sorts of psychic experiences to which they ascribe the dignity of mystic holiness, which they peddle in the bookmarket.

It is unlikely that Weber had in mind religious studies when he added that such an activity 'is plain humbug or self deception'. His respect rests on those who make an intellectual sacrifice in favour of unconditional religious devotion. He adds 'in my eyes, such religious return stands higher than the academic prophecy, which does not clearly realize in the lecture-rooms of the university that no other virtue holds but plain intellectual integrity'.[69]

A belief in religious pluralism that disguises a confessional affiliation, offering an objective view of what is riddled with subjective meanings, can hardly claim the virtues of an intellectual integrity for proclaiming what it cannot explain, and affirming what it cannot understand. As a strategy for adherents of a religion, such as Catholicism, it reflects a liberal proclamation of a free market, in which the weak are dissuaded from competing, knowing how far they can go in a brave new theological world that owes more to Thatcher than to Marx. The rules of this new game of diversity seem concealed in an ideology appropriated by theologians to liberate the marginal, but which sends them packing to an attractive fundamentalism lurking on the ecclesiastical fringe. As a sociological concept, pluralism has entered the textbooks as being about the issue of power. If liberal theologians deceived themselves in their genuflections to the concept, there might be little to worry about, but when they render the plausibility structures of the weak implausible through a term such as 'pluralism', then there is a basis for sociological intervention.

A pluralism that bears on a common richness of faith is acceptable where an opening to the issue of a diversity of meanings is made in a theological manner that includes all and excludes none. Stress on the incarnational in liturgy has to be complemented by the availability of the transcendent in its performance. The one is implicated in the other, and a genuine pluralism requires reference to a diversity of strands that seem to contradict. There is a creative theological tension involved in effecting a link between the incarnational and the transcendent.

If a progressive theology affirms an opening to the cultural, a regressive version is needed to supply a contrasting closure that specifies and locates that which is bound into authority and tradition. Without these elements of contradiction, Catholicism would lose its capacity to attract through the mysterious and it would become emptied of the need to journey beyond the limits of the cultural. Relocating rites in their sacralizing tradition is to re-hallow them in a way that admits hermeneutic considerations and a need to understand *before* a diversity of encounters. It is to place pluralism where it belongs, in a way that admits a theological and a sociological understanding. It is to rescue the issue of a diversity of meanings from the breath of culture and to place it in the depths; to remove it from the ideological and to locate it where it belongs, in the theological, where doubt can be overcome and a selective closure can lead to an opening to the holy.

What is to be avoided is what Ratzinger aptly terms a 'ruinous pluralism' that emerges when people have 'lost the ability to re-unite the great tensions internal to the totality of the faith'.[70] To do otherwise, and not to try to find what Ratzinger has termed a 'fruitful pluralism', would be to abandon the market-place to those who make reckless knock-down arguments that push the weak off the wall, and leave them unwilling and unable to struggle back. It would be to abandon them to the fate of the Laodiceans, where the angel of the church was to tell them 'I know thy works, that thou art neither cold nor hot: I would thou wert cold or hot. So then, because thou art lukewarm, and neither cold nor hot, I will spue thee out of my mouth' (Rev. 4: 15–16).

Notes

1 John Hick (ed.), *The Myth of God Incarnate*, London: SCM Press Ltd (1977); John Hick, 'Religious pluralism and absolute claims', in Leroy S. Rouner (ed.), *Religious Pluralism*, University of Notre Dame Press (1984), 197. See also Alan Race, 'Truth is many-eyed', in Eric James (ed.), *God's Truth: Essays to celebrate the twenty-fifth anniversary of* **Honest to God**, London: SCM Press Ltd (1988), 177–90. For an incisive account of the theological issues raised by pluralism for Christianity, see Gavin D'Costa, *Theology and Religious Pluralism*, Oxford: Basil Blackwell (1986).

2 Rodger Van Allen, 'Catholicism in the United States: some elements of creative inculturation', in Arij A. R. Crollius (ed.), *Creative Inculturation and the Unity of Faith*, Pontifical Gregorian University (1986),

57–76. See also Kenneth Smits, 'Liturgical reform in cultural perspective', *Worship*, 50 (Mar. 1976), 98–110.

3 For a useful discussion of the misuse of the term in Catholicism after Vatican II see Andrew Greeley, 'Religious symbolism, liturgy and community', in Herman Schmidt (ed.), *Liturgy in Transition*, New York: Herder & Herder (1971), especially 66–9.

4 A vast literature has been developed on the rationality debate in sociology. See, for example, Martin Hollis and Steven Lukes (eds.), *Rationality and Relativism*, Oxford: Basil Blackwell (1982).

5 Hans Urs von Balthasar, *A Short Primer for Unsettled Laymen*, San Francisco: Ignatius Press (1985), 43.

6 Steven Lukes, *Power: A Radical View*, London: Macmillan (1974). For a useful summary of the literature on the debate on politics and pluralism, see the entry in Vernon Bogdanor (ed.), *The Blackwell Encyclopaedia of Political Institutions*, Oxford: Blackwell Reference (1987), 426–8; and Geraint Parry, *Political Elites*, London: George Allen & Unwin Ltd (1969).

7 Pierre Bourdieu and Jean-Claude Passeron, *Reproduction in Education, Society and Culture*, London: Sage Publications (1977).

8 Henry S. Kariel, 'Pluralism', in the *International Encyclopedia of the Social Sciences*, New York: Crowell & Macmillan (1968), vol. 12, 168.

9 Tony Bilton *et al.*, *Introductory Sociology*, London: Macmillan (1982), 185–205.

10 See Crawford Young, *The Politics of Cultural Pluralism*, University of Wisconsin Press (1976), chs 1–2, pp. 3–65.

11 Ninian Smart, 'Religious studies in the United Kingdom', *Religion*, 18 (Jan. 1988), 8.

12 Don Weibe, 'Postulations for safeguarding preconceptions: the case of the scientific religionist', *Religion*, 18 (Jan. 1988), 15.

13 Jacob Neusner, 'The theological enemies of Religious Studies: theology and secularism in the trivialization and personalization of religion in the west', *Religion*, 18 (Jan. 1988), 21–35.

14 Kieran Flanagan, 'To be a sociologist and a Catholic: a reflection', *New Blackfriars*, 67 (June 1986), 256–70.

15 Aidan Nichols, 'The habit of theology, and how to acquire it', *Downside Review*, 105 (Oct. 1987), 248.

16 ibid., 257.

17 Robert Bellah in his introduction to Mary Douglas and Steven Tipton (eds), *Religion and America: Spiritual Life in a Secular Age*, Boston: Beacon Press (1983), ix.

18 Peter L. Berger, 'From the crisis of religion to the crisis of secularity', ibid., 15.

19 Phillip Hammond, 'Religion in the modern world', in James Davison Hunter and Stephen C. Ainlay (eds), *Making Sense of Modern Times: Peter L. Berger and the Vision of Interpretative Sociology*, London: Routledge & Kegan Paul (1986), 148–9.

20 Peter L. Berger, *The Social Reality of Religion*, Harmondsworth: Penguin (1973), 132, see also ch. 6.

21 Flannery O'Connor, *Wise Blood*, London: Faber & Faber (1968).
22 Peter L. Berger, *The Heretical Imperative: Contemporary Possibilities of Religious Affirmation*, London: Collins (1980), see especially ch. 1, 1–31.
23 Monica Furlong, *Thérèse of Lisieux*, London: Virago Press (1987), 88.
24 Bill McSweeney, *Roman Catholicism: The Search for Relevance*, Oxford: Basil Blackwell (1980), 171.
25 ibid., 168.
26 Giovanni Barberini, 'Pluralist content in the IInd Vatican Council', in Stanislaw Ehrlich and Graham Wootton (eds), *Three Faces of Pluralism: Political, Ethnic and Religious*, Farnborough: Gower (1980).
27 Joseph Cardinal Ratzinger with Vittorio Messori, *The Ratzinger Report*, Leominster, Herefordshire: Fowler Wright Books Ltd. (1985), 36–7.
28 For a liberal theological defence of pluralism as an option, see Claude Geffre, Gustavo Gutierrez, and Virgil Elizondo (eds), *Different Theologies, Common Responsibility: Babel or Pentecost?* Edinburgh: T. & T. Clark (1984).
29 A sound account of the need for discernment in theological relationships with cultures of the Third World appears in Rosemary Goldie, 'The Christian experience of women in the midst of cultural change', in Arij A. R. Crollius (ed.), *Cultural Change and Liberation in a Christian Perspective*, Pontifical Gregorian University (1987), 27–46.
30 Anscar J. Chupungco, *Cultural Adaptation of the Liturgy*, New York: Paulist Press (1982), 75.
31 See, for example, Kevin Seasoltz, 'Anthropology and liturgical theology: searching for a compatible methodology', in David Power and Luis Maldonado (eds), *Liturgy and Human Passage*, New York: The Seabury Press (1979), 3–24; and David Martin, John Orme Mills, and W. S. F. Pickering (eds), *Sociology and Theology: Alliance and Conflict*, Brighton: The Harvester Press (1980).
32 Anscar J. Chupungco, *Cultural Adaptation of the Liturgy*, 73–4.
33 Victor Turner, 'Ritual, tribal and catholic', *Worship*, 50 (1976), 504–26.
34 Brian Morris, *Anthropological Studies of Religion: An Introductory Text*, Cambridge University press (1987).
35 Kieran Flanagan, 'Ritual form: liturgy's sociological dimension', *Modern Theology*, vol. 2 (July 1986), 341–61.
36 Anscar J. Chupungco, *Cultural Adaptation of the Liturgy*, 62.
37 ibid., 41.
38 Quoted in Marcel Dumais, 'The church of the Acts of the Apostles: a model of inculturation?', in Arij A. R. Crollius, *Cultural Change and Liberation in a Christian Perspective*, 4.
39 Arij A. R. Crollius, 'Inculturation from Babel to Pentecost', in *Creative Inculturation and the Unity of Faith*, 3–7.
40 Robert Hardawiryana, 'Building the church of Christ in a pluricultural

situation', in Arij A. R. Crollius (ed.), *Building the Church in Pluricultural Asia*, Gregorian University (1986), 26.

41 George A. De Napoli, 'Inculturation as communication', in Arij A. R. Crollius (ed.), *Effective Inculturation and Ethnic Identity*, Pontifical Gregorian University (1987), 71–2.

42 Peter Winch, *The Idea of a Social Science in its Relation to Philosophy*, London: Routledge & Kegan Paul (1963).

43 For an excellent account of the debate and its implications for the application of hermeneutics to sociology see Richard J. Bernstein, *Beyond Objectivism and Relativism*, Oxford: Basil Blackwell (1983).

44 Anscar J. Chupungco, *Cultural Adaptation of the Liturgy*, 70.

45 Peter L. Berger, *The Social Reality of Religion*, 56.

46 Alan Race, *Christians and Religious Pluralism: Patterns in the Christian Theology of Religions*, London: SCM Press (1983), 143.

47 Robert J. Schreiter, *Constructing Local Theologies*, London: SCM Press (1985), 16–20.

48 Hans Urs von Balthasar, *A Short Primer for Unsettled Laymen*, 46.

49 Robert J. Schreiter, *Constructing Local Theologies*, 142–3, and Anscar J. Chupungco, *Cultural Adaptation of the Liturgy*, 75–80.

50 Robert Hardawiryana, 'Building the church of Christ in a pluricultural situation', in Arij A. R. Crollius (ed.), *Building the Church in Pluricultural Asia*, 26.

51 Hans Urs von Balthasar, *A Short Primer for Unsettled Laymen*, 1–19.

52 Hans Urs von Balthasar, *Truth is Symphonic: Aspects of Christian Pluralism*, San Francisco: Ignatius Press (1987), 13.

53 Joseph Cardinal Ratzinger, *The Feast of Faith*, San Francisco: Ignatius Press (1986), 123. See also his essay, 'Liturgy and sacred music', *Communio* 13 (Winter 1986), 377–91.

54 Mark Horst, 'The problem with theological pluralism', *Christian Century*, 103 (Nov. 1986), 973.

55 Ian Hamnett, 'Idolatry and docetism: contrasting styles of proclamation', in Denise Newton (ed.), *Liturgy and Change*, Birmingham: Institute for the Study of Worship and Religious Architecture (1983), 21–37.

56 Dean M. Kelley, *Why Conservative Churches are Growing: A Study in Sociology of Religion*, New York: Harper & Row (1972).

57 Mary Douglas, *Natural Symbols*, Harmondsworth: Penguin (1973), ch. 3, 'The Bog Irish', 59–76.

58 This was first noted in the USA in Garry Wills, *Bare Ruined Choirs: Doubt, Prophecy and Radical Religion*, New York: Delta Books (1972).

59 Antony Archer, *The Two Catholic Churches: A Study in Oppression*, London: SCM Press Ltd (1986).

60 'Class and Church: After Ghetto Catholicism', *New Blackfriars* 68 (Feb. 1987). There had been some critical arguments that warned of the consequences of an ill-thought-out reform in the early seventies in the USA: see, for example, Ralph A. Keifer, 'Ritual makers and poverty of proclamation', *Worship*, 46 (1972), 66–76, and James

Hitchcock, *The Recovery of the Sacred*, New York: The Seabury Press (1974).

61 Antony Archer, *The Two Catholic Churches*, 98–9 and 133–46.

62 See the two essays by R. W. Franklin, 'Guéranger: a view on the centenary of his death', *Worship* 49 (Nov. 1975), 318–28; and 'Guéranger and pastoral liturgy: a nineteenth century context', *Worship* 50 (Mar. 1976), 146–62.

63 Romano Guardini, *Sacred Signs*, London: Sheed & Ward (1930), ix.

64 Kieran Flanagan, 'Competitive assemblies of God: lies and mistakes in liturgy', *Research Bulletin*, Birmingham: Institute for the Study of Worship and Religious Architecture (1981), 20–69.

65 Kieran Flanagan, 'Liturgy, ambiguity and silence: the ritual management of real absence', *British Journal of Sociology* 36 (June 1985), 193–223; and 'Liturgy as play: a hermeneutics of ritual representation', *Modern Theology* 4 (July 1988), 345–72.

66 Hans Urs von Balthasar, *Truth is Symphonic*, 65.

67 See Aidan Nichols, *The Theology of Joseph Ratzinger: An Introductory Study*, Edinburgh: T. & T. Clark (1988), and Louis Roberts, *The Theological Aesthetics of Hans Urs von Balthasar*, Catholic University of America Press (1987).

68 John Habgood, *Church and Nation in a Secular Age*, London: Darton, Longman and Todd (1983).

69 Max Weber, 'Science as a vocation', in H. H. Gerth and C. Wright Mills, *From Max Weber: Essays in Sociology*, Oxford University Press (1946; repr. 1958), 154–6.

70 Aidan Nichols, *The Theology of Joseph Ratzinger*, 290–1.

8

Towards a 'materialist' critique of 'religious pluralism'

An examination of the discourse of John Hick and Wilfred Cantwell Smith

Kenneth Surin

The fact that thinkers of such different theological persuasions as David Tracy and John Hick regard themselves as 'religious' and/or 'theological pluralists' serves to indicate that 'pluralism' must itself be irreducibly 'plural'. In this chapter I shall confine my attentions to the version of 'pluralism' advertised in the writings of John Hick and, to a lesser extent, in those of Wilfred Cantwell Smith. I am proposing, in other words, to make two assumptions. First, that what Hick and Cantwell Smith say, and assume tacitly, about 'pluralism', is acceptable as a prima-facie characterization of this concept; and second, that anything that I have to say about this 'pluralism' will apply, *mutatis mutandis*, to other versions or manifestations of 'pluralism' which have features in common with the position espoused by Hick and Cantwell Smith.

John Hick has written movingly about the 'spiritual pilgrimage' (his term) which brought him to the kind of Christian self-understanding that came to be articulated in his 'Copernican theology of world religions', a self-understanding in which a 'Christ-centred' picture of the universe of faiths has given way to one that is 'God-centred'.[1] It is Hick's contention that the diversity of religious and cultural traditions necessitates 'a paradigm shift from a Christian-centered or Jesus-centered to a God-centered model of the universe of faiths'.[2] In making this paradigm-shift, 'one . . . sees the great world religions as different human responses to the One divine Reality, embodying different perceptions which have been formed in different historical and cultural circumstances'.[3] Given Hick's espousal of the autobiographical mode when prefacing his many presentations of the third 'Copernican revolution', it could plausibly be argued that these presentations are perhaps best seen as a kind of narrative, in this case a secondary narrative – one constituting an abstract second-order discourse – whose typical and primary function in this instance is that of a theological or philosophical 'sense-making'. Hick's philosophy of religion, we are suggesting, is a 'sense-making' narrative which ranges over the more immediately personal, first-order narratives recounting his decisive encounter with the cultural and religious realities that prevailed in Birmingham when he went to live there a couple of decades ago. The themes, categories, arguments, etc., of Hick's 'theology of world religions' can thus be said to constitute him as a narrative character, in this case a character who of course features in his own narratives. Now the emergence of narrative characters requires historical and social preconditions, and my purpose in this paper will be to conduct an examination of the particular historical and social preconditions that have to be assumed if 'religious pluralists' in general, and John Hick in particular, are to emerge as narrative characters.[4]

In his 'Author's Introduction' (1920) to the 'Collected Essays on the Sociology of World Religions', Max Weber addresses himself to the problem of the cultural specificity of modern 'western' civilization. Speaking as a child of this civilization, Weber says:

> A product of [this] civilization, studying any problem of universal history, is bound to ask himself to what combination of circumstances the fact should be attributed that in Western civilization, and in Western civilization only, cultural phenomena have appeared which (as we like to think) lie in a line of development having *universal* significance and value.[5]

As manifestations of the 'west's' self-advertised universality, Weber cites a wide range of cultural phenomena: systematic methods of experimentation in the natural sciences, the elevation of rationality to a canonical status in philosophy, rational harmonious music, the widespread utilization of lines and spatial perspective in painting, systematic theology, bureaucratic administration in the political and social spheres, a wholly capitalistic economic order, and rational industrial organization. Weber does not, of course, wish to suggest that these cultural phenomena emerged at the same historical moment. The central thrust of Weber's 'Introduction', however, is that the above phenomena are variables which progressively combine to constitute a comprehensive 'mind-set', an *epistēmē*, which Weber designates by the category of 'rationalization'. Rationalization and its concomitant ideological manifestation, cultural rationalism, emerged in the so-called 'early modern' period – that is, over the course of the fifteenth, sixteenth, and seventeenth centuries. However, as Jürgen Habermas has argued, this process reached its culminating-point in the eighteenth century, when traditional society was decisively and irrevocably supplanted by its modern successor.[6] In this transition there was a fundamental shift from societies governed by cosmological world views to those governed by de-centred or differentiated world-views.[7] As a result, society ceases to be based on a single homogeneous value-system which pen-etrates and orders its component subsystems. Each subsystem is then able to function according to its own 'inner logic'. The upshot is the creation of a whole range of autonomous and non-absolute 'value-spheres', each legitimized and rendered plausible by rad-ically contextualized criteria that are internal to the 'value-sphere' in question. This, as Weber sees it, is the inevitable outcome of the 'rationalization' of 'value-spheres'. I do not wish to get em-broiled in questions of Weberian scholarship. Nevertheless, I want to make the rather trivial point that the phenomenon of 'religious pluralism' is on all fours with those other items, unique to the 'west', which Weber takes to be illustrative of its self-avowed universality. Without the intellectual legacy of modernity, in other words, the notion of 'religious pluralism' would lack historical grounding in any kind of socially supported code or public dis-course. Or to put it bluntly: the categories of 'religious pluralism' are dialectically constituted, in that they are constructed through intellectual and practical activities which have concrete temporal, historical, and political conditions. The names 'John Hick' and 'Wilfred Cantwell Smith' *can* denote characters in a narrative that purports to be 'about' a 'religiously plural' reality precisely because historical – dare one say 'material?' – circumstances have generated a quite specific political economy of relations between individuals, classes, and nations; an economy which allows the self-professed universality of the 'west' to be articulated and sus-tained. Admittedly, everything that I have said about this econ-omy has been put in a rough-and-ready, somewhat programmatic, way. Nevertheless, this rudimentary account does specify the gen-eral lines of an approach which enables us to understand how 'religious pluralism' comes, historically, to be constituted as a discourse.

Now I must acknowledge that none of the foregoing consider-ations are even remotely mooted by Hick in his writings. Of Weber there is no mention. Troeltsch is mentioned once or twice. But he is invoked only in connection with his 1923 Oxford lecture on the place of Christianity in the world religions, and even here his position is that of a purely titular figure, the revered patron saint of the brand of 'religious pluralism' promoted by its exponents. Of Troeltsch's profound interest in the historical tra-jectory of 'western' civilization, and the philosophico-historical problems generated by this trajectory – an interest which Troeltsch shared with Weber – there is absolutely no discussion. Instead, we are told that the 'Copernican revolution' is 'demanded by the facts of religious experience'.[8] The 'facts' in question coalesce round the fundamental 'pluralist' insight

> that the great world faiths embody different perceptions and conceptions of, and correspondingly different responses to, the real or the ultimate from within the major variant cultural ways of being human; and that within each of them the transformation of human existence from self-centeredness to Reality-centeredness is manifestly taking place – and taking place, so far as human observation can tell, to much the same extent. Thus the great religious traditions are to be regarded as alternative soteriological spaces within which, or ways along which, men and women can find salvation / liberation / fulfillment.[9]

There appears to be no realization that this acknowledgement of our 'religious ethnicity' (to use Hick's term) *can* be articulated from Hick's 'Copernican' standpoint precisely because certain quite specific social, political, and cultural configurations provide the requisite 'grid of intelligibility' (to use a technical term of Michel Foucault's) for the 'religious pluralist's' discourse. The phenomenon of plurality (as opposed to 'pluralism') is of course not new. After all, the early church had to confront Marcion's heretical affirmation of an absolute antagonism between the two covenants, an antagonism in which the creator God of the Old Testament is subordinated to the redeeming God of the New Testament, and it is clear that the problem of 'alternative soteriological spaces' to which Hick and Cantwell Smith address themselves was the very one which confronted Tertullian and Irenaeus (the principal theological adversaries of Marcion). And yet Tertullian and Irenaeus did not, or could not, avail themselves of the linguistic and conceptual resources integral to contemporary 'religious pluralism'. To say, as the 'pluralist' might be inclined to say in response to this kind of objection, that theologians such as Irenaeus and Tertullian were creatures still constrained by the imperatives of a benighted Christian 'exclusivism', is simply to reintroduce the problem that confronts us: this rejoinder fails to indicate, in a way that is even remotely plausible, why it is that historical forces generate certain discursive practices at quite specific times and places; practices which permit the enunciation of this rather than that set of canons (canons which are determinative of such matters as intelligibility, truth, relevance, propriety, conviction, and so on). Our 'religious pluralist' seemingly fails to recognize that his theories commit him to a number of quite distinctive signifying practices, practices which he can engage in only because a certain immensely complex tissue of interests and relationships places him thus, and thereby enables him to be precisely the kind of signifier that he happens to be. The signifying practices of the 'religious pluralist' are by any standards a form of impressive human activity, and so these practices must perforce be correlatable with other forms of historically and geopolitically situated human activity.[10] In Hick's (and Cantwell Smith's) writings, the requirement, integral to any historically situated reflection, that we 'map' the materially-determined possibilities of a signification, is totally displaced. It is displaced by the necessity, imposed by a 'morality of knowledge' (if I may be forgiven for putting to another use a phrase of Van Harvey's), that we curb our inclinations towards a 'religious ethnicity': an 'ethnicity' which Hick and Cantwell Smith take to be incompatible with (and here I quote Hick) 'the awareness of a common human history and a common human relationship to the mysterious transcendent reality which we in the west call God'.[11]

The time has come for me to venture a few wildly speculative remarks. The high-point of the 'Christian triumphalism' decried by Hick is associated by him with the organized church's assertively apologetic and aggressively missionary attitude towards the non-Christian religions, an attitude which received its decisive, and some would say its most virulent, expression in the period which extends roughly from the time of the Islamic threat to European Christendom in the Middle Ages up to the first half of the present century. This somewhat combative stance on the church's part was paralleled by the rise and growth of a number of discourses in specifically non-religious spheres, new discourses which have as their explicit focus of enunciation a geographical entity that is non-western and non-Christian, namely, that part of the globe which is designated as 'the east'. The two discourses in question are those spoken by the practitioners of ethnography and orientalism. If religion and commerce are two dimensions of a common historical process which enables the alien reality of the unChristian, barbarous east to be distanced, separated, and then subjugated, the discourses of orientalism and ethnography must be seen as the third component of this self-same historical process. It is being suggested, in other words, that religion, trade, and knowledge operate conjointly to confine non-Europeans to their position as non-whites, in order to make the notion of whiteness – a notion threaded seamlessly into the fabric of European culture and so-called Christian civilization – superior, purer, stronger.

I am well aware that I am trafficking in ideas that are highly controversial, and which have generated a lot of bad-tempered discussion in the last decade or so. The thesis I have just outlined has been argued for most persuasively by a number of scholars, most notably Edward Said, Bryan Turner, and Johannes Fabian.[12] To their credit, Hick and Cantwell Smith are fully cognizant of Christianity's massive complicity with the political and economic forces which occupied, ruled, and exploited almost all of the non-European world. Indeed, one of the primary motivations behind their adoption of a 'theocentric' or 'Copernican' theological standpoint is precisely the desire to discredit and to undo the theological legacy of this shameful complicity. The criticism that I wish to direct at Hick and Cantwell Smith (and, all else being equal, their fellow 'religious pluralists') in this: in seeking to dismantle the dogmatic and institutional framework which reflects and reinforces Christianity's tacit and overt collusion with those structures of colonial power and authority that enabled the European powers to occupy 85 per cent of the earth's surface by 1918, they are addressing themselves to only one (or perhaps two) of the three dimensions of the historical process which culminated in the subjection of the East. I want to argue now that, as a discourse, 'religious pluralism' is at depth hardly different from the discourses of enthnography, anthropology, and orientalism. That is to say, when it comes to presenting other cultures, societies, histories, etc., the 'political economy', the 'imaginative geography'[13] presupposed by Hick's 'global theology' and Cantwell Smith's 'world theology' is not materially different from the similar economies and geographies sponsored by anthropology and orientalism. If the discourses of the anthropologist and the orientalist are sectarian, coercive, and dominative, in that they effectively override the historical reality of that part of humanity which is non-western and non-white, then Hick's and Smith's 'pluralism', its protestations to the contrary notwithstanding, is essentially such that it is unable to remedy and to subvert the exclusions, discriminations, separations and absences which lie at the heart of these discourses. In the discourse of orientalism the orient serves as the anti-type of Europe and everything that Europe purports to represent. In the discourse of 'religious pluralism' we have what is fundamentally the liberal corrective to orientalism. For the orientalist, the orient is the occident's 'silent Other'.[14] For the 'religious pluralist', however, the non-European and non-Christian are incorporated into a common humanity having, in Hick's words, 'a common human history and a common human relationship to the mysterious transcendent reality which we in the west call God'.[15] The first point to note about this ahistorical affirmation of 'a common human history' is that it is irredeemably ideological. There can be no 'common human history' as long as the existing political and economic order constitutes a 'world-system' whose structures, group members, rules of legitimation, etc., require the systematic consignment of masses of human beings into political and economic subjugation.[16] To say that the hungry nomad in Chad and the prosperous investment-banker in Zurich have a 'common human history' is to veil the political and economic forces and relationships which maintain the nomad in his or her poverty and the well-off citizen of Zurich in his or her affluence. To dress up the imperatives of a one-way history in the garbs of a universalistic 'pluralism' is effectively to maintain reality in its existing unredeemed form. In transcending or obscuring the radical historical particularly of the situation of the nomad in Chad, the 'religious pluralist', despite his or her best intentions, succumbs inevitably to a most profound illusion, an illusion which has been characterized thus by T. W. Adorno:

> The familiar argument . . . that all people and all races are equal, is a boomerang . . . Abstract utopia is all too compatible with the insidious tendencies of society. That all men are alike is exactly what society would like to hear. It considers actual or imagined differences as stigmas indicating that not enough has yet been done; that something has still been left outside its machinery, not quite determined by its totality . . . An emancipated society, on the other hand, would not be a unitary state, but the realization of universality in the reconciliation of differences. Politics that are still seriously concerned with such a society ought not, therefore, to propound the abstract quality of men even as an idea. Instead, they should point to the bad equality today, . . . and conceive the better state as one in which people could be different without fear. To assure the black that he is exactly like the white man, while he obviously is not, is secretly to wrong him still further. He is benevolently humiliated by the application of a standard by which, under the pressure of the system, he must necessarily be found wanting, and to satisfy which would in any case be a doubtful achievement. . . . The melting-pot was introduced by unbridled industrial capitalism. The thought of being cast into it conjures up martyrdom, not democracy.[17]

I am suggesting, in other words, that it is no mere coincidence that 'global' theologies have appeared at the precise historical moment when capitalism has entered its global stage; a stage in which (and here I quote Peter Worsley):

> These [multinational corporations] operate, by definition, at a new, 'transcendental' global level, . . . their operations are worldwide. The largest, Exxon, has some 300 subsidiaries in over fifty countries. Political influence apart, the sheer scale of their operations means that the decisions they take are often more important to a country than those taken by its government, and not only in the case of the smaller countries. Even large, developed countries are losing the capacity to control their own economic future. Today, General Motors spends more than the Japanese government (and Japan is the world's fourth largest industrial Power); Ford spends more than the French government's defence expenditure; and Imperial Chemical Industries has a budget larger than that of Norway. In the Third World, in 1970, only three Latin American countries – Brazil, Mexico and Argentina – had a GNP superior to the annual sales of General Motors, Standard Oil, Ford and Royal Dutch Shell. The capacity of governments in societies with a GNP of less than $450 *per capita* per annum to exercise sovereign choice is thus extremely limited.[18]

But we need to look a little more closely at Hick's theological method if we are to see how exactly it is that 'religious pluralism' is a comprehensive and homogenizing historical scheme which assimilates to itself, and thereby tames and domesticates, the practices and beliefs of the different religious traditions. The bare bones of the Copernican theology can be specified thus: the ultimate and transcendent divine reality which is common to all the world religions is a *noumenon* that 'is schematised or concretised in a range of divine images', phenomenal 'images' which are culturally conditioned and hence culture-specific.[19] From the standpoint of the Copernican theology, these culture-specific claims are of course claims that have to be 'bracketed': they merely 'concretize', in culturally specific ways, abstract 'Copernican' theological principles such as 'the ultimate divine reality is the uncreated creator of the universe' and 'salvation occurs when the individual abandons self-centredness for Reality-centredness', and so forth. Now quite a few theologians and philosophers of religion have dealt with Hick's delineation of the relationship between the universal (and 'pluralist') 'Copernican theology' and the various particular ('exclusivist') 'Ptolemaic theologies', and I do not think that there is much more that can be added to the great deal that has already been said on this matter.

It would perhaps be more profitable if we attended instead to the political cosmology which underlies the ideology that is 'religious pluralism'.

Our starting-point in this enterprise is Hick's conviction that it is in the nature of an ('exclusivist') 'Ptolemaic theology' to be saturated by mythological elements that are culturally conditioned. (The 'Copernican theology', by contrast, is quite free of such problematic elements.) In this scheme of things, the adjective 'mythological' and its cognate expressions are used as part of a process of temporal distancing: 'once upon a time there were Christians who really believed that God was *in* Jesus', 'once upon a time there were Christians who really believed that Jesus' death was a vicarious atonement for human sin', and so on. Hick's qualified espousal of the thesis of 'cultural relativism' therefore serves two purposes. First, it justifies the supersession of the ('exclusivist') 'Ptolemaic theologies' by the global 'Copernican' theology. Hick, after all, believes that there is a world-historical sanction for this supersession – we now live in 'the post-colonial era', etc. Second, it facilitates the 'translation' of 'Ptolemaic' religious images, symbols, dogmas, etc., into the 'Copernican' idiom. Thus, for example, to say, as a certain kind of Christian would say, that Christ's death was a ransom for my sin is, in Hick's terms, a 'culture-specific' way of saying that Jesus has an unsurpassable significance for me when I endeavour to make the transition from self- to Reality-centredness. It is hard to know whether one is doing Hick justice here. He gives the impression in his writings that the term 'culturally specific' is virtually coextensive with the adjective 'mythological'. But regardless of this difficulty, the thrust of Hick's strategy is quite evident: the category of 'myth' and, by implication, the underlying thesis of 'cultural relativity' function in Hick's theology as distancing devices. They are used by him in a way which effectively petrifies the doctrinal components of the different religious traditions, a petrification that is a necessary preliminary to their subsequent integration or 'translation' into the 'common soteriological structure' posited by the 'Copernican theology'.[20] The strategy pursued is, despite Hick's best intentions, that of Procrustes: the global discourse that is the 'Copernican theology' – that is, a typically European-Atlantic discourse – regiments or 'irons out' the somewhat messy, idiosyncratic, and recalcitrant historico-cultural features of the particular religions. The discourse of the 'religious pluralist' appropriates and displaces the signifying and representing functions of the various religious traditions. It creates an optic which gently overrides their historical reality. Orientalism imposed, and still imposes, a muteness on its (oriental) objects. Hick's position can be seen as an essentially liberal corrective to the discourse of orientalism – his own discourse gives the members of all 'non-western' religious and cultural traditions a voice and a hearing, on one unexpressed condition – namely, that they acquiesce in his homogenizing world-historical scheme, a scheme which sedately but relentlessly uses its distancing devices to assimilate histories, cultures, peoples, and religious traditions to itself. In this scheme, the different religions are only different ways of saying or experiencing or striving for the 'same' thing, that is, 'Reality-centredness'. In the process, the 'otherness' of the Other is traduced, and the real possibility of any kind of dialectical confrontation between the different religious traditions is extinguished. The faiths have the structure of commodities: they are fungible, homogeneous entities which are to be consumed according to the preferences of the individual consumer. 'Pluralism', thus conceived, shamelessly reinforces the reification and privatization of life in advanced capitalist society. Such is the political cosmology of 'religious pluralism'. As you would probably have gathered by now, I am inclined to the view that this cosmology, and the discourse in which it is articulated, need to be overturned. To accomplish this, however, we need a discourse that will fragment, dislocate, decentre, and dissolve the experiential and linguistic terrain covered by 'religious pluralism'. I shall conclude by indicating, in a crude and grossly schematic way, how this overturning might in principle be accomplished.

Intrinsic to the 'Copernican theology' is a vulgar historicism: one that is sweepingly classificatory, empathizing, and relativist, and thus concerned above all with the 'average' characteristics of the different religions. This historicism evinces no real understanding of the central problematic which confronts anyone who is concerned about the relation between religion and truth: namely, how can something enduring and ineffable (which is what truth itself is), emerge from something sensuous and time-bound (which is what religion is)? The historicist outlook, by valorizing the latter aspect to the exclusion of the former, merely dissolves this problematic. What we need, therefore, is an approach that will accept that religions are historically conditioned, while seeking at the same time to preserve what is enduring in them – their truth-content, shall we say; a truth-content that is distorted by the capricious idealism of the historicist outlook. The historicism of the 'religious pluralist' prompts him or her to look for commonalities of theme and structure, the 'average traits' of the religions as it were; and in the process the religions, which should themselves be the object of critical analysis, are degraded into mere examples and illustrations of the pervasive themes of the 'Copernican theology'. An approach which seeks to dismantle this historicism will focus on the intrinsic make-up or 'natural history' of the religions. It will focus in particular on the extreme or 'non-average' features, that is, the unique material content, of each religion. It will be an approach which realizes, with Adorno, that

> the matters of true philosophical interest at this point in history are those in which Hegel, agreeing with tradition, expressed his disinterest. They are nonconceptuality, singularity, and particularity – things which ever since Plato used to be dismissed as transitory and insignificant, and which Hegel labelled 'lazy *Existenz*'.[21]

Against the seamless and totalizing arrangement of concepts that is the 'Copernican theology', this non-heteronomous alternative approach will rivet itself on that which qualifies as 'lazy *Existenz*'; that is, that which is particular and peculiar. In so doing, it will conform to Walter Benjamin's injunction that 'truth is not a process of exposure which destroys the secret, but a revelation which does justice to it'.[22]

Hick employs the noumenal-phenomenal distinction, and insists that the noumenal divine reality is 'schematized' or 'concretized' in the phenomenal realm. But he does not really tell us how access to the noumenal sphere is in principle to be secured. He observes the Kantian injunction that theology should remain within the bounds of phenomenal experience, but he has not, as far as I am aware, said anything about the modalities whereby the phenomenal sphere yields noumenal truth. At any rate, there is no specification in his work of the way (or ways) in which noumenal truth can be extracted from concrete objects, but without transcending their historical particularity.

In Benjamin's 'materialist' hermeneutic, the material-content of an object originates at a specific, transient moment in history, and so the noumenal truth locked in objects can be released only when historical truth contained in the concrete particular is released. And this truth is released only when the interpreter refrains from seeking to justify, to homogenize reality. To quote Benjamin:

> The structure of truth . . . demands a mode of being which in its lack of intentionality resembles the simple existence of things, but which is superior in its permanence. Truth is not an

intent which realizes itself in empirical reality; it is the power which determines the essence of this empirical reality.[23]

Truth lies beyond all intention. The universal is not to be accorded primacy over the self-contained particular, the hypostatized general concept over the concrete object. The universal must be deduced from within the boundaries of the particular. The truth embodied in the idea has to emerge from the concrete particular in purely immanent, non-coercive, intentionless fashion. The essentially heterogeneous object cannot be reduced to a function of the conceptual system, it cannot be constituted by the thinking subject. The particular has an isolated singularity, it has certain concealed contours, which resist assimilation by the cognizing subject. Or as Adorno, who was profoundly influenced by Benjamin, puts it:

> Contemplation without violence, the source of all the joy of truth, presupposes that he who contemplates does not absorb the object into himself: a distanced nearness.[24]

'A distanced nearness': this should be the motto of anyone who seeks to overturn the deep-rooted monism of those who profess to be exponents of 'religious pluralism'. 'A distanced nearness' would express the conviction of someone who believed that a true philosophy of the relationship between the faiths would be one that safeguarded the 'otherness', the 'strangeness', of the Other, and this precisely by not incorporating the various faiths into the comprehensive, totalizing framework of the 'Copernican theology'. The 'Copernican' theological paradigm evinces a profound idealism (in the pejorative sense of the term); an idealism which shows itself in Hick's programme – where the different world faiths are unrelentingly assimilated by an abstract and a historical theoretical superstructure – with an outcome that is potentially just as insidious as the 'exclusivism' of the old 'Ptolemaic' theologies. There are some who might go further, and say that the 'Copernican theology' is even more baneful than its 'Ptolemaic' alternatives precisely because this homogenizing tendency is obscured by the 'pluralist's' loud disavowal of 'exclusivism'. The compromised record of political liberalism *vis-à-vis* the so-called 'post-colonial' world should serve as a salutary reminder to those who are spellbound by the 'religious pluralism' that is the theological companion of this ambivalent political liberalism. The Christian who is seeking to feature as a character in any narrative featuring other faiths is perhaps best advised to avoid the narrative framework supplied by the 'religious pluralist'. This framework is incapable of sustaining negation, the real negation that betokens a true 'Copernican turn' to the disturbing, intractable 'otherness' of the Other. The 'pluralist's' narrative, in rendering this 'otherness' tractable, subverts it in the very process of affirming it. In truth, it is no 'Copernican revolution'.

Notes

1 For Hick's account of his 'spiritual pilgrimage', see *God Has Many Names*, London: Macmillan (1980), 1–5; and the essay 'Three controversies' which introduces his recently published collection, *The Problems of Religious Pluralism*, London: Macmillan (1985). A similar 'God-centredness' is evinced in Wilfred Cantwell Smith, *The Meaning and End of Religion: A Revolutionary Approach to the Great Religious Traditions*, London: Macmillan (1963); repr. London: SPCK (1978), 170–92. Note especially the remark which concludes the chapter titled 'Faith': 'The Traditions evolve. Men's faith varies. God endures' (192). The subtitle to this book is somewhat misleading, because there is nothing recognizably 'revolutionary' about it. Smiths work is a tepid liberal corrective to the 'exclusionary' discourses sponsored by certain strands of Christianity and the hegemonic 'western' culture in which these strands are socially legitimated.

2 *God Has Many Names*, 6.

3 *ibid*. A similar emphasis on religious traditions as 'historical constructs' is to be found in Cantwell Smith, *The Meaning and End of Religion*, 154 ff.

4 The reader who is interested in the theoretical underpinnings of what I am proposing to undertake is referred to Fredric Jameson's quite brilliant *The Political Unconscious: Narrative as a Socially Symbolic Act*, London: Methuen (1981).

5 The English version of this 'Introduction' is to be found in *The Protestant Ethic and the Spirit of Capitalism*, trans. Talcott Parsons, London: Unwin (1930), 13–31. Quotation taken from p. 13.

6 See Habermas, *The Theory of Communicative Action*, 1. *Reason and the Rationalization of Society*, trans. T. McCarthy, London: Heinemann (1984). See especially pp. 173–271.

7 On this see Richard Wolin, 'Modernism vs. postmodernism', *Telos* 62 (1984–5), 10. I am much indebted to Wolin's essay for my presentation of Weber's seminal contribution to our understanding of the constitutive features of 'modernity'.

8 See John Hick, 'Christ and Incarnation', in *God and the Universe of Faiths*, London: Fontana/Collins, (1977), 148. In his *Towards a World Theology: Faith and the Comparative History of Religion*, London: Macmillan (1981), Cantwell Snith confidently announces that the 'new categories' he espouses mean that 'the line that led from Schleiermacher to Troeltsch . . . can be transcended now, if not indeed dismantled' (120). While I am inclined to share this estimation

of the tradition of nineteenth-century liberal theology (albeit on grounds that are entirely different from Smith's), I none the less believe that two caveats are in order: (1) that, whether he likes it or not, the brand of 'pluralism' espoused by Cantwell Smith *is* the direct theological descendent of the very liberal theology that he purports to subvert and supplant; and (2) that any denigration of liberal theology (such as Smith's) should not blind us to Troeltsch's profound, and still germane, insights into the historical trajectory of 'Western' culture.

9   John Hick, 'Religious pluralism and absolute claims', in *The Problems of Religious Pluralism*, 47. Cantwell Smith makes a similar point in *Towards a World Theology*: 'Of this I *am* sure: that the cosmic salvation too is the same for an African tribesman and for a Taoist and for a Muslim as it is for me, or for any Christian' (170). Both Hick and Smith thus espouse what Philip Almond has called 'the principle of the soteriological equality of all faiths'. See his 'Wilfred Cantwell Smith as theologian of religions', *Harvard Theological Review*, 76 (1983), 335–42; and 'John Hick's Copernican theology', *Theology*, 86 (1983), 36–41.

10   The reader of Edward W. Said's 'Problem of textuality: two exemplary positions', *Critical Inquiry*, 4 (1978), 673–714; and 'The text, the world, the critic', in Josue V. Harari (ed.) *Textual Strategies: Perspectives in Post-Structuralist Criticism*, London: Methuen (1980), 161–88, will be only too aware of how deeply indebted I am to Said's essays.

11   *God Has Many Names*, 9. This 'morality of knowledge' is very much the motivational dynamo of Hick's theology. It has an undeniable affective power, a power which will be acknowledged by anyone who has some awareness of Hick's tireless and unstinting efforts to combat the endemic racism of present-day British society. Smith subscribes to the same universalizing 'morality of knowledge' in adumbrating his flagrantly ideological personalism. It is better to keep silent than to utter such platitudes as 'the truth of all of us is part of the truth of each of us' (*Towards a World Theology*, 79). See also his *Faith of Other Men*, New York: Harper & Row (1962), 11. Such platitudes can only bring comfort and satisfaction to those who do not want the screams of our society to be heard. For a similarly ideological affirmation of an 'increasingly common history', see George Rupp's contribution to Smith's *festschrift*, titled 'The critical appropriation of traditions: theology and the comparative history of religion', in Frank Whaling (ed.), *The World's Religious Traditions: Essays in Honour of Wilfred Cantwell Smith*, Edinburgh: T. & T. Clark (1984), 165–80. See also the section titled 'Pluralism in an emerging world culture', in Rupp's *Beyond Existentialism and Zen: Religion in a Pluralistic World*, Oxford University Press (1979), 13–16. We shall see later why this affirmation of an 'increasingly common history' is ineluctably ideological.

12   See Edward W. Said, *Orientalism*, Harmondsworth: Penguin (1985); Bryan S. Turner, *Marx and the End of Orientalism*, London: Allen

& Unwin (1978); and Johannes Fabian, *Time and the Other: How Anthropology Makes its Object*, Columbia University Press (1983).

13 To use a phrase of Said's in his 'Orientalism reconsidered', *Race and Class*, 27 (1985), 2.

14 Said, 'Orientalism reconsidered', 5.

15 Quoted above, p. 118.

16 On the modern economic 'world-system', see Immanual Wallerstein, *The Modern World-System: Capitalist Agriculture and the Origins of the European World-Economy in the Sixteenth Century*, New York: Academic Press (1974); Fredric Jameson, 'Postmodernism, or the cultural logic of late capitalism', *New Left Review*, 146 (1984), 52–92.

17 *Minima Moralia*, trans. E. F. N. Jephcott, London: Verso (1974), 102–3.

18 Peter Worsley, *The Three Worlds: Culture and Development*, London: Weidenfeld & Nicolson (1984), 317. Cantwell Smith exults that 'evidently the new way that we are beginning to be able to see the global history of human kind is presumably the way that God has seen it all along' (*Towards a World Theology*, 18). This is a 'global history' in which 67 per cent of the population of Africa, Asia, and Latin America are designated as 'seriously poor' and 39 per cent as 'destitute' by the ILO; in which Africa's debt-burden multiplied 20 times between 1960 and 1976 (figures quoted from Worsley, *The Three Worlds*, 203, 317). One can only hope that Smith is mistaken in his presumption, and that God sees the world somewhat differently from the author of *Towards a World Theology*.

19 On this see Hick's 'Towards a philosophy of religious pluralism', *Neue Zeitschrift für systematische Theologie und Religionsphilosophie*, 22 (1980), 142–3.

20 On this 'common soteriological structure', see Hick, 'On grading religions', in *The Problems of Religious Pluralism*, 67–87. Cantwell Smith explicitly endorses the principle of such a structure in the passage quoted in n. 9 above. Also significant in this context is Smith's resolutely Bultmannian stress on the 'presentness' of the faith-event. For this see *Towards a World Theology*, 176 ff.

21 T. W. Adorno, *Negative Dialectics*, trans. E. B. Ashton, London: Routledge & Kegan Paul (1973), 8 (translation slightly altered).

22 *The Origin of German Tragic Drama*, trans. John Osborne, London: NLB, (1977), 31. The alternative approach that I am seeking to expound is essentially an application of a number of ideas developed by Benjamin in his famous 'Epistemo-critical prologue' to the *Trauerspiel* study. Central to Benjamin's position is the thesis that 'truth-content is only to be grasped through immersion in the most minute details of material-content' (29) (translation slightly altered). I must emphasize that it is simply not possible to do justice to Benjamin's recondite theory of knowledge in such a brief discussion. Politically, one is reminded of Foucault's injunction that 'a progressive politics is one which recognizes the historic conditions and the specified rules of a practice, whereas other politics recognize only ideal

necessities, univocal determinations, or the free play of individual initiatives'. See his 'Politics and the study of discourse', *Ideology and Consciousness*, 3 (1978), 24.

23 *The Origin of German Tragic Drama*, 36. I have chosen to read Benjamin as the exponent of a 'materialist' hermeneutic, but accept the need to qualify this reading by agreeing with Susan Buck-Morss that the 'Epistemo-critical prologue' was not intended to be a 'materialist' text. See her 'Dialectic of T. W. Adorno', *Telos*, 14 (1972), 137–44. However, I believe that the 'completion' of Benjamin's text requires the reader to construe it as a text that is 'dialectical' and 'materialist'.

24 *Minima Moralia*, 89.

9

'Extra ecclesiam nulla salus' revisited

Gavin D'Costa

Introduction

Christians are faced with profound missiological, ecclesiological, and Christological questions raised by the presence of other religions. Roman Catholic Christians must take account of their tradition in reflecting upon this issue, and part of that tradition includes the *extra ecclesiam nulla salus* axiom – 'no salvation outside the church'.[1]

At first sight it would seem that this teaching, which has a long and venerable tradition, precludes further reflection in its apparently straight-forward denial of the possible value and salvific efficacy of non-Christian religions. It would also seem to imply that all non-Christians are unredeemed. Indeed, this is the way in which many Catholics and non-Catholics alike have persistently understood, or rather misunderstood, the teaching.[2]

The purpose of this paper is to revisit the axiom and argue that, far from precluding further questions, the axiom discloses an important starting-point for Christian reflection on the existence of religious pluralism and the concomitant question of salvation outside the church. There are a number of points which I shall try to demonstrate. First, the axiom affirms that all grace, and thereby salvation, is related to Christ and thereby to his church. This is the most positive and valuable insight enshrined within the teaching. Second, the proper context of the early development of this axiom bears no explicit relationship to the status of non-Christians or their religions. Therefore the axiom cannot be indiscriminately applied to this question. Furthermore, in examining the development of the axiom, we will also see its potentiality for misuse and abuse. This history is a salutary reminder of the dangerous triumphalist manner in which the axiom can be applied. Third, those who propounded the axiom often acknowledged, without contradiction, that some non-Christians before Christ were saved. For a number of reasons, which are not today permissible, many theologians held that after Christ the situation had changed so that there were either Christians – or those who in various ways rejected the gospel. Fourth, given this suggested acknowledgement of salvific grace operative outside the explicit boundaries of Christianity, the phenomena of religious pluralism need not be negatively evaluated by Catholic theologians.

An underlying assumption of this paper is that theological archeology can help recover some of the profound insights within the traditions of the church and incorporate these regulative and grammatical rules within new hermeneutical horizons.[3] These rules may help us speak more authentically and appropriately as Christians faced by contemporary religious pluralism. I do not wish to suggest that there is or should be a historical continuity of attitude towards non-Christians. If anything, such an attitude is decidedly negative. What I do wish to suggest is that the traditions of the church can provide resources for a more positive evaluation – which inspires, rather than precludes, further critical discussion on the existence of religious pluralism.[4]

To focus my discussion, I will briefly outline the criticisms of the *extra ecclesiam* axiom made by Professor John Hick. I am not interested here in Hick's own theories concerning other religions, but his comments exemplify many current misunderstandings of this teaching and its implications.

The criticisms

Hick characterizes most of Christian history as 'Ptolemaic', which he defines as a theology 'whose fixed point is the principle that outside the church, or outside Christianity, there is no salvation'.[5] He argues that this teaching, by implication, consigns most human beings to eternal perdition. According to Hick, within the Catholic tradition this attitude is epitomized in the *extra ecclesiam* teaching which reached its high-point with Boniface VIII in 1302 and was formally established in the Decrees of the Council of Florence (1438–45), which affirmed that:

> No one remaining outside the Catholic Church, not just pagans, but also Jews and heretics or schismatics, can become partakers of eternal life; but they will go to the 'everlasting fire which was prepared for the devil and his angels', unless before the end of life they are joined to the Church.[6]

This position is characterized by Hick as the 'first phase – the phase of total rejection' which is 'as arrogant as it is cruel'.[7]

Hick sees official Catholic restatements of this position, from Pius IX in 1854 up until the Second Vatican Council (Vatican II 1962–5), as slowly coming to terms with the wider religious life of humankind but in a 'characteristically Catholic way . . . continuing to pay allegiance to the original dogma but at the same time adding an epicycle of subsidiary theory to change its practical effects'.[8] (He uses the term 'epicycle' in a way analogous to that in which the Ptolemaic world-view was said to be defended through complex elaborations – epicycles – against counter-evidence.) He protests that Pius IX's Allocution, stating that those in 'invincible ignorance' of the Catholic faith may be saved outside the church, is hopelessly vague for 'only God himself knows to whom this doctrine applies'.[9] He criticizes the doctrine of 'implicit faith' and 'implicit desire' as a sleight of hand, rendering those who are 'consciously outside the church' as 'nevertheless unconsciously within it'.[10] Furthermore, since presumably only theists can have a sincere desire to do God's will, the doctrine of implicit desire does not extend to adherents of the non-theistic faiths, such as Buddhism and an important part of Hinduism'.[11] These developments within the Catholic tradition are characterized by Hick as the 'second phase . . . the phase of the early epicycles'.[12] While acknowledging Vatican II's *Declaration on the Relationship of the Church to the Non-Christian Religions* as 'magnificently open and charitable', Hick thinks that it fails to move forward out of this theological impasse.[13] Hick and many others thereby dismiss much of the Catholic tradition pertaining to the question of religious pluralism.

Two questions arise from Hick's criticisms which will focus my investigation. Is his understanding of the *extra ecclesiam* teaching correct: does the doctrine imply that the majority of human beings are eternally lost? Secondly, what was the reason for the retention of this axiom despite the fact that the 'second phase of Ptolemaic Christianity' acknowledged that 'outside Christianity there is salvation'?

The first phase

As Hick indicates, the *extra ecclesiam* axiom precedes Boniface and the Council of Florence. The axiom was developed at least ten centuries earlier by Origen (*c.* 185–254) and Cyprian (*c.* 206–58).[14] Augustine (*c.* 354–430) took up Cyprian's axiom, and was followed in this by his disciple Fulgentius (*c.* 467–553), from whom the teaching entered into the theology of the Middle Ages. The

Council of Florence text quoted by Hick cites Fulgentius' *De fide liber ad Petrum* (38, 79).[15]

As Cyprian is cited by Augustine and Fulgentius and has exercised a considerable influence upon ecclesiological concepts, he is a useful starting-point for my investigation.[16] I exclude Origen because, despite his 'outside the church, no one will be saved' teaching, Baker argues that 'the terms in which he [Origen] describes the true Church preclude identification of it with the outward visible Church'.[17] Although Baker minimizes Origen's grasp of the church as an organized community with its own laws and constitution, Kelly agrees with Baker in noting that according to Origen's mystical sense of the church, 'Christ's body comprises the whole of creation; for according to Origen's teaching all creatures will ultimately be saved'.[18] Clearly Origen does not fit Hick's category of the first phase of Ptolemaic theology, although his is one of the earliest formulations of the *extra ecclesiam* axiom!

Cyprian's teaching at first sight seems to correspond to Hick's categorization of the first phase of Ptolemaic theology. As bishop of Carthage, Cyprian had to deal with many lapsed Christians who had offered sacrifice to the emperor during the Decian persecution (in 249). Cyprian opposed two contrasting solutions: the easy reconciliation of the lapsed and the rigorism of Novatian – who had also been consecrated rival bishop of Rome opposing Pope Cornelius. Novatian's rigorism precipitated schism. Cyprian's axiom was developed in his debate with Novatian, not in relation to non-Christians, and reflects his concern for the unity of the church.

Another factor is also important in appreciating the context of Cyprian's *extra ecclesiam* teaching. Daniélou writes that 'in contrast to the apocalyptic writings of the Judaeo-Christians and the idealism of the early Greek Fathers, the work of the early Latin theologians is characterized by [an] extremely *concrete concept* of the Church.'[19] This stress on the concrete and visible arose partly with the church being contrasted as an alternative society in 'opposition to a hostile pagan world';[20] and was further accentuated in this case by Cyprian's use of 'analogies borrowed from Roman law'.[21]

This brief historical background illuminates Cyprian's use of the *extra ecclesiam* axiom. His unquestioned theological premiss was 'that the Catholic Church not only ought to be, but in fact is, one,'[22] and this one body represents the unity of the Godhead and of Christ.[23]

Consequently, the unity of the church has its analogue in the unity of the three divine persons of the Godhead.[24] In this respect,

Cyprian's indivisible linking of Christ and his church is a fundamental feature of both earlier and later ecclesiology.[25] Without the latter, the former is only an idea, not a celebrated saving presence. Without the former, the latter could not exist. Christ was considered founder and also head of his mystical body, the church. It was through Christ, and therefore through the church and its sacraments that a person received salvific grace. The Novatian schism threatened the fundamental unity of the church. Irenaeus' earlier criterion for valid membership (unity in doctrinal matters) failed to deal with Novatian, whose doctrinal works on the Trinity was orthodox. Cyprian therefore argued against Novatian that the church's true unity is based on the collegial authority of the bishops operating in unity with the episcopate of bishops. (There is also a controversial text in which Cyprian may have accorded the Roman bishop special primacy over the episcopate.)

The logical corollaries of Cyprian's theory are lucidly summarized by Kelly:

> The criterion of church membership is . . . submission to the bishop himself. Rebellion against him is rebellion against God, and the schismatic, however correct his doctrine or virtuous his life, renounces Christ, bears arms against His Church and resists God's ordinances. In effect he is a heretic, so that Cyprian can write of Novatian himself: 'We are not interested in what he teaches, since he teaches outside the Church. Whatever and whatsoever kind of man he is, he is not a Christian who is not in Christ's Church'. And, since 'he cannot have God for his Father who has not the Church for his mother', there is no salvation outside the Church.[26]

We may note the following significant points. First, Cyprian's use of the axiom bore reference to schismatics, not to the adherents of the great world religions. Second, the theological grounding of the axiom lay in the intrinsic connection between Christ, the mediator of salvation, and his mystical body, the church. The way in which this insight was employed through history would vary considerably. The concern behind Cyprian's teaching was the body of Christ torn in two through what he perceived to be a lack of charity and obedience. This lack of charity, Cyprian believed, confirmed the lack of grace to the schismatic – hence 'there is no salvation outside the church'. Third, the use of such an axiom, although expressing a positive insight, was liable to theologically rigorist and politically manipulative interpretation. The latter will be encountered later in this essay. It is to the former that we now turn.

There is an important development in Cyprian's career, adding further nuance to the proper understanding of the *extra ecclesiam* axiom. Cyprian's thesis, if taken in an exclusively literal and negative fashion, entailed the view that grace was restricted to the juridical church. Consequently, outside the church, within schismatic groups, sacraments were invalid. Benson thinks that Cyprian's lack of 'distinction between a Visible and an Invisible Communion upon earth . . . in his next great crisis placed Cyprian himself in some danger of separatism'.[27] This crisis was precipitated by the strong papal reaction against Cyprian's teaching of the invalidity of sacraments outside the church. Pope Stephen argued for certain supernatural effects of baptism even among heretics and schismatics, as the minister's role was instrumental, not substantial. The character of the minister did not affect the sacrament. The significance of Stephen's position was the acknowledgement of grace outside the visible church – and it was Stephen's view that was eventually endorsed at the Council of Arles in 314.[28] Küng correctly notes that 'when the axiom was both formulated negatively and taken literally, it led to heresy'.[29]

In relation to this issue of grace outside the visible church, it should be noted that the Catholic Church later condemned the teaching exemplified in Jansenism: 'outside the church no grace is granted'.[30] De Lubac shows that, with varying emphasis, some of the Fathers (Irenaeus, Cyprian, Hilary, Ambrose, John Chrysostom, Origen, Cyril of Alexandria, the early Augustine) and Aquinas have all maintained the principle 'that the grace of Christ is of universal application, and that no soul of good will lacks the concrete means of salvation'.[31] This principle was used primarily for those before Christ who had not been confronted with the gospel.

Two related factors support my reading of the history and implications of the axiom. Firstly, generally the Fathers (and many of the medievals) viewed the world as 'gospel-saturated'.[32] They assumed that everyone who had come into contact with the church had been confronted by the gospel. Furthermore, they also believed that 'the *echo* of the Gospel preaching had already reached the furthest limits of the earth'.[33] Consequently, those who were not Christians were in bad faith, having, it was believed, rejected the truth of the gospel.[34] Heretics, schismatics, and Jews belonged to one category – those who had properly heard of and rejected Christ, each in a different manner. In this sense it was clear to the Fathers that for those 'outside the church' there was no salvation. Later, it has also been made clear that this was not primarily a personal judgement upon the fate of anyone,[35] – and the axiom could therefore be seen as a grammatical rule, not a condemnatory proposition.

A second and related factor is the special position of the just who lived before Christ. Many of the Fathers devoted considerable time to the question of how the just and good before Christ were saved.[36] This category is significant, as it is applicable to a person who has not heard the gospel objectively proclaimed. It also tended to be restricted to the saints of the Old Testament, although some Fathers extended this category to include the just from the beginning of creation.[37] This category was understandably not extended by the Fathers to apply after Christ. However, logically, this category can be extended to those after Christ who have never been confronted by the gospel historically and existentially. I add 'and existentially', because it is not clear that a person who simply hears the gospel proclaimed can be said to be truly existentially confronted by it.

This may be for a variety of non-culpable reasons.[38] With this qualification in mind, let me return to the development of the axiom and my argument that the axiom does not bear a negative implication regarding non-Christian religions.

In Augustine's development of Cyprian's *extra ecclesiam* axiom, the question of the salvation of those before Christ is addressed more explicitly. Before proceeding, it must be acknowledged that Augustine's thought developed over a long period of time and is not easily characterized. Furthermore, only some of his teachings have been accepted by the church.[39] I wish to investigate Augustine's response to the special problem of those before Christ in the context of the *extra ecclesiam* doctrine, in order to shed further light upon the two questions I have addressed to Hick.[40]

Some brief contextualizations are in order. Baker points out that (as with Cyprian) the *extra ecclesiam* doctrine in Augustine is applied in relation to 'heretical or schismatic societies of Christians'.[41] Augustine's main works were aimed at the Manichaeans, Donatists, and Pelegians. Furthermore, Augustine, as all the Fathers, indivisibly related the church to Christ. (Here again, he is in keeping with Cyprian.) For Augustine, Christ held a triple mode of existence: as eternal Word, as God-Man Mediator, and 'as the Church, of which He is the Head and the faithful the members'.[42] For Augustine, the essential unity of the church is love – just as the Holy Spirit is love personified, the mutual product of love between Father and Son. Consequently, schismatics, such as the Donatists, were excluded from the church for they lacked, according to Augustine, love and charity in precipitating separation in the one body of Christ.[43] As with Cyprian's case with Novatian, Augustine could not attack the Donatists on the orthodoxy of their doctrinal belief.

Augustine's stress on love as entirely dependent on grace led him (in controversy with the Donatists,[44] and in the aftermath of Rome's fall) to develop his notion of the visible and invisible church. The visible church (communio sacramentorium) contained both sinners and the just, whereas the invisible church (communio sanctorum) contained only the just, 'the congregation and society of saints', the 'holy church'.[45] Kelly minimizes the importance of the visible church for Augustine. He rightly says that, for Augustine, even those who are 'heretics or schismatics, or lead disordered lives or even are unconverted pagans, may be pre-destined to the fullness of grace', thereby transferring the 'whole problem of the Church's nature to an altogether different plane'.[46] However, Kelly fails to point out, as Baker does, that Augustine assumed 'that the elect who were outside the Church were des-tined to come inside *before* their death'.[47] However, this still left the problem of those before Christ unresolved.

Given this context, we may turn to the question of the salvation of those before Christ. Augustine believed that the communio sanctorum exists 'from the beginning of the human race until the end of the world.[48] Augustine recognized the just and righteous within the pagan and gentile 'saints' of the Old Testament up to the time of Abel. In this, we have noted, he was not alone.[49] Consequently, in the *Retractationes* he writes of his summary of an argument in *De vera religione* ('This is the Christian religion in our day. To know and follow it is the safest and surest sal-vation', 10, 9):

This I said, bearing in mind, the name [religion] and the reality underlying the name. For the reality itself, which is now called the Christian religion, was already among the ancients. It had never been wanting from the beginning of mankind until the incarnation of Christ, and from then on the true religion, which had already been in existence, began to be called Christian. For when the Apostles began to make him [Christ] known after his resurrection and the ascension into heaven, and when many believed in him, his disciples were called Christians for the first time in Antioch, as is it written (Acts 11:26). That is why I said: 'This is the Christian religion in our times', not because it did not exist formerly, but because it received this name only later on.[50]

Clearly Augustine, a 'Ptolemaic' theologian in Hick's eyes, is optimistic about the just before Christ, explaining theologically that they are included in God's providential plan, despite his retention of the *extra ecclesiam* axiom.[51] Furthermore, Augustine, like Cyprian before him and Fulgentius after him, uses the axiom in relation to schism within the church and not in relation to the major world religions. Like both, he also uses it to maintain the primary insight that all salvific grace comes through Christ – and thereby, through his mystical body, the church.

Similar contexts for the axiom's use are evident when we examine the later texts cited by Hick and others.[52] Boniface uses the axiom in his Bull *Unam Sanctam* (from which Hick quotes) which should be viewed in the context of his long-running dispute with Philip the Fair of France over the temporal power of the pope and 'the threat . . . the king's policies posed to the church's essential unity'.[53] Boniface's formulation of the axiom reflects the development of medieval papal theory, so that in his time it was possible to view the authority of the pope as synonymous with that of the church. In this respect, there is some continuity with the earlier tradition investigated above and with a number of strands of medieval theology, not all of which are acceptable today.[54] The proper controversy about *Unam Sanctam* does not concern its applicability to non-Christians as Hick and others imply, but concerns whether the final binding statement about salvation outside the church was pertinent to the church-state controversy raging at the time. Theologically, it 'treated above all the divinely willed unity of the Christian Church and the role of the Roman see as guardian of that unity'.[55] It is also significant that the document was prepared a few days after only 36 out of 70 French bishops came to Rome for Boniface's council. Philip's pressure on the bishops to remain in France and thereby disobey the pope certainly raised the issue of church unity in a dramatic fashion. Nevertheless, the wider political context of *Unam Sanctam* would be difficult to deny. Boniface constantly intervened on the international political scene which had seen a decisive shift of temporal power away from the papacy. That Philip interpreted *Unam Sanctam* as political and spiritual blackmail is evident in his forcing Clement V to annul *Unam Sanctam*. Pope Nicholas V similarly resorted to the use of this axiom in his controversy with Charles VII regarding the pragmatic sanction of Bourges. However, even in this instance, the issue of church unity was at stake and not a decision on non-Christians.

The medieval use of this axiom, while still bearing some organic continuity with the axiom's positive teaching (that salvation comes through Christ and his church), became an alibi for a sometimes unchecked papal ideology and demonstrates the possibility of the misuse of an essentially positive insight, applied in a negative and literal fashion. Coupled with the dubious exegesis of Jesus' teaching in Luke 14:23 ('Compel them to come in'), the axiom was liable to be used as an ideological instrument of oppression.

The final document for inspection is the Decree for the Jacobites (1442) issued during the Council of Florence. Once again, the *extra ecclesiam* axiom is not used in reference to 'the great religions of mankind' as is often claimed.[56] The Council was preoccupied with the question of schism and separation, and during its seven-year duration decrees of union between Roman and several churches were issued – the Greeks, Armenians, Syrians, Chaldeans, and Maronites.[57] The Decree for the Jacobites concerned union with the monophysitic Copts of Egypt. ('Jacobites' derived from Bishop Jacob Baradaeus (*c*. 500–78) who renewed the monophysite church.) The use of Fulgentius' quotation in the decree (cited by Hick) is once more with reference to the necessity of church unity and is applied to schismatics and heretics. Interestingly, the Copts still retained a number of Jewish rites, such as circumcision. This and other practices occasioned an indirect statement on the validity of Judaism before the coming of Christ,[58] – keeping with the patristic reflections mentioned above.

To summarize: I have been arguing that the axiom has been developed over the ages and applied to certain very concrete situations – to the cases of those perceived to be responsible for schism, revolt or betrayal. Cardinal Bea's remarks to the Fathers of the Second Vatican Council, when introducing the *Declaration on the Relation of the Church to Non-Christian Religions*, supports this view of the application of the *extra ecclesiam* doctrine: 'About these [world religions] it is, as far as I know, the *first time* in the history of the Church that a Council has laid down principles in such a solemn way.'[59]

It would appear that the first question (whether Hick has correctly understood the *extra ecclesiam* doctrine) must be answered negatively. Therefore the implication that he derives from it (that the doctrine consigns the majority of non-Christians to perdition) must also be denied. The Fathers, contrary to Hick's suggestions, *did* 'stop to think about . . . the human race who have lived and died up to the present moment . . . before Christ'.[60] Although there is truth in Hick's comment that the church neglected the problem of salvation 'outside the borders of Christendom',[61] it must also be remembered that it was often assumed that the world was 'gospel-saturated' in the way defined above and that consequently, after Christ, no one really lived outside the borders of the gospel. Furthermore, it may also be noted that Christianity's long and bloody engagement with Islam during the Crusades was not always viewed as an encounter with a major world religion, as Islam was often considered a Jewish-Christian heresy, following the teachings of John of Damascus (*c.* 675–749). Of course the political threat of Islam and its distraction from internal social and political problems also determined the prevailing negative view to a great extent.[62]

A highly developed analysis of implicit faith and invincible ignorance was in existence by the time of the Middle Ages.[63] However, due to the reasons outlined above and others, the theories of implicit faith and invincible ignorance were on the whole not applied to the question of salvation in non-Christian religions. This application characterizes what Hick called the 'second stage' of Ptolemaic theology.

The second phase

The second question to Hick must now be briefly considered: why was the axiom retained, despite the later acknowledgement that salvation was possible outside the explicit church? I have argued that the *extra ecclesiam* doctrine did not address the particular problem of salvation in the major world religions and thereby did not consign the majority of human beings to perdition. Therefore it is questionable whether 'epicycles' have been introduced to *change* the doctrine's 'practical effects', as Hick suggests. Rather, the introduction of theories of implicit faith, while retaining the *extra ecclesiam* axiom, represents a legitimate deepening of insight into the axiom's concerns. The 'epicycles' delimit the regulative application of the axiom within the new hermeneutical horizon of religious plurality.[64] The axiom is an expression of faith that the sole source of grace is God, and equally affirms that this truth is indivisibly revealed and mediated through Jesus Christ, who is the founder and head of the church, his mystical body. While thereby maintaining the axiom's primarily positive insight, these theological developments ('epicycles') account for those who have never been historically and existentially confronted with the truth of the gospel, but who must nevertheless retain a relationship to the church and Christ in so much as they are saved.

The theory of implicit faith, contrary to Hick's contention, does not require the explicit formal profession of theism,[65] neither is it a 'sleight of hand' boosting membership-numbers (unconsciously!). It is employed to maintain the axiom's stipulation that when the Christian speaks of salvation he or she must at the same time speak of God, Christ, and his church. Finally, Hick's criticism that 'only God himself knows to whom this doctrine applies' must surely be a benefit rather than a shortcoming. The affirmation that God's grace cannot be manipulated by and restricted to the church results in the acknowledgement of the universality of the offer of grace.[66] Where and when particular men and women respond to this grace is not ultimately accessible to others. The doctrine of implicit faith attempts to formulate conditions for the reception of salvific grace for one who is not a full visible member of the church, rather than to specify who precisely fulfils these conditions.[67]

Concluding reflections

In this paper I have been primarily concerned with revisiting the ancient *extra ecclesiam* axiom which has been widely misunderstood in its application to non-Christian religions. Besides arguing against this misunderstanding, while not denying the existence of negative attitudes to non-Christian religions, I have tried to show why the axiom was in fact so important to the Christian tradition in its essentially Christological and ecclesiological insights. I have also tried to point out how the axiom is susceptible to misuse when applied negatively and literally as an instrument of oppression. In relation to non-Christian religions these negative ideological implications are as detrimental and dangerous as they were in earlier times when the axiom was utilized within a different context. The history of missions is partial testimony to this danger. However, I also want to suggest that the positive rule stipulated in the axiom is as valuable today as it was in past times. Not surprisingly, then as now, it requires and raises a number of difficult but important theological questions.

The axiom's basic theological *raison d'être* was to maintain the Christian conviction that God is the source of all salvific grace, and that Christ, through his mystical body, the church, is the prime mediator of that grace. As a regulative rule, it stipulates that when a Christian speaks of salvation he or she cannot do so without at the same time speaking of Christ and his church. A major stream of Christian tradition has, nevertheless, maintained that salvific grace was operative before the time of Christ and sought to explain – as Augustine did – the relationship of those before Christ to the church. The later utilization of the theory of implicit faith is a hermeneutical corrective, aligning many after the time of Christ as if they existed in the same logical space as those before the time of Christ – those who have never historically and existentially been confronted with the gospel. These later qualifiers do not alter the fundamentally evangelistic mission of the church or the positive insight of the *extra ecclesiam* axiom, but regulate this axiom within a different hermeneutical horizon.

What then are the parameters for further Catholic reflection on religious pluralism in the light of this study? The following are tentative suggestions. They may help rather than hinder Christian reflection on religious pluralism. I would also suggest that this regulative grammar may act as a criterion in evaluating and criticizing various proposals in the theology of religions.

First, Christian reflection on non-Christian religions should begin from a thoroughly *Christocentric* and *ecclesiological* starting-point. This would mean that grace could properly be acknowledged as operative outside the visible church, but must be causally related to Christ and his church. Here there are questions for the dogmatic theologian regarding the nature of 'membership' of the church and the appropriate corresponding models of the nature of the church;[68] the nature of the atonement and the sense in which theology can articulate the claim that Christ is the mediator of all salvific grace; and the relation of the church to Christ. Clearly, these questions are interrelated. The underlying theme informing the answer to these questions in the light of the *extra ecclesiam* axiom is that of the final causality of Christ and his church in the order of salvation. The existence of religious pluralism poses sharp Christological and ecclesiological questions.

Second, given this starting-point, the following may also be stated as possibilities without contradicting the *extra ecclesiam* axiom. Non-Christians can be saved while remaining explicit non-Christians. The religion of the non-Christians may thereby contain the instrumental means of grace in varying degrees.[69] In this respect, Christians have much to learn through their encounter with non-Christian religions. This is already exemplified in the way in which the history of the church is a partial history of indigenization. The extent to which these possibilities are true remains an open question, and the collaborative efforts of historians of religion, sociologists, philologists, and others is of vital consequence. And, in so much as this process deals with living religious traditions, the self-designation and self-understanding of non-Christians must be allowed its proper autonomy. While the appropriate methodology for pursuing the question of these possibilities is left open, the guiding theological principle will none the less obviously determine the presuppositions of Christians involved in this 'dialogue'. Hence, the understanding of

Christology and ecclesiology will be interrogated inter-religiously as well as intra-religiously.

Elsewhere I have tried to develop these suggestions.[70] What I have tried to argue in this paper is that the traditions of the church should guide our reflection rather than be insensitively abandoned. While our hermeneutical horizons have distinctively shifted from those of our ancestors, the regulative grammar embedded in their doctrines may well indicate the paths for future reflection. This I believe to be the case with the *extra ecclesiam* axiom.[71]

Notes

1 From now on the axiom is abbreviated as *extra ecclesiam*.
2 See for example: (Catholics) J. Mahoney, 'On the other hand . . .' (response to Ratzinger), *New Blackfriars*, 66 (1985), 289; P. Knitter, *No Other Name?*, London: SCM (1985), 121: R. McBrien, *Catholicism*, vol. 1, London: Geoffrey Chapman (1980), 274; (non-Catholics) K. Cracknell, *Towards a New Relationship*, London: Epworth (1986), pp. 9 and 166n. 2; A. Race, *Christians and Religious Pluralism*, London: SCM (1983), 10.
3 See G. Lindbeck, *The Nature of Doctrine: Religion and Theology in a Postliberal Age*, London: SPCK (1984), 79–88.
4 See Vatican II's *Declaration on Religious Liberty*, (1965).
5 J. Hick, *God and the Universe of Faiths*, London: Collins, Fount (1977), 125.
6 Hick, 120; citing *God and the Universe of Faiths*, Denzinger, *Enchiridion Symbolurum, Definitionum et Declarationum de rebus fidei et morum*, Freiburg in Breisgau (1953), para. 1351. All subsequent references to Denzinger are to paragraphs in this work.
7 J. Hick, *God Has Many Names*, Philadelphia: Westminster (1982), 29.
8 Hick, *God and the Universe of Faiths*, 123.
9 ibid., 123; citing Denzinger, 1647.
10 Hick, *God and the Universe of Faiths*, 123.
11 Ibid., 124.
12 Hick, *God Has Many Names*, 31.
13 Hick, *God and the Universe of Faiths*, 126.
14 Origen, *In Jesu nave*, 3, 5; Cyprian, *De unitate ecclesiae*, 6. The roots of the axiom go even further 'back to Ignatius of Antioch, Irenaeus, Clement of Alexandria, and others' – H. Küng, *The Church*, London: Search Press (1981), 313.
15 See Denzinger, 1351 n.1.
16 See E. Benson, *Cyprian: His Life, His Times, His Work*, London: Macmillan (1897), 200–20, 432–37; G. Walker, *The Churchmanship of St. Cyprian*, London: Lutterworth (1968), ch. 5.

17 J. Baker, *An Introduction to the Early History of Christian Doctrine*, London: Methuen (1903), 363.

18 J. Kelly, *Early Christian Doctrines*, London: A. & C. Black (1980), 202.

19 J. Daniélou, *The Origins of Latin Christianity*, London: Darton, Longman & Todd (1977), 429 (my emphases).

20 Daniélou, *Origins*, 441.

21 Kelly, *Early Christian Doctrines*, 204. However, Cyprian's prime analogy for the church was Noah's ark: A. Dulles, *The Resilient Church*, Dublin: Gill & Macmillan (1978) 134, calls this model of the church juridical, as opposed to organic (Origenist) or participatory.

22 Kelly, *Early Christian Doctrines*, 204.

23 Benson, *Cyprian*, 185.

24 Cyprian, *De unitate ecclesiae*, 23.

25 See Daniélou, *Origins*, 436; Benson, *Cyprian*, 186–200; Kelly, *Early Christian Doctrines*, 204–7; this continues right up to Vatican II – see (Vatican II), *Dogmatic Constitution on the Church* (1964), paras 1–8. This is not to deny the important teaching that the church is also a church of sinners.

26 Kelly, *Early Christian Doctrines*, 206; citing from Cyprian's *De unitate ecclesiae*, 17, 6, and *Letters*, 55, 24, 73, 21.

27 Benson, *Cyprian*, 186; see also Greenslade's perceptive commentary on this issue in S. Greenslade, *Schism in the Early Church*, London: SCM (second edn. 1964) 168–89. There are ironic parallels in Leonard Feeney's controversy in 1949 about the axiom, where he was placed outside the church by the Holy Office for insisting that salvation was only possible inside the church – see n. 64 below.

28 See K. Rahner, *Theological Investigations*, vol. 3, London: Darton, Longman & Todd (1963), 42. This Stephanic tradition is admittedly not without problems: see Greenslade, *Schism in the Early Church*, 170 ff.

29 Küng, *The Church*, 314.

30 Denzinger, 1379. Before Clement's condemnation, see also Pius V (Denzinger, 1025) and Alexander VIII (Denzinger, 1295). Admittedly these are not assertions of the positive counter-view, but condemnations of the restrictive negative view. However, see Vatican II statements expressing a positive view: *Declaration on Religious Liberty; Dogmatic Constitution on the Church*, para. 16; *Declaration on the Relation of the Church to Non-Christian Religions*, paras. 7, 9; *Decree on the Church's Missionary Activity* (1965), para. 16.

31 H. de Lubac, *Catholicism*, London: Burns & Oates & Washbourne (1950) 108.

32 Y. Congar, 'Salvation and the non-Catholic', *Blackfriars*, 38 (1957), 290–300, at 297 ff.; for an examination of this assumption in medieval theology see N. Abeyasingha, *A Theological Evaluation of Non-Christian Rites*, Bangalore: Theological Publications of India (1979), 117–22. There are of course exceptions, and this is not to deny that

the Fathers vehemently condemned paganism and the contemporary cults and philosophies.

33 M. Eminyan, *The Theology of Salvation*, Boston: St Paul's (1960), 19 (my emphasis), and see also his n. 13.

34 Y. Congar, *The Wide World My Parish*, London: Darton, Longman & Todd (1961), 119; Küng, *The Church*, 513; Rahner, *Theological Investigations*, 41.

35 Congar, *The Wide World*, 135. Pius IX (in *Singulari Quadam* (1854) and Denzinger 2865–67: *Quanto Conficiamur Moerore* (1863)) affirms that no comment can be legitimately made upon the personal salvific status of anyone.

36 See J. Daniélou, *Holy Pagans of the Old Testament*, London: Longman, Green & Co. (1957), 22–4; M. Cyriac, *Meeting of Religions*, Madras: no publisher named (1982), ch. 3, tends to have an over-optimistic interpretation of the Fathers on this question. J. Daniélou, *Gospel Message and Hellenistic Culture*, London: Darton, Longman & Todd (1973), 39–74, and C. Saldanha, *Divine Pedagogy: A Patristic View of Non-Christian Religions*, Rome: LAS (1984), contain the most balanced assessments.

37 See especially Daniélou, *Gospel Message*, 39–74; Saldanha, *Divine Pedagogy*, 160–80.

38 See Congar, *The Wide World*, 121–7.

39 For example, the Council of Orange (529) affirmed Augustine's teaching on the priority of grace to human response, but not his doctrine of predestination.

40 Clement of Alexandria, Origen, Ambrosiaster, Cyril of Alexandria, John of Damascus, and Oecumenius were some of the Fathers who reflected on Christ's descent into hell as a means of union with those who did not explicitly know him – see Congar, *The Wide World*, 136–7; H. Vorgrimler (ed.), *Commentary on the Documents of Vatican II*, London: Burns & Oates (1969), 75–81; and for the early Jewish-Christian development of this tradition see J. Daniélou, *The Theology of Jewish-Christianity*, London: Darton, Longman & Todd (1964), 233–48.

41 Baker, *An Introduction*, 368. The same is true of Fulgentius' use of the axiom, see J. Neuner, 'Votum ecclesiae', in G. Gispert-Sauch (ed.) *God's Word Among Men*, Delhi: Vidya Jyoti (1973), 149.

42 Kelly, *Early Christian Doctrines*, 413.

43 St Augustine, *Civitus Dei* (The City of God), trans. D. Knowles, Harmondsworth: Penguin (1972), 1007–10; Kelly, *Early Christian Doctrines*, 414, n. p. 11; E. Portalié, *A Guide to the Thought of St. Augustine*, Westport, Conn.: Greenwood Press (1975), 233, 244–5, 270–6.

44 The Donatists claimed that the church must be sinless and rejected the Catholic Church for accepting sacraments conferred by 'traditores'. Augustine held to the notion of a sinless church which was only visibly manifested in an eschatological time.

45 Cited in Kelly, *Early Christian Doctrines*, 415–16. See also Augustine, *The City of God*, 45–6, 593, 831–32, 998–9.
46 Kelly, *Early Christian Doctrines*, 416.
47 Baker, *An Introduction*, 370 (my emphasis). See also Portalié, *A Guide*, ch. 13. By 'inside' is meant 'visible'.
48 Daniélou, *Holy Pagans*, 10.
49 Hence the *Ecclesia ab Abel* doctrine, which is also found in the writings of Justin, Irenaeus, Origen, and (later) Eusebius, Jerome, and Ambrosiaster – see Neuner, 'Votum Ecclesiae', 149; and Y. Congar, 'Ecclesia ab Abel', in M. Reading (ed.), *Abhandlungen über Theologie und Kirche: Festchrift für Karl Adam*, Dusseldorf, (1952); and see n. 40 above. The doctrine is affirmed in Vatican II, *Dogmatic Constitution on the Church*, para. 2.
50 St Augustine, *Retractationes*, trans. R. Defarrai, Washington: The Catholic University of America (1968), bk 1, ch. 12, para. 3. This organic notion of the church is developed by Aquinas – see C. O'Neill, 'St Thomas on membership in the church', in A. Lee (ed.), *Vatican II: The Theological Dimension*, Washington: Thomist Press (1963), 88–140. For the relation of 'unbelievers' to the church, see Aquinas, *Summa Theologiae*, III, q. 8, a. 3, in the Blackfriars edn, London: Eyre & Spottiswoode, 60 vols (1964–81).
51 See also Augustine, *The City of God*, 828–32; *Selected Sermons*, ed. Q. Howe, London: Victor Gollancz (1967), 135–42, 113–17; Portalié, *A Guide*, 233.
52 Hick does not mention the fourth Lateran Council (1215), where Cyprian is cited (Letter 73), and where this axiom is directed against the Albigensian, Cathar, Amalrician, and primarily Waldensian heresies – see Denzinger, 802.
53 J. Muldoon, *Popes, Lawyers and Infidels*, University of Pennsylvania Press (1979), 70; see also B. Tierney, *The Crisis of Church and State. 1050–1300*, Englewood Cliffs, NJ: Prentice-Hall (1964), 172–9; T. Boase, *Boniface VIII*, London: Constable & Co. (1933), 313–38.
54 See J. Riviere, 'Boniface's theological conservatism', in C. Wood (ed.), *Philip the Fair and Boniface VIII*, New York: Holt, Rinehart & Winston (1967), 66–71. Certainly Boniface's view of the papacy and papal authority does not fully square with Vatican II, *Dogmatic Constitution on the Church*, paras. 22–5!
55 Tierney, *The Crisis of Church and State*, 182.
56 Hick, *God and the Universe of Faiths*, 120.
57 See J. Gill, *The Council of Florence*, Cambridge University Press (1959), and his *Eugenius IV: Pope of Christian Unity*, London: Burns & Oates (1961).
58 See Denzinger, 1348, 1350.
59 Cited in Cyriac, *Meeting of Religions*, 111 (my emphases).
60 Hick, *God and the Universe of Faiths*, 122.
61 ibid.
62 Cyriac, *Meeting of Religions*, 144. Wolfram von Eschebach's *Willehalm* (1220s) marks an important shift in the High Middle Ages'

attitude towards the 'good pagan'. The two doctrines underpinning this work are that God will not punish people for their ignorance, and that 'a pagan who leads a good life not merely may receive, but merits God's grace' – C. Brooke, *The Twelfth Century Renaissance*, London: Thames & Hudson (1969), 161. See also Foster's study of Dante's treatment of the good pagan in the context of thirteenth-century scholasticism – K. Foster, *The Two Dantes*, London: Darton, Longman & Todd (1977), chs. 10–12; and Dante, *Paradiso*, canto 19, ll. 70–8.

63 Suarez's post-Tridentine reflections are the most developed. See also the Council of Trent: Denzinger, 1379; Congar 'Salvation', 299 ff.; Rahner, *Theological Investigations*, ch. 1; Foster, *The Two Dantes*, ch. 10.

64 See J. Nuener and J. Dupuis (eds), *The Christian Faith*, London: Collins (1982), 282, 285–300, for official statements on this issue, and 241–2 for the Holy Office letter to Feeney.

65 See Congar, *The Wide World*, 93–155; C. Journet, *The Church of the Word Incarnate*, London: Sheed & Ward (1955), 31–40.

66 See Vatican II, *Declaration on Religious Liberty*, para. 1, and biblical texts.

67 Originally, however, the theory of implicit faith was developed with reference to catechumens.

68 See Dulles, *The Resilient Church*, ch. 7; Rahner *Theological Investigations*, ch. 2; Eminyan, *The Theology of Salvation*, ch. 2.

69 Traditional non-religious movements may also be considered as they occupy the same logical space in this context.

70 See G. D'Costa, *Theology and Religious Pluralism*, Oxford: Basil Blackwell (1986); *John Hick's Theology of Religions: A Critical Evaluation*, New York: University Press of America, 1987; and (ed.), *Christian Uniqueness Reconsidered*, Maryknoll: Orbis, 1990.

71 I am indebted to Christopher Seville, Dr Gerard Loughlin, Robert Ombres OP, and Professor Christopher Brooke for their helpful criticisms and suggestions. My gratitude does not imply their agreement with the contents of this paper.

10

Evangelicals and religious pluralism

Christopher Sugden

Introduction

I have been asked to share on the subject of how those Christians who define themselves as evangelicals (and I count myself among them) address the issues raised by religious pluralism. My chapter will seek in part to be a report, not of how everyone who calls themselves 'evangelical' would address the question, but of how a significant body of informed evangelicals who are members of mainline churches address them. Their opinion has recently found expression in a section on 'Evangelism in the Context of Other Faiths' in a statement produced in March 1987 by a Consultation on Evangelism convened by the Commission on World Mission and Evangelism of the World Council of Churches. The paper will not expound this statement, but will be a map-making exercise, giving a background to the way these evangelicals address the questions, before giving the statement at the end.

What counts as an evangelical?

First, it might be helpful to outline what is meant by 'evangelical'. There are many caricatures of evangelicals about. The images identify evangelicals with the TV evangelists of the electronic church in the USA; or with those who are insensitive detractors of other people's serious religious convictions; or with those who are ignorant of the relation and interaction between the gospel and culture and impose a western middle-class understanding of Christianity on the rest of the world. These aspects of some people's Christian faith make others stumble. But many people who stumble in this way have unfortunately not seen what informed evangelicalism is like around the world.

I would like to share with you how a range of evangelicals from around the world – many themselves in situations of religious pluralism – understand Christian faith in relation to religious pluralism. They understand themselves as evangelicals to affirm that Jesus Christ is Son of God, true God and true man, crucified and risen from the dead, God's anointed messiah to inaugurate his kingdom in his ministry and consummate it on his return. They affirm the scriptures as God's revelation of himself to humanity, and the only authority in all matters of faith and practice, and the church as God's agent to bring salvation to the world. From this perspective of claiming an exclusiveness for the person of Jesus Christ and an authority for the Christian scriptures, how do they understand and address religious pluralism?

A vision of pluralism

First, the Bible gives us a perspective of a pluralist humanity. Humanity is pluralist both in present fact and in future vision. The scriptures assert that humanity comes from one origin, one primal couple. It asserts that humanity has one goal, to bow the knee to Christ either in humble submission to him as Lord or in recognition of his final judgement. Paul in Romans sums up this unity as being in Adam and in Christ. But humanity is not inherently united, theologically. Though humanity may be identified as a species biologically and psychologically, theologically its unity is fragmented. It is divided up into different groups, often in conflict with one another. The Bible takes these divisions seriously. Some divisions are inherent in creation (male/female), but they are infected by human sin so that divisions become barriers rather than complementary parts. Thus men oppress women. Other divisions are the product of the principalities and powers of evil, producing the enmity that divides, for example, Jews and Gentiles.[1]

A gospel of reconciliation

In this context of a pluralist world, the result both of creation and of the fall, the gospel is a gospel of reconciliation. In Ephesians a chief sign of the gospel is to declare to the principalities and powers of evil that bring and reinforce division that in Christ the dividing wall of hostility between Jews and Gentiles has been broken down. The new community of God's people in Christ is to demonstrate that the Gentiles are 'fellow citizens with God's people and members of the family of God'. 'With his own body, he broke down the wall that separates Jews and Gentiles and kept them enemies . . . by his death on the cross Christ destroyed their enmity; by means of the cross he united both races into one body and brought them back to God' (Eph. 2: 15–16). Thus in scripture the sign of these divisions being overcome is not the openness of Christians or Jews to the fact that God may have revealed himself to other non-Christian (or non-Jewish) groups. The sign is when Jews and Gentiles come into one people through Christ: 'It is through Christ that all of us, Jews and Gentiles, are able to come in the one Spirit into the presence of the Father. So then, you Gentiles are not foreigners or strangers any more, you are now fellow-citizens with God's people and members of the family of God.' (Eph. 2: 18–19)

In Romans and Galatians Paul insists that the church is to be made up of both Jews and Gentiles on an equal footing. Jews can learn from Gentiles the meaning of 'being saved by faith', which was how Abraham was saved, and Gentiles can learn from Jews that God's work of saving people by faith did not start with Paul's preaching but with the Jew, Abraham. In Romans and Corinthians Paul stresses that in the body of Christ each has different gifts to contribute to the good and well-being of the whole. In Galatians he stresses that the work of the Spirit is to overcome the three major barriers that are the expressions of sin in the world, the barriers of race (Jew/Gentile), class (slave/free), and gender (male/female) (Gal. 3: 28).

In such a reconciled community, people are to serve one another. Power exercised in domination over others is to be opposed (Mark 10: 42–5). The teaching on the mutual sharing of gifts expresses this. This teaching reflects a particular bias to the poor and powerless: if domination is opposed and if all are to be recognized as having gifts, then the dominant patterns of surrounding culture are to be resisted. In surrounding culture, some groups have power over others, and some groups are excluded and have no opportunity to make a contribution. Therefore a genuine pluralism requires a bias to enable those excluded and demeaned by the dominant culture to make a contribution to the Christian community.

It is unfortunately true that this perspective of a church in which people from different cultures and backgrounds share together on the basis of mutuality is more a vision than a reality in today's world. The history of western Christian mission in the nineteenth century was, in the words of Bishop Michael Nazir Ali, probably the first time that Protestant Christian mission was elided with the spread of wealth and power. The combination of Christianity with the 'civilizing mission' of western imperialism, education, medicine, and technological culture meant that little (if any) value was paid to the cultures and the histories of the peoples to whom the gospel came. H. Kraemer, in *The Christian Message in a Non-Christian World*,[2] gave a theological rationale based on Barthian rejection of natural theology for dismissing any contribution that a people's own history and religious culture could bring to their understanding of the Christian faith. This effectively removed people's identity from them and gave them a new western Christian identity. Thus (for example) in Indonesia, Christians were known as Black Dutch. So the western Christian church has a history to live down in its international relations. The reaction to this history was that when many of the erstwhile colonies of western nations became independent they sought to establish their identity through reaffirming their historic religious culture.[3]

The Protestant church in Britain has not done much better at home. While there are Christian churches within many of the cultures in Britain – urban priority areas, suburban, Afro-Caribbean, Asian – one would be hard pressed on entering a church building in Britain during Sunday worship to note how the Spirit had broken down the barriers of race, class, and gender. Christians from different races worship mainly in their racial and sociological groupings. Power in the church resides mainly in a priestly caste that is almost exclusively male.

The biblical vision of pluralism in which people from the rich variety of different groups in God's world make up a community reconciled to one another and learning from and sharing with one another in Christ is thus a long way from the reality of the Protestant churches in Britain at the moment. I would suggest that one reason why it is such a long way off is that the cultural spectacles through which we view the Bible, the Christian faith, and our world focus on individual experience. They do not give the same weight as the Bible gives to the need for reconciliation between groups of people. Therefore they do not give adequate consideration to the power of vested interests, the reality of insecurity, and the exercise of power through domination. They do not interpret the plight of humanity in the corporate terms of divisions between groups. Thus they do not express the work of Christ or the life of the church in these terms.

By contrast the New Testament focuses particularly on the relations between groups as a key area of the expression both of human sin and of God's salvation. The issues of status – of the relations between Jews and Gentiles, men and women, Jews and Samaritans, rich and poor, religious leaders and the people of God, the well and the sick, adults and children – dominate its pages. Thus Stephen Mott writes:

The status boundaries that Jesus crossed are crucial to the stability of a society. That is why he provoked hostility. Status is one of the basic elements of a social system. It is a way of controlling people. Because of it some are weak and some are powerful. This inequality is socially useful. The existence of roles is inherent in being social . . . When Jesus by his actions and words challenged the existing status system, he defied a major requirement for operating a social system . . . he could not have done anything more basic to challenge institutions and social structures. The leadership, with vested interests in maintaining society as it was structured, were threatened by his actions. They responded with enmity against him . . . A priority for the early church was to determine if the relationships among its members would be characterised by the status distinctions of the surrounding culture. In the new reality made present by Jesus the major status distinctions of the culture – slavery, nationality and sex – were considered null and void (Gal. 3: 28). When Paul argues in Romans that the Gentiles (who according to Ephesians had no rights in the commonwealth of Israel) have been made participants in God's community through his righteousness (or justice, *dikaiosunē*) not by works – a category of status – but by faith, he draws upon the biblical sense of justice which involves bringing people back into community.[4]

The scriptural context of the claim that Jesus is unique

The New Testament affirms that God's righteousness or justice, his right relationships, are established through the work of Jesus Christ (Romans 1: 16–17). He was the anointed bringer of the kingdom of God in which these right relationships exist and will one day be established for ever in a new heaven and earth. The cross of Jesus was the only place in human history where God has intervened to break down these barriers between human groups, to overcome the power of the principalities and powers. The resurrection of Jesus affirmed that the kingdom he claimed to have brought was indeed a reality and that he was God's anointed one to bring the kingdom.

Thus the claims of scripture that Jesus is the Messiah, the one Son of God, the only Saviour, do not focus on whether he mediates an authentic personal religious experience. The context of that claim is history. Jesus is presented as the climax of God's action in history to redeem humankind. His ministry demonstrates the nature of that kingdom which will one day fulfil God's purposes for all creation in a new heavens and a new earth where peace and justice are at home. The decisive evidence that he was not the Messiah was his death. Yet the Jewish expectation of the final kingdom of God at the end of the world included resurrection. The persuasive argument in scripture that Jesus had indeed brought the kingdom into history before the end of the world was this: while this world still stood, one person had entered into the resurrection-state of the kingdom of God. It was on the basis of the resurrection that the disciples could claim that Jesus had indeed brought the kingdom 'ahead of time' into history. It was on the basis of the resurrection that they could call on the Jewish people to repent for killing Jesus, for the resurrection had vindicated Jesus' role as God's servant. This is why the resurrection from the tomb in history is so important. Merely to claim an abiding influence of Jesus on people after his death neglects the context of the fulfilment of God's purpose to bring the kingdom into history.

Working back from the resurrection, Jesus' disciples had then to explain his death. It was explained as being caused by human sin, focused in the Jewish rejection of God's Messiah; his death was a representative death on behalf of his murderers; dying to make victory available to his own people who had rejected him; it was a substitutionary death dying the death which God's people deserved for the gross insult to God of rejecting his Messiah; it was a death so that they might not die but enter into the resurrection life of the kingdom of God.

Jesus' death had historical causes in the reaction of the Jewish leaders to his claim to bring the kingdom of God. It had historical results in issuing in the resurrection. This demonstrated both God's reversal of the decision of the Jewish leaders and that Jesus had indeed brought the invasion of the kingdom of God.

History is the context in scripture of the claim that Jesus was unique. History is the arena for the expression of reconciliation between different human groups. The means whereby God made this possible was the historical incarnation, death, and resurrection of Christ. The fulfilment of his purpose will be in a new heavens and a new earth. On this basis Christians are to be motivated to seek reconciliation between groups in society as a whole, knowing that this is an expression of God's purpose, that it has been made possible in Christ, and that it is to find its fullest expression in this world in his church.

While reconciliation and understanding between different religious groups remaining within their religious traditions is not the final expression of the New Testament purpose, to the extent that it represents a degree of reconciliation, it points towards the full reconciliation which God purposes in Christ. But if full reconciliation can only occur within the church, does not this represent a Christian supremacy and imperialism? It seems churlish and extreme to declare that the true reconciliation and unity of divided groups is brought about according to the scriptures by Jesus Christ. But the Bible leaves no other option. How can we understand it?

Christian relations with people of other faiths

First, we must not confuse questions related to what we could describe as 'race relations' with questions of religious pluralism. Christians may have authentic and respectful relations with those of other faiths, but this does not depend on affirming the equal validity of all religions. The biblical basis for affirming the unity of humanity is that the divisions between different groups have been overcome in Christ. The biblical basis for affirming that people from different cultures have gifts to share with each other is that Christian people from different cultures have much to learn from each other, having gifts to share. This is not to say that there have not been occasions when Christians have confused questions of race relations with those of religious pluralism, to the detriment of both. Thus Graham Houghton documents how western Protestant missionaries in India in the nineteenth century adopted as their main apologetic the task of discrediting and ridiculing the faiths of the Hindus as irrational.[5] In the twentieth century Kraemer argued that non-Christian religions were not truly religious in the western sense of the word, being more concerned with getting benefits from God than with responding to truth.[6] We have noted how this process inevitably demeaned people's sense of identity and led to a resurgence in the post-colonial period of national-culture religions as the basis for national identity.

Second, we must not confuse a biblical view of the relation to other faiths with a view that denies that God is at work among them. Evangelical mission theologians from Africa and Asia have been exploring recently ways in which Christian theology must begin to affirm the identity of people of other religious cultures. For example, in the context of African traditional religions Kwame Bediako has done extensive work on the issue of African Christian identity.[7] He writes:

> By failing to view man-in-African 'heathenism' as *man* in the same terms as man-in-Christianity, they [western missionaries]

deprived themselves of adequate means for discerning the activity of God in the lives of Africans. They also tended to confuse their particular institutionalisation of western Christianity with Christ, and to present the former as the giver of salvation. The truth is that it is 'not Christianity that saves, but Christ'.[8]

Bediako perceives that western Christians identified Christianity with their cultural interpretation of Christianity, and by identifying salvation with Christianity rather than with Christ devalued the work of God in African pre-Christian history, and thus seriously affected the African Christian's sense of identity. Bediako writes:

It was the generally negative missionary attitude to African religious life which most profoundly influenced African understanding of the Christian faith as presented by missionaries . . . [as a result] Africans could only receive and articulate the faith insofar as they kept to the boundaries and models defined by the Christian traditions of Europe. Christ could not inhabit the spiritual universe of the African consciousness except, in essence, as a stranger. It is difficult not to link our missionary connection with the problem of identity which came to weigh so heavily on the Christian conscience of many an African; must we become other than African in order to be truly Christian? . . . Instead of producing a real meeting at the specific level of religious apprehension and theology, the missionary enterprise produced what can be called an African Christian identity problem.[9]

Bediako discovers precedent for the approach of reinterpreting one's past in the early church Fathers:

Such coming to terms with one's past, and the interpretation, even reinterpretation of it, with the aid of the new understanding and commitment, has outstanding precedent in Christian history. It was crucial for laying the foundations for the vigorous patristic theology of the second and third centuries AD in the context of Gentile Christianity. Therefore the well-known 'quest for an African theology' by this generation of theologians must be understood as a quest in which African Christian identity could inhere, in terms meaningful also for the demands of African integrity; for without such integrity African Christian theology would be impossible.[10]

Bediako argues against the traditional and dismissive Christian view of the non-Christian past in Africa on two grounds. First, he notes that the primal (animistic) religions in Africa have been a very fertile ground for the spread of Christianity and therefore asks, with H. W. Turner, whether there may be some affinities between Christianity and the primal traditions. Second, he mounts a biblical argument that, because of the universality of Christ,

> our Lord has been, from the beginning, the Word of God for us as for all men everywhere. He has been the source of our life, and illuminator of our path in life, though like all men everywhere, we also failed to apprehend him aright.[11]

Through Jesus everyone has access to the history of the people of God:

> Through our faith in him [Jesus], we show that we are also the children of Abraham, who was the spiritual father of all who put their faith in God (Rom. 4: 11). Consequently, we have not merely our own 'natural' past; we also have an 'adoptive' past, the past of God, reaching into the biblical history itself.[12]

But this adoptive past does not obliterate the natural past. For Bediako gives a strong redemptive thrust to that natural past. He rejects a weak doctrine of creation as 'nature'.

> The beginning of the Gospel (of John) echoes the early verses of Genesis 1. We are meant to appreciate the close association of our creation and our redemption, both effected in and through Jesus Christ (Col. 1: 15 ff.). We are to understand our creation as the original revelation of God to us, not as it is often taken, in the rather weak and abstract sense of the realm of 'nature'. Rather, it was in the creation of the universe and especially of man, that God first revealed his Kingship to our ancestors, and called them and us freely to obey him. Working from the perception of our creation as the original revelation to and covenant with us, we, from an African primal tradition, are given a biblical basis for theologising within the framework of the high doctrine of God as Creator and Sustainer, which is deeply rooted in our heritage. More significantly, we are enabled to discover ourselves in Adam (cf. Acts 17: 26), and come out of the isolation which the closed system of clan, lineage and family imposes, to recover universal horizons.[13]

Bediako insists on the redemptive value of creation. He insists on salvation through Christ, not through Christianity, and that Christ is a universal Christ who is Lord of the African's history: 'He has been the source of our life'.[14] Bediako thus finds identity a crucial category for developing theological reflection, and suggests that a proper understanding of the relation of the pre-Christian history of the African people to the Messiah is critical for developing an authentic African Christian identity. To recover this Bediako strongly suggests a re-examination of the mission history of Africa, viewed through the eyes not of western missionaries but of African Christians.

Bediako's work shows that it is possible to accord proper dignity and respect for people's pre-Christian past and non-Christian culture and at the same time commend the uniqueness and exclusive claims of Jesus Christ.

Reconciliation in Christ without religious imperialism

How can the unique and exclusive claims of Jesus be expressed as the grounds for true human reconciliation without a religious imperialism? We have to recognize at the outset that any world-view that claims to be comprehensive will be imperialistic, in the sense of offering an interpretation of other views within its own terms. Christianity is no better and no worse than (for example) Marxism or secularism in this regard. However, particular dangers have not always been avoided in commending the claims of Jesus Christ. So we proceed to suggest how those exclusive claims can be best expressed with proper sensitivity to religious pluralism.

First, they are not to be commended as delivering the only true experience of God. Once religious experience is chosen as the ground of commonality of comparison between religions, we have moved out of the arena of biblical theology into the arena of (for example) Hindu religions. Within that arena, the content of religious experience can only be known and authenticated by the individual who experienced it. It cannot be evaluated by anyone else. Some evangelical Christian apologetic has increasingly focused on the superiority of Christian religious experience. This is to move in a framework within which any claim to uniqueness implies an unacceptable arrogance. Indeed, such arrogance must contradict the very claims being made for the value of the Christian religious experience.

Second, we turn to the practice of Jesus in discussion with the religious leaders of his time. He did not discuss the fields of religious experience or religious philosophy. He began with questions and judgements of the marginalized within his own religious culture, especially the women and the poor. It was with the questions of these groups that Jesus began to explain the good news. Vinay Samuel writes in India:

Not all human questions point to the realities and answers of the gospel. The questions of the untroubled rich did not lead them to appreciate the answers of Jesus. It was those rich who experienced the questions of the marginalised, Zaccheus the outcast and the prodigal son who experienced degradation, who found in Jesus the answer to their quest. When they found themselves victims of oppression, they asked the right questions and came to Jesus for the answers. That is part of what is meant by repentance.

A crucial area therefore for Christian witness to Hindus is to begin with the questions of the marginalised within Hinduism, the women and the poor, and to share the answers of Jesus which affirm the validity of their questions and of their judgements. The aim of Christian witness is not to enable the literate sophisticated Hindu to have a religious encounter with a mystical figure from another religious tradition. The gospel comes with questions. It enables the questions of the marginalised Hindus to be affirmed, and addressed by the gospel, and addresses these questions to the socially elite Hindu.[15]

Samuel makes a further point that the nature of this witness is not primarily the witness of an individual to the superiority of an experience or of the rationality of a theological system. It is the witness of a community.

The Christian gospel is about breaking down barriers between God and man and between man and man and so addresses issues such as the barriers between rich and poor, caste and outcaste. So the Christian witness cannot be the witness of an individual alone testifying to his own personal religious experience. It must be the witness of the life of a Christian community in which the new life of reconciliation is being expressed. A person's Christian witness . . . must be to witness to his participation in the reality of reconciliation which his Christian community is experiencing and which he is convinced is mediated to them and offered to all through Jesus Christ.[16]

In the New Testament the pattern of witness is the pattern of event and explanation. In the Acts of the Apostles, events of healing were followed by explanations. In the epistles the event to be explained is the existence of a community within which the barriers of race, class, and gender are overcome. C. J. Wright points out that while our western way of approaching the issues is

to begin at the personal level and work outwards . . . the Bible tends to place the emphasis the other way round. Here is the kind of society that God wants . . . what kind of person must you be to be worthy of inclusion within it, and what must be your contribution to the furthering of these overall objectives.[17]

There is a large body of evidence that in the Indian subcontinent the relation of Christianity to those within the Hindu religions has been at this level of social significance. For example, M. M. Thomas writes:

The outcastes, the poor and the orphans saw Christian faith as the source of a new humanising influence and the foundation of a human community. Where conversion was genuine, whether of individuals or of groups, the converts saw salvation in Christ not only in terms of individual salvation, of heaven after death, but also as the spiritual source of a new community on earth in which their human dignity and status were recognised. It was the promise of humanisation inherent in the gospel of salvation which led to the influx of the oppressed into the church.[18]

The evidence comes not only from Christians. V. T. Rajshekar, a leader of the untouchables in India, and not himself a Christian, writes:

Christians have rendered such a signal service to the liberation of Untouchables as can be written only in letters of gold when we re-write Indian history . . . conversion to other religions has become popular among the Untouchables, not because after conversion to Christianity and Islam the problem of poverty is solved. To them property is not their number one problem. People cannot live by bread alone. They want the self-respect which is denied under Hinduism. They will get it the moment they get out of Hinduism and convert to other religions.[19]

This perspective on evangelicals contrasts for example, with the view that would suggest that, since people comprehend what they comprehend within the concepts and categories given in their context, and since each religion is culturally expressed and culturally relative, each religion is necessarily most appropriate to the particular culture it is at present found in. It contrasts with this view on the ground that this view denies the unique role of Jesus Christ in breaking down the barriers between different groups, and also on the ground that if our Christian witness is to make a Hindu a better Hindu, the question remains 'what is a better Hindu?' If it is a Hindu who is liberated from caste, to what extent has he ceased to be a Hindu and moved towards becoming a Christian? The exclusiveness and uniqueness of Jesus pose the question 'what other religion in its revelation and best expressions presents itself as good news to the poor and affirms those elements in other religions as the work of God?'

Third, it is important that in formulating a Christian expression, adequate attention is given to the context in question, for example in the way outlined by Bediako above. The wholeness of Christian expression is not found when people in one situation discover the totally adequate and true formulation, but when Christians from different cultures share their understanding of the faith in their context with one another. While affirming the uniqueness of Jesus and his exclusive claims, we must resist the imperialism of any one cultural view of Jesus over others.

Fourth, it is important to recognize the possibility that people outside the Christian church can be saved in their own religious context through God's mercy in Christ. Sir Norman Anderson expresses a view held by many evangelical Christians:

> multitudes of Jews . . . in Old Testament times, turned to God in repentance, brought the prescribed sacrifice, and threw themselves on his mercy. It was not that they earned that mercy by their repentance or obedience, or that animal sacrifice could ever avail to atone for human sin. It was that their repentance and faith (themselves, of course, the result of God's work in their hearts) opened the gate, as it were, to the grace, mercy and forgiveness which he always longed to extend to them, and which was to be made for ever available at the cross on which Christ 'gave himself as a ransom for all to be testified in due time'. May we not believe, then, that the same would be true of the follower of some other religion in whose heart the God of all mercy had been working by his Spirit, who had come in some measure to realise his sin and need for forgiveness, and who had been enabled, in the twilight as it were, to throw himself on the mercy of God? Is not this, perhaps the meaning of St. Peter's words in the house of Cornelius: 'I see now how true it is that God has no favourites, but that in every nation the man who is godfearing, and does what is right is acceptable to him'? This cannot mean that the man who tries to be religious and strives to be moral will earn salvation, for the whole Bible denies this possibility. But does it not mean that the man who realises something of his sin or need, and throws himself on the mercy of God with a sincerity which shows itself in his life (which would always of course be a sure sign of the inward

prompting of God's Spirit, and especially so in the case of one who had never heard the Gospel), would find that mercy – although without understanding it – at the cross on which Christ 'died for all'.[20]

Anderson adds that such people would still lack the knowledge of salvation and the assurance of sins forgiven, of 'the experience of joy, peace and power, which a conscious knowledge of Christ, and communion with him, alone can bring' and would have no clear message to pass on to others. So this understanding can never replace the need to share the gospel explicitly with others or build a visible Christian community.

In summary, for evangelicals the context of the exclusive claims of Christ is history. In history the purpose of God is to bring right relationships between groups and thus enable each group to make its contribution to the whole in an authentic pluralism. This requires an especial bias to the poor. This purpose has been established through Christ. This purpose is one criterion for identifying his activity outside the Christian community, and is also part of the mission of the church. The questions that Christian faith poses to other religions concern the way in which women, the poor, and the powerless within them experience the operation of the faith. This question must also be addressed to empirical Christianity. This question sets the agenda for dialogue and relationships with those of other faiths. In such a situation the basis of Christian faith and hope that such a process is not a fruitless task is that the barriers between different human groups have already been broken down in Christ.

In a book co-ordinated by a department of sociology it might not be out of place to suggest that the mission-practice of Christians in contexts of religious pluralism, such as those of Bediako in Ghana, Samuel in India, and Mastra in Indonesia, would make appropriate topics for study of the way in which the church expresses its belief through its work in such societies.

Conclusion

This background will, I hope, illuminate the most recent international evangelical statement on the relation of Christian faith with other faiths. The statement is dated 27 March 1987 and forms part of the Statement of the Stuttgart Consultation on Evangelism convened by the Commission on World Mission and Evangelism. Among those who participated in this consultation and drew up the statement are the authors quoted, Bediako and Samuel, and

161

the author of this chapter. The section is headed 'Evangelism in the Context of Other Faiths':

We acknowledge and affirm that authentic witness to Jesus Christ should be carried out in a spirit of respect for the beliefs and devotion of others. It can never be simply a 'telling' but must also be a sensitive 'listening'. It must, furthermore, always respect the freedom of others and should not be coercive or seductive in any way. We acknowledge that God has not left himself without witness anywhere (Acts 16: 17) and we joyfully recognise a knowledge of God, a sense of the transcendent, among many human communities, including many faith-communities. At the same time, it needs to be pointed out that humankind's knowledge of God is vitiated by sin and God's gracious revelation in Christ is needed to call us all back to an authentic vision of God. We agree with the *Ecumenical Affirmation on Mission and Evangelism* (para. 43) that the Spirit of God is at work in the world convincing humankind of God's righteousness and convicting them of their own sin (John 16: 8). As we enter into dialogue with those of other faiths we should keep in mind both the knowledge of God which is available to all and the work of the Spirit ahead of our own witness. We recognise also the figure of Christ in the poor, the needy, the ill and the oppressed (Matt. 25: 31–46).

Christians, nevertheless, owe the message of God's salvation in Jesus Christ to every person and to every people (*Ecumenical Affirmation*, para. 41). As we have already said, the proclamation of the Gospel includes an invitation to each person to recognise and accept in a personal decision the saving Lordship of Christ (para. 10). This might be seen as a fulfilment of the aspirations of humankind expressed sometimes in religious traditions but at other times in non-religious movements. Such proclamation may also be understood as a making explicit of an implicit knowledge; or as bringing assurance and certainty of salvation to all those who, without prior explicit knowledge of Jesus Christ, the only Saviour and Lord, have nevertheless realised their own inadequacy and sin and have thrown themselves on the mercy of God. While the proclamation of the Gospel will affirm and confirm certain aspects of a person's or a people's previous religious experience, it will also challenge and judge other aspects of such experience. It is always, therefore, a call to repentance and new life. We recognise that dialogue is not to be used for cheap proselytism but we believe that it can be a medium of authentic witness, though we are

aware that there are other reasons for the necessity of dialogue
with those of other faiths. Such reasons would include the building up of community, common witness about the dignity and
rights of human beings and addressing human need.

As Christians we welcome the fact that many societies are
moving towards greater openness and pluralism. In some cases
the emergence of a plural society makes the existence of
Christian churches, in a predominantly non-Christian culture,
possible. In others, societies which have hitherto been largely
'Christian', become increasingly plural with many different old
and new faiths represented in them. We recognise both
phenomena as within God's providence and as giving Christians
fresh opportunities to love, serve and witness to their neighbours. We are concerned that some societies remain closed and
continue to deny freedom of belief, of conscience and of free
expression to their members. As Christians, we are committed
to the promotion of these freedoms in our respective societies.[21]

It is my hope that this chapter has served to show to some
extent some of the background to the thinking in this statement
which represents where a significant body of evangelicals stand
on the issue of Christian faith and religious pluralism. To that
extent I hope my chapter has served the purpose of being a map-
making exercise.[22]

Notes

1 See Ephesians 2–3. For a discussion on principalities and powers see
   for example H. Berkof, *Christ and the Powers*, Scotdale: Herald Press
   (1962), and Ronald J. Sider, *Evangelism, Salvation and Social Justice*,
   Nottingham: Grove Booklets on Ethics (1975).
2 Hendrik Kraemer, *The Christian Message in a non-Christian World*,
   New York: Harper (1938).
3 See Wayan Mastra, 'The Salvation of Non-Believers' Ph.D. thesis
   presented to Dubuque University, Iowa, (1970), 206–7.
4 Stephen Mott, *Jesus and Social Ethics*, Nottingham: Grove Booklets
   on Ethics (1984), 13–14.
5 See Graham Houghton, 'Late nineteenth century Protestant Christian
   attitudes towards Hinduism', in V. Samuel and C. Sugden (eds),
   The Gospel among our Hindu Neighbours, Bangalore: Partnership in
   Mission Asia (1983).
6 See, for example, Kraemer, *Christian Message*, 144 and 294.
7 His main work is so far in his Ph. D. Thesis, 'Identity and Integration:
   An Enquiry into the Nature and Problems of Theological Indigenis-
   ation in Selected Early Hellenistic and Modern African Christian
   Writers', Aberdeen (July 1983), Oxford: Regnum (forthcoming). He

has published material from this in his one published study, 'Biblical Christologies in the context of African traditional religions', in V. Samuel and C. Sugden (eds), *Sharing Jesus in the Two Thirds World*, Grand Rapids: Eerdmans (1984).

8 Kwame Bediako, in 'Biblical Christologies in the context of African traditional religions', 92. The quote is from Andrew Walls, 'The first chapter of the epistle to the Romans and the modern missionary movement', in W. Ward Gasque and Ralph P. Martin (eds), *Apostolic History and the Gospel*, Exeter: Paternoster Press (1970), 356.

9 Bediako, 'Biblical Christologies', 87–8.

10 ibid., 88.

11 ibid., 101.

12 ibid.

13 ibid., 102.

14 ibid., 101.

15 'Dialogue with other religions', in *The Gospel among our Hindu Neighbours*, 207–8.

16 ibid., 208.

17 Christopher Wright, 'The use of the Bible in social ethics', in *Transformation*, vol. 1, no. 1, p. 14, Nottingham: Grove Booklets on Ethics (1983).

18 M. M. Thomas, *Salvation and Humanisation*, Madras: Christian Literature Service (1971), 14. See also Leslie Newbiggin, *Unfinished Agenda*, London: SPCK (1985), 142: 'The Gospel was doing what it has always done, making it possible for those who were formerly "no people" to become God's people'.

19 V. T. Rajshekar, 'How India's Untouchables view Hinduism', in *The Gospel among our Hindu Neighbours*, 124 and 131–2.

20 J. N. D. Anderson, *Christianity and Other Religions*, Leicester: Inter Varsity Press (1970), 101–2.

21 'The Stuttgart statement on evangelism', in V. Samuel and A. Hauser, op. cit., 221–2.

22 Examples of further writings that express the point of view expressed in this paper are:
Michael Nazir Ali, *Islam: a Christian Perspective*, Exeter: Paternoster (1983); 'That which is not to be found but which finds us', in *Towards a Theology for Inter-faith Dialogue*, 2nd edn., London: Church Information Office (1986), 41–50; *Frontiers in Muslim Christian Encounter*, Oxford: Regnum (1987).
'Fidelity, freedom and friendship: Christians in plural societies', in V. Samuel and A. Hauser (eds), *Proclaiming Christ in Christ's Way*, Oxford: Regnum (1989), pp. 85 ff.
Evangelical Alliance, *Christianity and Other Faiths: An Evangelical Contribution to our Multi-Faith Society*, Exeter: Paternoster (1983).
Vinay Samuel and Chris Sugden (eds), *Sharing Jesus in the Two Thirds World*, Grand Rapids: Eerdmans (1984).
Christopher Sugden, *Christ's Exclusive Claims and Religious Pluralism*, Nottingham: Grove Booklets (1985); 'A Critical and Compara-

tive Study of the Practice and Theology of Christian Social Witness in Indonesia and India between 1974 and 1983 with Special Reference to the Work of Wayan Mastra in the Protestant Church of Bali and Vinay Samuel in the Church of South India', Ph.D thesis presented to the Council for National Academic Awards (1987).

The papers of 'Mission in Plural Contexts', London: Consultation of Partnership in Mission (1986), available from Partnership in Mission, c/o In Contact, St Andrews Vicarage, St Andrews Road, London E13.

11

Religion, science, and symbolism

Mary Hesse

(The paper on which this chapter is based was read at the Colloque Chantilly, 30 September–2 October 1985, and published in French in 'Le Symbole religieux et l'imaginaire dans la littérature Anglaise', by Groupe de Recherche sur Littérature et Religion dans les Pays de la Langue Anglaise, Université Paris-Nord, 1987.)

Our society is familiar with the idea of the 'pluralism' of religious and moral belief – a situation in which such beliefs are regarded as more or less necessary for social health, but in which there is confusion about their rational basis, and general scepticism about the possibility of any specific belief-system being uniquely true. Such a situation is not perceived to be the case with scientific beliefs. Here there are supposed to be clear rational foundations and a well-understood method of acquiring and extending truth. The distinction between science and religion is seen most sharply in their uses of *language*, and in this respect there is a pluralism which goes much deeper than the diverse symbolisms which characterize different religious belief-systems. It is this pluralism of language-use that I shall try to analyse in this paper.

In the English-speaking philosophical tradition it has generally been held that there is a radical difference between scientific and symbolic uses of language. Science is literal and empirical, and has a unique relation to truth. Scientific theories exhibit continually progressive accumulations of objective knowledge. Symbolism, on the other hand, employs irreducibly metaphorical language, is holistic in meaning, and is typically the vehicle of subjective world-models, whether the worlds of literary texts, or of physical systems or religious cosmologies. Science is objective and representational; symbolism is subjective expression of psychological and social 'realities', and does not attain to knowledge of reality, properly speaking.

The success of natural science has appeared to make this

conclusion too easy. The argument goes something like this: to know the truth we must investigate according to scientific methods; these yield true statements that correspond to the real, and moreover are the only sure way of attaining true statements; hence the real is exhausted by science. To those who object that the conclusion is a *non sequitur*, the reply comes: if the real is not so exhausted, then tell us how to speak truly of it, for we know of no way but the scientific. Thus scientific naturalism becomes scientific positivism, or rather scientific imperialism. The argument is not cogent, but the challenge is fair and pertinent, and is neglected at our peril if we wish to commend religion in a scientific culture: 'If there is reality beyond science and the natural, tell us how to speak of it.'

In the history of religion there have been two kinds of answer: the symbolic and the metaphysical. From Aristotle to Aquinas to Heidegger these have been seen as conflicting alternatives. But both have presupposed that there is something beyond the natural to talk about; while under the dominance of naturalism this pre-supposition has gone bankrupt, and therefore both the symbolic and the metaphysical have been made redundant. The symbolic has, however, somewhat unexpectedly found employment recently in the heart of the scientific enterprise itself. First, the linguistic literalism and correspondence-theory of truth implied in the representational view of science has become untenable, and science has been shown also to weave metaphorical world-models. Second, the realist view of scientific theories has been undermined by new sensitivity to the historically contingent character of these world-models. And third, the 'progressive' nature of science has come to be seen in terms of success in empirical application, which is itself a contingent choice of demarcation-criterion for what we call 'science'. But this is not enough to give science a specially privileged status *vis-à-vis* knowledge.

I shall draw on some of these developments to suggest how we use metaphoric and symbolic language as the proper vehicle of truth for realities that go beyond the natural. And first I shall show how it has found application even in natural science, and how its use there already takes us beyond a simple-minded theory of the relation between language and reality.[1]

Naturalism and naked speech

It is impossible to understand the close association that has always held between science and naïve realism without considering the context in which the association arose in the seventeenth century.

Aristotle had defined what it is to state a true proposition in a way that does not yet amount to naïve realism: 'To state of what is, that it is; and of what is not, that it is not'. Thus he asserted at the outset of Western philosophy the assumption that the real somehow parallels the true; ontology and language are isomorphic. But his statement does not specify what kind of 'reality' is referred to: there may be worlds of mathematics, or of morals, or of aesthetic values, whose being might be the subject-matter of true statements. In seventeenth-century natural philosophy, however, the isomorphism that is claimed is between descriptive language and the natural world. This is how it was taken up in the concepts of an ideal or universal language, an 'alphabet of nature' in which all general terms would correspond with the essences of natural things, and the grammar of the language would correspond with the laws of things.

In the early years of the Royal Society it was held that this ideal implied that language should be cool and prosaic. The society's official historian, Thomas Sprat, wrote that the society's aim was to confirm its writing and talking to a 'close, naked, natural way of speaking' in contrast to what one of the society's founders, Seth Ward, called the 'windy impostures of magic and astrology, of signatures and physionomy'. Since then both literary language in general and theoretical and metaphysical language in particular have shared with magic and astrology the condemnation of being 'windy apparitions' signifying nothing. Descriptive language succumbed to an empiricist myth, namely that truth-value inheres only in the literal, the univocal, the exact, the cool, the impersonally objective.

Almost every assumption underlying this seventeenth-century realism has been subjected to damaging criticism. It was realized from an early stage in the scientific revolution that there is an epistemological problem about the inference from observations to theories which are supposed to describe the real, because this cannot be made logically conclusive. There is in principle always an indefinite number of theories that fit the observed facts more or less adequately. Since renewed attention has been paid to this problem by Duhem and Quine, it has come to be called the 'underdetermination' of theory by empirical data.

A second epistemological problem concerns the particular theoretical language and conceptual structure within which scientific results are expressed. In even the most apparently elementary observational situations, we are bound to bring to our description the categories our language provides, and these may reflect unconscious 'common sense' theories, or consciously held background beliefs which have already been structured by previously accepted theories. For example, the professors at Pisa, according to Galileo's report, could not describe their observations through the telescope in terms of imperfections in the spherical form of the heavens, because their theories did not permit this category to be applied in that domain – they had to describe sunspots, the phases of Venus, and Jupiter's moons as distortions due to the telescope itself. Moreover, the background knowledge and belief that conditions what we see and how it is described is not *a priori* knowledge, independent of observation, but is itself vulnerable to similar ambiguities in the way observations are described in the light of theory. Even apparently immediate descriptions of what we observe are theory-laden – they presuppose the way in which we make our fundamental classification of objects and events in the world.

It follows that the very meanings of the concepts we use in descriptive sentences, whether observation-sentences or theories, are at least partly conferred by the whole context of theory, and they vary from theory to theory. What Newton means by 'force' is to be understood as that which is related to mass and acceleration in Newton's laws of motion. Its meaning cannot be exhausted by talking about tugs-of-war or falling bodies or impacting billiard balls. But to say that force is just that concept that satisfies Newton's laws appears to lead into a circle of meanings, for the same has to be said about the other concepts of those laws – mass and motion – which also have to be understood as implicitly defined by the laws, as well as having reference to actual bodies moving in space and time. Thus Newton's force, mass, and motion are different concepts from Einstein's force, mass, and motion, because the implicitly defining laws are different. This has come to be called the 'meaning-variance' thesis, according to which the meanings of concepts are holistically related to theoretical networks, and hence change from theory to theory.

I shall not here go into the detailed debates about realism, theory-ladenness, and meaning-variance as they have developed in the philosophy of science literature. Rather, I shall suggest an alternative view of natural science that is both consistent with the theses of underdetermination and theory-ladenness, and that indicates better than the standard view how scientific cosmologies may be continuous with metaphoric and symbolic worlds. The basic metaphor for this alternative view is that scientific theories are imaginative narratives: they tell a story about the natural world, within a particular set of categories and presuppositions which are subject to historical change, and which usually develop from local metaphysical and social world-models.

Thus, for example, in the seventeenth century the generally accepted model of the universe was mechanical: everything was interpreted as *really* the product of matter-in-motion, the universe as a great piece of clockwork. This was not an obvious perception of the surface nature of things: as Galileo put it, it committed violence upon the senses even to contemplate the solar system as a sun-centred system with the earth as just one of the planets freely orbiting in space. Nor was it a deduction from surface observations, since these seem obviously to contradict it. Its origins lie in a complex mixture of many factors, including increasing familiarity with man-made clockwork mechanisms, and the linguistic analogy of the alphabet of nature, together with theological objections to the notion of capricious powers operating by arcane magic accessible only to the initiated. The twentieth-century revolution in physics has required a different story, another fundamental re-description of the ontological elements of nature, of the categories of space, time, matter, motion, and causality, and of the interaction of observers with the observed. All these categorial systems are imaginative hypotheses, for ever beyond direct verification or refutation by empirical facts alone.

Revolutionary changes in ontologies and categories cannot, however, be the whole story, for there must also be some sense in which science progresses through revolutions, and this seems to be the feature which distinguishes science from other metaphysical and symbolic cosmologies. There is indeed instrumental progress, in the sense that we now have vastly increasing pragmatic possibilities of predicting and controlling empirical events by means of experiment and theory-construction. The human species employs the 'test and empirical feedback' method of science as a natural extension of animal learning, in order first to survive in its environment, and later to change and exploit it. The method yields 'objective' knowledge in this pragmatic sense. But, contrary to the traditional realist claims for science, it is knowledge of local rather than universal reality, of particulars rather than universals, it is approximate rather than exact, and it refers to the immediately describable and verifiable rather than the theoretically deep and real. It is not the theoretical frameworks as such that validate the claim of science to be a distinctive and reliable body of knowledge, but rather the way in which they are used to further the feedback method of prediction and control. Science refers to the real world by modelling its accessible features in terms of some categorization or classification which bears a relation of *analogy* to the world, not an identical correspondence with it. The model does not *state* what the analogy is, it *shows* it in the form of the language. Reality is therefore never exactly or comprehensively captured in explicit speech.

In Kantian terms we may say that science 'objectifies' the world, rather than reveals its structure by realistic description. Objectification is an active but controlled process – a corporate decision so to represent the world that its structure can yield instrumental facts. Objectification is the projection upon the world of the classificatory presuppositions of the language of a scientific culture for a particular purpose – namely, instrumental prediction and control. In carrying out this goal it strips the world of all intrinsic meaning and purpose, except that of 'objective' truth and usefulness, and even the objectivity of truth is seen to be dependent on instrumental goals.[2] This view undoubtedly conflicts with a widespread ideology of science, which holds that scientific theory is its *raison d'être*, and values science for its 'truth' rather than its usefulness. If this ideology is, in the instrumental view, a 'false consciousness', we have to go on to ask, what then is the status and function of theory in the instrumental view?

There is no doubt that increasingly complex, yet unified, theoretical constructions provide overwhelming fascination for laymen and unending motivation for practising scientists. It would be too simple to ascribe this fascination purely to the instrumental success of science and its technological application. In view of the profound aesthetic appeal that scientific problem-solving has for those who pursue it, we might put its non-instrumental aspects in the same category as 'art' or 'play', which are regarded in positivist philosophy as having no direct social or epistemological function except in their by-products of challenges and pleasure.[3] A great deal of scientific theorizing, especially in fundamental physics and cosmology, is not too distant from the creation of science fiction, which might indeed be said to be speculative theory without the full rigour of experimental control.

But the aesthetic appeal of science indicates something deeper than this, of which the claim to 'discover reality' is but a misleading hint. It is quite clear that for the lay public in educated western society, scientific accounts of the origin and destiny of the universe, and of the status of human beings within it, have replaced the traditional mythical accounts given in various forms of religion, including in particular biblical religion. In other words, whatever other significance scientific theory has, it certainly has the status of cosmological myth[4] in our society, as can be seen in the way 'origins' are taught in schools, and in the popularity of

171

media presentations of fundamental science, both of physics and biology.

It would be a mistake, however, to take this mythic function of science as a mere by-product, or as a vestigial influence of long-running 'science and religion' controversies. It is rather of the essence of the relation between science and society. Recent studies of the social history of science have amply shown a two-way influence: the categories of scientific theory are partly determined by surrounding social forces and cultural ideas, and theories can, intentionally or unintentionally, be used to reinforce or revolutionize cultural forms.[5] Scientific theory, as it is accepted within the scientific community and hence by the wider public, is the result of a complex of decisions and persuasive arguments of individual scientists which reflect their ideological and evaluative commitments as well as their instrumental motivations. Scientific theory has its place in the dynamically interacting mythologies of western culture just as cosmologies have in primitive cultures, and without input from cultural needs there would be no motivation for instrumental science to flower into the universal world-models that have always been part of its social goal.

Religion and symbolism

Scientific models, then, may be seen as prototypes for imaginative creations which are based on language and experience, but go beyond them by analogical extension to permit the meaningful description of worlds that become mythical realities in the surrounding culture. They are prototypes for a general category of narrations including myths, symbol-systems, metaphysics, and theologies. In these cases meanings are also freely extended from natural and social experience into descriptions of possible worlds, but their appropriate validations are other than those of empirical science – that is, other than the objectification of the empirical world for instrumental purposes.

My application of these ideas to religion will be all-too brief, but the essence of the matter has already been laid out in relation to science. Once the spell of scientific objectification as the only route of true descriptions is broken, the way is open to consider new theories of meaning and truth for alternative modes of relating to the social and religious worlds. In order to understand how language functions in these non-objectified ways we have to break not only with the seventeenth-century 'alphabet of nature', but also with Aristotle's conception of the isomorphism of propositions with any world of being that the propositions describe.

Aristotle's ontology may have been more liberal than that of the scientific naturalists, but his theory of language was not. Our discussion of scientific models, however, has suggested that even these models do not capture reality univocally and isomorphically. It remains to draw out the implications of this conclusion for language and symbolism in general.

Models are concrete and systematic metaphors. Like models, metaphors rely on resemblances between different structures of experience to find new modes of expression, and to keep language and meaning in a state of constant, but controlled, change. This flux of meaning introduced by metaphor and other linguistic tropes, is what led both Aristotle and the seventeenth-century theorists to regard metaphoric language as imperfect and deceptive. It does indeed prevent the construal of language in terms of logic, for a word-token that changes its meaning with time or context cannot be a formal element satisfying the requirements of reidentifiability and substitutability of a logical system. But once the isomorphism of language and the world is abandoned, the notion of ideal language as a static logical system falls with it, and makes room for a view of language as a constantly changing holistic network of metaphors, striving to capture various orders of reality by the resemblances, tensions, and interactions of metaphor, metonymy, and other poetic devices. It is indeed possible to argue that since all general descriptive terms in language depend on perceived resemblances and differences for their concrete application, something like metaphor is essential for all linguistic expressions.[6] We have seen that metaphor is indispensable in scientific narratives, and it would be a mistake to suppose that such metaphor becomes static and 'dead' as soon as it is incorporated into an acceptable theory. For example, metaphors such as 'electric current flow' or 'charged conductor' are not reducible to the naked, natural, literal prose of positive theory. Maxwell found to his cost that the seductive model of electric fluid, which had become entrenched in the language, was merely the deposit of a previous atomic theory, from which he was attempting to liberate himself. The metaphors were not dead, but only lurking ready to deceive, and required to be consciously replaced by a new metaphoric system – that of continuous fields instead of discrete particles.[7]

The question now arises as to what can be meant by the 'truth' of metaphoric expressions. In the case of scientific models 'truth' is construed in terms of an adequate fit with the whole network of empirical applications, and in terms of their success in satisfying predictive expectations in the natural world. As we have seen, this does not guarantee the truth of high-level theories, but it conforms to what we generally mean by the truth of low-level regularities in limited space-time domains. In any case, metaphoric expressions have no discrete or stable meanings, but are controlled as 'meaning-in-use' by their holistic context. We shall therefore not expect the notion of 'truth' to have the clear-cut character of a propositional logic. For non-scientific contexts, however, the key to 'truth' lies in the nature of this 'control' where the criterion of empirical predictive success is inappropriate. This question will arise in connection with poetic metaphor and all kinds of social and religious myths, rituals, and symbolisms, which seem to have the function of communicating and maintaining socially relevant beliefs.

To extend the notion of 'truth' in this way, to 'what functions as true' in social groups, is no doubt a radical departure from philosophical orthodoxy, but it can be justified by looking at the orthodox scientific conception of truth from a different perspective. The constraints on truthful expression in language and in metaphor and symbol system must be relativized to the function of the type of communication intended. This suggestion is not new. For example, Durkheim and subsequent social anthropologists have relativized their conceptions of 'truth' and 'knowledge' to the accepted social representations of different cultures, and have examined how the symbol-systems function in maintaining social solidarity, in persuasive rhetoric, and in adaptation to change. Habermas has distinguished three 'knowledge interests' corresponding to the empirical-technical interest of natural science, the interest in understanding and communication served by history and the human sciences, and the critical and emancipatory interest in unmasking false consciousness, as in the theories of Marx and Freud. More recently he has added the function of self-expression served by aesthetic interests.[8]

There has as yet been little discussion of how this generalized conception of truth might apply to religious expressions, except in so far as religion is regarded as reducible to one or other of the other social functions: to poetic self-expression, or social opium or cement, or to early magical attempts to control the natural environment, which are now superseded by science. None of these reductions has been notably compelling or successful in assimilating the vast variety of religious myths, symbols, beliefs, and practices. It is surely time that religious expression should be looked at as being *sui generis* (to use Durkheim's description of religion).[9] In particular, it may be suggested that the common identification in our society of the religious with the aesthetic and subjective is a mistake. There are some respects in which a religious metaphor is more like the scientific model than like poetry, because it appears to involve descriptive statements and to make claims on the cognitive beliefs of its adherents. Like scientific models, religious myth and symbol constitute narrative accounts of worlds going beyond our everyday world, by emphasizing significant resemblances and differences in everyday experience, and endowing the whole with coherence, meaning, and purpose.[10] Religious symbols, again like scientific models, are perennial, though ever-changing and ever-renewable. We may say, perhaps, that the function of pure poetry is to create the perception of resemblances where none existed before, whereas religion also has the function of reflecting permanences in the human condition. 'The Lord is my Shepherd' can never become a dead metaphor: it can be used again and again in different contexts, developed in meaning, and extended throughout a whole network of associated metaphors of care and comfort, the lost and the found, sin and redemption. Any attempt to replace it by paraphrase, as in many modern renderings of scriptures and liturgy, is caught in the literal expression of a particular transient and quickly dating culture. Something like this insight seems to lie behind Lévi-Strauss's dictum that, far from being a species of poetry, myth is at the opposite end of a linguistic spectrum, for it can be told and retold, paraphrased and reparaphrased, without losing its meaning. What is conveyed by religious myth and symbol is part of the deep structure of human experience and the human psyche.[11]

What, then, are the tests of a religious symbolism which justify us in speaking of the possibility of the metaphoric truth of a religion? The tests are as various as are religious institutions and religious experiences. They will include coherence with acceptable systems of morality and with human psychological and social needs. They will answer to the perennial human dissatisfaction with things as they are, and the longing for salvation. They will endow human life with a framework: meaning and purpose, a beginning and an end. They will satisfy the need for prayer and worship of something other than the world. They will create and mould communities of believers. How these and other criteria of truth work for a religion is the subject-matter of theology and apologetics. What I am attempting to do here is to set up a framework within which conceptions of knowledge and justification can be extended from objectifying to non-objectifying domains.

The argument so far may seem to lead to an extreme pluralism and relativism of belief. 'Truth', even in scientific theory, is

175

relative to social functions and goals, and acceptable beliefs are controlled by holistic systems of symbol and metaphor which are intrinsic parts of the social fabric. Some societies exhibit more or less uniform religious belief-systems; some contain radically different systems, sometimes in violent conflict with each other; and some, like our own, seem to be held together by a basic ideology of science, together with some vestigial common moral principles, and a variety of religions whose distinctive tenets are increasingly superficial and non-functional relative to the general operations of our society.

There are two sorts of epistemological response to such pluralism. We may say that constraints on belief are wholly relative to local conditions and that there are no external rational criteria for choice either between societies or within a pluralist society. This relegates the interactions of beliefs to irrational and perhaps violent forces. Or we may take seriously the analogy with science and look for the relevant types of social constraint on belief that may reveal our common humanity. In so far as science is a unity, I have argued that this is because there is universal acceptance of an empirically instrumental goal for science. The difficulty in looking for a similar unity among the plurality of religious symbols is that goals and values are also relative to symbol-systems – values are bound up with facts in the holistic networks of symbolic belief. If the symbols reveal diverse and conflicting goals as well as diverse beliefs about facts, how can there be external criteria of truth?

There certainly cannot be any syncretic global religion, and even the pressures towards a liberal ecumenism that flourished in the mid-twentieth century now look over-simplistic. Our immediate refuge from relativism must be a less individually orientated immersion into our own symbol-system, whatever that may be. Such an immersion is not inconsistent with a critical stance towards it, nor with a deeper understanding of it by means of social and historical analysis and comparison. The process is analogous with what Kuhn describes as the exploitation of a given scientific paradigm in 'normal science', even while keeping in mind the possibility of revolutionary change.[12] And just as the natural world does have a real structure which we exploit by means of our various models of it, so we may retain a faith in an ultimate 'real structure' of the human world, whether that be merely biologically conditioned, or, as religious belief would have it, a transcendental destiny of the human under the providence of God.

Pluralism need not mean that religious truth is identified with psychology, sociology, or the various pragmatic effects with which religion has always been accompanied. Nor does it run counter to the claims of religion to be representative of a reality beyond this world. As we saw, even Aristotle's classic definition of the correspondence-theory of truth does not specify what sort of 'reality' is involved, nor what sort of criteria for such truth there should be. 'God is' may be true, because God is, but what Aristotle (and Aquinas) lack in their 'analogy of being' is a good theory of how to speak truly of God in ordinary – that is to say, metaphorical and symbolic – language. Religious models will always be plural and diverse, and no 'truth' within them will exactly mirror reality here any more than scientific models exactly mirror natural reality. Religious language may, however, be more or less adequate to its purposes, and more or less controlled by the variety of human experience religious and secular. A religious believer may want to say also that it is controlled from without by revelation, mistily and imperfectly perceived. Such a theory of metaphoric truth is still awaited, both in the analytic and hermeneutic philosophical traditions.

Notes

1 For more detailed accounts, see my *Revolutions and Reconstructions in the Philosophy of Science*, Brighton: Harvester (1980), especially Part II, and M. A. Arbib and M. Hesse, *The Construction of Reality*, Cambridge University Press (1987), chs. 1, 8, 10, 11.

2 Cf. C. Taylor, *Hegel*, Cambridge University Press (1975), 14.

3 For a more positive view of art and play, see M. G. Gadamer, *Truth and Method*, London: Sheed & Ward (1975), pt. 1.

4 'Myth' is used to mean 'significant story', in the sense distinguished by Northrop Frye (*The Great Code*, London: Routledge (1982), 32): 'Certain stories seem to have a particular significance: they are the stories that tell a society what is important for it to know, whether about its gods, its history, its laws, or its class structure'. 'Myth' is not of course meant here in its more popular sense of merely fictional tale, or downright untruth.

5 For examples from the history of physics (which might be thought to be most distant from the possibility of social influence), see P. Forman, 'Weimar culture, causality and quantum theory 1918–1927', in R. McCormack (ed.), *Historical Studies in Physical Science*, 3, University of Pennsylvania Press (1971), 1, and B. Wynne, 'Physics and psychics: science, symbolic action, and social control in late Victorian England', in B. Barnes and S. Shapin (eds), *Natural Order*, London: Sage (1979), 167.

6 See my 'Cognitive claims of metaphor', *Journal of Speculative Philosophy*, 2 (1988), 1–16.

7 See 'Maxwell's logic of analogy', in my *Structure of Scientific Inference*, London: Macmillan (1974), ch. 11.

8 J. Habermas, *Knowledge and Human Interests*, London: Heinemann (1972), appendix, and *Communication and the Evolution of Society*, Boston: Beacon (1979), ch. 1.

9 E. Durkheim, *The Elementary Forms of the Religious Life*, London: Allen & Unwin (1915), 424.

10 'Symbolism' may be regarded as a generalization of metaphor, including ritual actions, sacred objects, social roles, and all kinds of speech-acts, as well as metaphoric sentences. In all these cases 'meanings' are context-dependent and subject to rules of correct performance like the semantic rules of a language, and they constitute acted narratives of possible worlds: see M. A. Arbib and M. Hesse, *The Construction of Reality*, ch. 8, especially pp. 169–70.

11 C. Levi-Strauss, *Structural Anthropology*, New York: Basic Books (1963), 210.

12 Cf. T. Kuhn, *The Structure of Scientific Revolutions*, Chicago University Press (2nd edn 1970).

Judaism and pluralism
The price of 'religious freedom'

Paul Morris

> The best way to feel oneself no longer a Jew is to reason
> (J. P. Sartre, *Anti-Semite and Jew*, 124)[1]

In this chapter I intend to highlight some of the limitations of pluralism and enter a plea for a more far-reaching, extensive pluralism. We[2] all live in, at least nominally, democratic liberal nation-states, and it is against this political background that I wish to raise questions as to the nature and limits of contemporary religious freedom.

The term 'pluralism' in the title refers to religious pluralism. Religious pluralism[3] along with ethnic pluralism[4] are recent expressions based analogously upon and intimately related to the older expression 'political pluralism'.[5] Like the older expression, religious pluralism is used both descriptively and prescriptively. Descriptively, it claims to describe contemporary religious realities with regard to the diversity of religious traditions and the increased contact between them.

Prescriptively, it outlines an ideal situation in which there are perfectly harmonious relationships between the different faiths, based on tolerance, dialogue, and mutual understanding. Both political and religious pluralism are only intelligible in terms of the framework of the liberal democratic state. It is not accidental that religious pluralism has developed in, and only in, states already commited to political pluralism. Both religious pluralism and political pluralism are variants of and correctives to the classical liberal relationship of the individual and the state. Religious freedom is dependent upon liberalism's conception of this relationship.

By 'liberalism', I am referring to the political ideology and programme[6] based on the philosophical and political revolution that began in the seventeenth century, and which gave rise to the democratic nation-state and the now prevailing technological-scientific world-view.[7] It should be noted that throughout this chapter the definition of 'liberal' (and 'liberalism') is far more comprehensive than as usually understood, by, say, political theorists, who contrast the liberal with the conservative tradition in politics. In a way, in which I hope will become clear in the course of this chapter, these so-called conservative political parties must also be seen as subscribing to the same ideology and programme that I have referred to as 'liberalism'. The cursory sketch that follows is solely to point to the two central cardinal principles of liberalisms, as they bear on the question of religious freedom. These two principles are the separation of the public and private spheres of life and the state's right to exercise its power of coercion.

The history of the separation of the public and private spheres of life is a long and complex one, and a full study would entail discussion of the ontological and political aspects of individualism, the rise of 'rational' Protestantism and the 'two kingdoms', the Enlightenment attack on religion, the development of 'civil society', and the theories of political economy. One important strand in this development is metaphysical dualism. Metaphysical dualism first finds modern expression in the writings of René Descartes (1596–1650).[8] This view distinguishes between two absolutely distinct realms of existence, that of the subject (mind or soul) and that of the object (matter). The realm of matter is 'out there', visible, external, and operates according to rational objective principles. It is a realm of logic and mathematics, where universally valid scientific truths can be discerned. It is a realm compelled by rational, natural laws. The natural world and the scientific knowledge of it are held to be neither good or bad, but neutral. Any knowledge of the world is independent of any particular subject. The subjective realm of mind and belief is a private, invisible, and inaccessible realm. Metaphysical dualism provides the foundations for a radically new doctrine of the nature of man. The new conception of the separate and ultimately isolated 'individual' is based upon this novel mythology of the two separate realms. The individual is a unique union of these two quite distinct and eternally separate realms of mind and body. This individual, as separate and atomic, is the basic unit of the liberal world-view. The liberal individual extends as far as his body, and it is his physical, material, mechanical body that provides the framework of his life. He owns his own body, together with his own thoughts, will, and mental life. Whilst the individual mind and its contents are his own concern, his visible external physical body is an objective political concern. Politics is the management of bodies. Politics is the external relationship between discrete individual bodies by association, consent, and covenant. The liberal views of freedom and violence are, likewise, based on this concern for the individual body.

Liberalism holds that a society is a voluntary association of self-determining individuals, who combine their will and collect their power for mutually self-interested ends. There are a number of views of this self-interest: for example, Spinoza (1632–77)[9] argues that individuals voluntarily surrender their own power to a sovereign authority, for the sake of increasing their self-preservation. The locus of power, in liberal theory, is this sovereign authority, the sovereign state. The individual is expected to have a total allegiance to the state. The individual and the state are the two poles of liberal political thinking.

Whilst not always subscribing to metaphysical dualism in a Cartesian sense, philosophers such as Hobbes (1568–1697), Spinoza, Locke (1632–1704), and later, in particular, J. S. Mill (1806–73)[10] developed the notion of this axiomatic separation of the two domains of human existence in the political sphere. This distinction between the objective, public sphere and the subjective, private sphere became one of the foundational principles of liberalism. This principle remains a cardinal liberal tenet although the extents of the spheres and their modes, if any, of relation, differ among individual thinkers. For example, the private sphere for Hegel (1770–1831) includes family life and civil society whilst the public is limited to the life of the state,[11] and even Marx (1818–83) recognized the (by then) realities of this distinction, even if only to advocate that it be overcome by the destruction of both the political state and civil society.

This distinction is the basis of all liberal religious toleration and religious liberty. The state was responsible for the rational organization of public life by law. The individual was to exercise his reason by his participation in the formulation of the laws to which he must adhere. The public aspect of the individual's life was as rational citizen of the state. This public aspect was held to be considerably more important than the merely private differences that distinguish one man from another. All men share their fundamental rationality, or, at least, have the potential to do so. All men share their status as 'man'. Moses Mendelssohn (1728–86), for example, wrote to Herder 'Moses, the human being [*mensch*] is writing to Herder, the human being, not the Jew to the Christian preacher';[12] or as a later Jewish writer advocated, 'Be a man abroad and a Jew in your tent',[13] a sort of schizophrenic existence, living without a connection between 'abroad' and your 'tent'. The individual was free to organize his private life according to his will, as long as there were no public implications.

The single most significant factor in the history of modern religions is that religion was thus included in the private sphere. It is also important to note that this was encouraged by a hostility, on the part of a major number of liberal thinkers, to the established churches.[14] The separation of the private and the public led to a transformation and almost total redefinition of religion, as religious life was reduced and all-but removed from the public life of the state. The nineteenth century saw the almost complete 'privatization' of religion in Europe and the United States, as noted with concern by Hegel and Marx.[15]

The democratic revolutions of the eighteenth century enshrined the distinction between the private and the public in the life of modern western culture and led to a programme for the complete separation of church and state. This distinction became established in the *Declaration of the Rights of Man and the Citizen* of the French National Assembly (August 1789):

> 10. No person shall be molested for his opinions, even such as are religious, provided that the manifestation of these opinions does not disturb the public order established by law.[16]

The same sentiments were even more forcibly proclaimed in the American *Declaration of Independence* (1776) and the *Virginia Act* (1785), which stated that civil rights are not dependent upon religious opinions and prohibited all forms of religious coercion. The private life of the individual was to have no bearing on or to be a barrier to public secular life. Freedom of religion was ensured unequivocally in Article VI of the *Constitution of the United States of America* (1789), in the famous First Amendment:

> Congress shall make no law respecting an establishment of religion, or prohibiting the free exercise thereof; or abridging the freedom of speech, or of the press; or the right of the people peaceably to assemble, and to petition the government for a redress of grievances.[17]

The significance of the sphere of religion was progressively reduced in importance and scope. Hegel, for example, in his *Philosophy of Right*,[18] included under the category of 'private personality' personality as such, freedom of will, ethical life, and religion. He argued that religious beliefs and the doctrines of religion were purely subjective and belonged to the sphere of the 'inner life' and had no place in the 'domain of the state' and he contrasts this inner 'content of a man's faith which depends on his private ideas' with the outer, objective 'real world and the truth present in it in the form of the universal i.e. the laws' of the state which is in possession of objective knowledge. Or, to take another example, Mill, in his essay *On Liberty*,[19] starts by clearly distinguishing the public from the private realms. Mill then asks what are the nature and limits of power which can be legitimately exercised by society (the state) over the individual? Mill argues that society had no power over the inner private sphere, but that in the public sphere power could be legitimately exercised over the individual, and that this coercion be based on the rational principle of utilitarianism. Mill excludes all actions from the private sphere. The private sphere is conceived of as the realm of actionless and bodiless belief.

The coercive power of the state is the second liberal principle that has profound implications for religious freedom. The great paradox at the heart of liberalism is that abuse and injustice are prevented, private rights ensured, and liberty guaranteed only by a strong state, and yet the stronger the power and authority of the state the greater the limits set on human freedom. Spinoza, Hobbes, and Rousseau (1712–88) all contend that once a man has given his power to the state he must abide by its laws, even to the point of being coerced to do so.[20] Kant (1724–1804) could be enthused by the French Revolution and yet still insist that he must accept the punishment of the state if motivated to act on the basis of his enthusiasm.[21] It is rational for the state to exercise its coercive power. In a liberal state the state itself is the supreme authority.[22] Liberalism entails state absolutism.

The state exercises its coercive power in relation to religion in a number of different ways. The limitation of religion to the private sphere is enforced by a network of disciplinary laws. Legalized private religion is combined with restrictive legislation.

More significantly, the state's control of education serves to reinforce this private model of religion. Contemporary liberal political ideology is coupled with a scientific epistemology and an evolutionary historicism. The first excludes even the possibility of almost all religious claims, and the second reduces all previous human endeavour to mere stages on the road to liberalism.[23] These factors, to which I will return below, make it all but impossible for religions or religious life to be comprehensible. Thus liberalism has a built-in protection against criticism of itself.

Christianity and (later) Judaism and (presently) Islam have responded by massive restructuring of their religions. Their liberal wings have sought to identify their traditions firmly with liberalism. Emphases are now on the private realms, and the public aspects have been left to wither, such as the breakdown of traditional religious welfare-provision. The full acceptance of the liberal framework resulted in the creation of 'private' theologies, such as that of Schleiermacher.

If we turn to the Jewish responses to liberalism, it is clear that after nearly two millenia of Christian persecution and enforced isolation from wider social and political life, many Jews enthusiastically embraced the prospect of being allowed to join civil society. This possibility, supported by liberals, became concretized following the French Revolution, when, for the first time, in Europe, the emancipation of Jews *qua* 'Jews', in terms of equal citizenship, was proposed.[24] The question of Jewish emancipation itself was a challenge to liberalism's two political poles of the individual and the state. The life of pre-liberalism Jewry was in self-governing, corporate societies, with their own culture, languages, traditions, criminal and civil legal systems and institutions. This corporate organization was a challenge to the liberal conception of the isolated individual, each of whom in the state was to be treated equally before the law. The breakdown of Jewish corporate life was required in order to integrate the Jews as individuals into the life of the state. As Jewish self-identity was essentially corporate, and Jewish notions of freedom were likewise corporate, they had to be redefined in terms of the individual and individual freedom. As the Count de Clermont-Tonnerre put it to the French National Assembly, 'Jews should be denied everything as a nation, but granted everything as individuals.'[25] That is, the price of citizenship was that Jews give up their cultural and religious corporate distinctiveness. This was enacted when the Assembly renounced all Jewish communal privileges of autonomy in 1791.[26]

Second, Jewish emancipation challenged liberalism's notion of the state. Jewish loyalty to the corporate Jewish structures ('the Jewish "state" ') was a threat to the power of the nation-state. Traditional Jewish expectations of a return to the land of Israel were also perceived as a challenge to the state. The question was whether a Jew could be loyal to the nation-state and hold messianic hopes linked with a potential second state of affiliation. These questions were raised in Napoleon's instructions to the Assembly of Jewish notables in 1806.[27]

These two issues of corporate autonomy and eschatological promise were addressed by Jewish thinkers in their attempts to demonstrate that adherence to Judaism was totally compatible with liberalism's conceptions of the individual and the state. A further charge to be answered was the alleged irrationality of

Judaism. Moses Mendelssohn, the Jewish philosopher, for example, wrote his major works on Judaism in response to these challenges. He subscribed to the private-public distinction, in terms of the individual and the universal society, manifest as the state. Whilst the individual and the state were natural rational categories, the Jewish autonomous community was not, and thus had to be rejected, in his call for the emancipation of Jews as individuals. Further, he argued that everything must be submitted to the state except matters of private religion. Mendelssohn interpreted the messianic redemption in terms of the universal brotherhood of man in the age of reason. He thus rejected Jewish peoplehood in terms of communal autonomy, although he foresaw that Jews would finally retrieve their rank as a nation in the community of nations, although this was to be subordinated to the task of the development of the universal society; he advocated the removal of distinctiveness in dress, language, and custom and reinterpreted traditional Jewish messianism in his claims for Jewish emancipation. One modern Jewish commentator writes, 'Mendelssohn made credible to Europe the existence of a rational Judaism and the possibility of a de-Judaised Jew.'[28]

The efforts of the liberal Jewish thinkers, who followed Mendelssohn in their presentation of Judaism as natural religion (that is, religion totally in accord with the dictates of reason), were developed by their responses to the criticism of Judaism by enlightenment thinkers – in particular, by Immanuel Kant. Kant could write:

> The function of the state is to guarantee every individual his freedom within the law, so that each remains free to seek his happiness in whatever way he thinks best, so long as he does not violate the lawful freedom and rights of his fellow subjects at large[29]

and yet could still call for the 'euthanasia' of Jews, as Jews, and of Judaism. He attacked and undermined the rationality and morality of Judaism by arguing that all revealed 'morality' was not, in fact, morality at all, by virtue of being revealed (that is, external to man). Kant further challenged the particularism of Judaism, which contrasted with his emphasis on the universal, and contended that Judaism was not a religion at all, on the grounds that, 'firstly, its commands relate morally to external acts' and that it was this-worldly and materialistic.[30] Kant's critique of Judaism, resonating with Pauline theological objections to Jewish 'legalism' and the distinctions between body and spirit, was echoed by almost all later liberal thinkers. Liberals were the inheritors of the long Christian tradition of falsely associating Judaism with the Old Testament, or rather of a reading in the New Testament and early church of the Old Testament, a reading that underlines the discourse of the positive transition from letter to spirit, works to faith, body to spirit, and from the national particularistic to the internationalistic and universalistic, and tended to find it impossible to recognize the Jewish claims for distinctiveness. In this regard many followed Kant in insisting that their 'caricatures' of Judaism were based ahistorically on its essentials – that is, its biblical foundations and not on later rabbinic developments. From Voltaire and his rabid antisemitism onwards the concept of rationality was contrasted with irrationality and superstition, with Judaism identified with the latter. If for no other reason than that the rationality of the majority was that of a Christian majority, the Jewish experience in their struggle for the removal of restrictive barriers to complete emancipation in civil society was that reason was not, in fact, neutral but permeated with Christianity. Rational universalism was rarely universal enough to subsume Jewish particularity. The rational universe, so ably constructed by Christian philosophers, such as Kant and Hegel, was in fact a rationalization of Christianity.[31] Further, at the core of liberalism is a paradox – the development of the nation-state, to which all individual citizens (including Jewish citizens) were to adhere, became during the nineteenth century, in accordance with its own inner logic, increasingly nationalistic; this growing self-determining nationalism emphasizing shared language, history, and traditions only served to alienate Jewish and other 'citizens', sometimes with awesome consequences and leading ultimately to disaster.

Jewish liberals during the nineteenth century in Europe and America developed a thoroughgoing Jewish private religion emphasizing its ethical components and its compatibility with reason and civic rights. This private model of Judaism, insisting on personal autonomy as the bench-mark, tended towards an evolutionary understanding of its own history and often distinguished between 'private' essentials and 'public' accretions. Although paradoxically the emphasis on the realized messianism of the age of reason led Jews into involvement in broader social actions (from the Pittsburg Platform (1885) to Rabbi A. J. Heschel marching with Martin Luther King and organizations such as JONAH (Jews for a Nuclear Arms Halt, affiliated to the Reform synagogues of Great Britain)),[32] this action tended to blur the private-public distinction.

A second Jewish strand took the liberal doctrine of the nation-state to a logical conclusion and advocated just such a Jewish state for the Jewish people. It is significant to note that they, too, tended to purge their public aims and activities of the private religious aspects of Judaism, although zionism has found itself facing many of the same issues as the western Christian nations with its own version of a rationalized liberalized state Judaism.

The orthodox response initially was to demand a retention of the unified public-private autonomous Jewish polity and most reacted to the liberal political reforms by rejecting both their claims and emancipation. Moses Sofer (1762–1839), the rabbi of Pessburg in Hungary, for example, perceptively recognizing that at the heart of Reform Judaism was the loss of belief in the world-to-come leading to concern for this world only, issued a rabbinical decree that instructed that 'the new is forbidden'. The widescale orthodox objections to zionism as both untimely and ultimately a secular movement antithetical to traditional Judaism, led the orthodox to become rooted in their nation-states. Orthodox thinkers came to subscribe to the privatization of religion by interpreting this to be in the interests of the preservation of traditional Judaism, notwithstanding the huge losses to Jewish life occasioned by the ending of Jewish communal autonomy, losses rationalized by extensions of the tradition of acquiescence in the laws of the state, as encapsulated in the talmudic maxim 'the law of the state is law'. Whilst Emil Fackenheim is surely right in his assertion that 'even orthodox Jews are secular liberals',[33] I would want to go further and claim that, paradoxically, the orthodox, with their emphasis on private religion coupled with degrees of indifference to the life of the state, more fully subscribe to the liberal model of the private-public distinction than do their Reform co-religionists.

Thus almost all Jews have come to accept the liberal understanding of religion as the price they pay for emancipation and a measure of security from a return to past persecution and capricious 'tolerance'.[34]

My own Jewish tradition becomes largely unintelligible when viewed in a liberal light. The first words of my Bible 'In the beginning God created the heavens and the earth' are unproven and unprovable and so it can only be a private opinion, and an opinion that runs counter to the scientific principle that matter is self-creating, self-sufficient, and eternal. A little later in the same chapter we read 'And God saw that it was good'; the public realm of matter is neutral, without value, according to the canons of liberalism. And finally, at the end of the very first chapter of my Bible, it is stated that man is created in God's 'image and likeness', as opposed to the modern claim that man is an accidental product of evolution. It is not that liberalism presents my tradition with unanswerable challenges but that it trivializes it and renders it unintelligible. My tradition does not hold knowledge to be neutral and makes important distinctions concerning the 'public' sphere, for example, between just and unjust wages, fair and unfair prices, and pure and impure wealth. The liberal model of creativity, individual originality, is hostile to my tradition of commentary. The liberal emphasis on the value of spontaneity challenges my tradition's overriding concern with routine.

Our religious traditions, traditions that are made up of cosmologies, politics, epistemologies, soteriologies, eschatologies, and mythologies are genuine and total world-views. These world-views are reduced by the liberal state to private spirituality. 'Spirituality', one of the most often used words in contemporary religious discourse, refers to the acceptance of the liberal reduction of religion to the private sphere. This century's obsession with mysticism and the mystical is based on the loss of the full dimensions of religious life.[35] This reduction leads to the understanding of Islam as essentially sufism, Hinduism as the spiritual traditions of vedānta and yoga. These views are essentially and profoundly distorted as they emphasize one single dimension of an entire religious tradition.[36] The liberal state, thus, imposes upon religions its model of private religion.

The liberal world-view is now so persuasive and so pervasive that we readily use the liberal 'private' language to talk of our religions: revelation, spirit, saints, etc. It is difficult even to begin to ask why we have such difficulty understanding our traditional texts. The Jewish thinker that I have been recently studying, Franz Rosenzweig, seeking to secure a view behind that of liberalism, eventually found himself immersed in the world of the twelfth-century poet, Judah Halevi. Emmanuel Levinas, the contemporary thinker, faced with this difficulty, writes that he chooses 'to speak Greek' in his phenomenological writings. In England, the liberal state imposes its view of liberal education, which includes science and liberal historicism, on every school. The recent experience of a Jewish school in London is a case in point. This school, run by the Belz hasidic community for its own children, had its grant (to which all taxpayers and local ratepayers subscribe) cut, ostensibly for spending a disproportionate amount of time on religious education. The very distinction of religious as opposed to other types of education is imposed universally on all subjects of the state. The current debates over the core curriculum and its list of foundational subjects, indicative of liberal priorities, with particular emphasis on marketable skills (to secure individual

autonomy) and including a heavy emphasis on science and technology, only serve to highlight this issue. The point that I wish to
make here is that all public issues, that is, all issues that concern
action or the physical, the bodily, anything in fact beyond individual private 'opinion', are, in the liberal state, to be decided in a
universal 'rational' way. This way is binding upon every subject
regardless of individual belief or conviction, and those whose
convictions happen to differ from those of liberalism are coerced
into following the law. I would like to illustrate the restrictions
on religious freedom by reference to three contemporary issues.

First, the Gillick case. Following the publication of a memor-
andum, from her local area health authority, allowing that a
doctor can prescribe contraceptives to a girl under 16 without
parental consent, Mrs Victoria Gillick asked for an assurance from
the authority that her own four daughters under 16 (later 5)
would not be given contraceptives without her consent. When the
authority were unable to do so, Mrs Gillick brought an action
against the authority and the DHSS on the grounds of the Sexual
Offences Act (1956), which makes it an offence to encourage a
girl under 16 to engage in unlawful sex (section 28 (1)), it being
an offence for a man to have sexual intercourse with a girl under
16 (section 6 (1)), and on the grounds of parental rights. Mrs
Gillick lost her case but won the case in the Court of Appeal.
The DHSS appealed to the House of Lords in 1985. Mrs Gillick
is a Roman Catholic, and made it clear in the media that her
concerns reflected her religious beliefs. It is significant that religion
is not mentioned at all in the Lords' report, and, if anything, Mrs
Gillick was hampered by having to fight the case on 'public'
grounds only. It is interesting that two of the five Lords found it
necessary to discuss whether her case fell into the sphere of private
or public law, a confusion reflecting the unclarity of the distinction
itself. The Lords considered it a public rather than a private issue,
that is, an issue to be decided by rational means in a universal
fashion, and decided (four in favour with one dissenting voice)
that the appeal should be allowed and that a doctor can lawfully
prescribe contraceptives to an under-age girl without the consent
of her parents.[37]

There has been a recent private member's bill on the question
of Sunday trading. A broad group, of Christians and others, concerned with the protection of the sanctity of the sabbath day, has
arisen in opposition to the removal of the present restriction
governing trading on the 'seventh' day. It should be noted that
Jewish traders, who object on religious grounds to trading on the
Jewish sabbath, may, after obtaining a licence from the British

Board of Deputies and registering with the local authority, trade on Sunday. This provision was later extended to factories and workshops, which may employ only Jewish staff on Sundays but cannot open to the public – all other forms of Jewish business are prohibited.[38] As trading is a public matter, that is, it involves the physical acts of exchange etc., the issue was decided by universal fiat, binding on all citizens of the state, and the restrictions on Sunday trading remain.

Finally, there has been a recent attempt in Parliament, supported by animal rights groups, to revoke the 1967 provision which permits Jews and Muslims to slaughter animals for food according to their traditional methods. The impetus behind this attempt was a report commissioned by the Ministry of Agriculture, and carried out by the Farm Animal Welfare Council in 1985. Neither that council nor the ministry felt that it was necessary to consult with representatives of the two communities concerned – and why should they, if one holds the notion that all men by the exercise of their reason will arrive at a unique rational solution? Their rational solution was that all animals should be stunned before slaughter – an action expressly forbidden by both these religious traditions. Such a decision if implemented would make it no longer possible for Jews and Muslims to obtain halal or kosher meats. But, as the slaughter of animals for food is a public issue, a political concern, it will be decided rationally and universally.

These three issues clearly illustrate that religions do have concerns in the public sphere and that the liberal state restricts and uses its power to restrict religious freedom by coercion. This issue of religious public life has arisen most recently with the churches' report, *Faith in the City* (1986), and the current statements by the clergy, up to and including the Archbishop of Canterbury, concerning the morality of government legislation. It is interesting that such phenomena can be read in two different ways: first, as a challenge to the public-private split and the consignment of religion to the private: and second, such statements and public concern on the part of the churches can be interpreted as stemming from, and based upon, this very distinction. Likewise, movements such as the house church-groups can be seen as accepting the private model of religion or, alternatively, by separating themselves from the public life of the state to a degree, as insisting upon a more complete, private *and* public religious life. To return to the issue above, it is possible for all three of these to be decided so as to ensure religious freedom. Rather than be decided by universal decision that necessarily entails coercion they might be decided differentially. It should be possible for the law to respect the beliefs and concerns of Mrs Gillick and her fellow Catholic parents (if she does, in fact, represent a majority Catholic view), by allowing Catholic parents to have the right to parental authority over the question of contraception. Whilst it would be coercive for all sectors of society to be bound by Catholic notions of the family, the place of sexuality in life, and of contraception, for the Catholics it is a public issue. Likewise, Christians should have the right to protect their sabbath, but then so should Jews and Muslims, as should those who do not subscribe to the concept of a 'sabbath' have the right to enjoy theirs as they see fit. All sectors of the community should have the right to slaughter and prepare their meats according to their religious traditions. The liberal solutions binding on the whole population (state) lead inevitably to religious coercion.

There must, of course, be a basic adherence to a shared code. In ancient Israel the *ger toshav*, the resident alien, was required to adhere to the seven commandments of the code of Noah, as a condition of residence. Although there is debate about whether these commandments are known 'naturally' or have to be pro-pounded, these laws are known as the Torah (law) for the gentiles and include prohibitions on idolatrous practices, murder, sexual immorality, theft (including the recognition of property rights) and enjoin every group to establish lawcourts in order to adminis-ter their own codes of justice. The early residents of the American state of Pennsylvania had to proclaim a belief in the one God. What I am here advocating is not the theory of the 'night-watchman state', most recently and forcefully revived by the liber-tarian liberal thinker, Robert Nozick,[39] but a degree of flexibility in the application of the law so as to minimize the coercive effects of legislation. Such a shared code must include a large number of legal injunctions binding on all citizens but should also allow for sub-legal frameworks based on the religious traditions to operate by the *consent* of those who subscribe to the tenets of these traditions. I will return to the issue of consent below. I am not suggesting that the state allow Jews, for example, to be removed from normal judicial processes and procedures but that parallel provisions could be instituted, the authority of which would be granted by both the state and those who consent to each semi-autonomous legal system. This canton system has parallels with the Ottoman *millet*-system, an inheritance of the Turkish empire, and in operation in Israel and other centres in the Middle East. This system grants religious rights to religious groups, in areas of self-definition, education, and family law, in the case of Israel, and the system is administered by a ministry of religion. The system in Israel has a most serious defect, in that it does not recognize the right of an individual to opt out of an existing group – for example it does not allow one to be a secularist – and so in the three legal areas above one is bound to the law of the recognized community of one's birth (or in special cases, conversion). So, for example, cross-tradition marriage cannot be conducted in Israel (although in such cases the couple can marry outside the state and have the marriage recognized under international law). There ought to be the real possibility of being a secularist or an adherent of a religious tradition, and there ought to be a shared code designed to minimize all coercion.

A most penetrating analysis of the modern liberal state and its powers of coercion, not just religious coercion, is offered in the examination of knowledge and power in the works of Michel Foucault. He rejects the Enlightenment claim that knowledge can be 'pure', that is, subject only to the dictates of reason, detached from social and political requirements. His concern is not with the private but with the public aspects of the modern liberal state and the public aspect of the individual – his body – as it is defined as it enters and is controlled by and in the public sphere. The state's power is both an individualizing and totalizing form of power, he writes,[40] in his attempt to explicate the structures of the liberal state. A state whose success is measured in terms of the introduction of modern mercantile economies requires the management of individuals, goods, family wealth, etc. to facilitate this economy. No aspect of life, customs, traditions, ways of thinking and doing, is exempt from this end and its attendant disciplines. These state disciplines or, as Foucault calls them, 'political or technological economies of the body', involve disciplinary processes and techniques for the manipulation, domination, and objectification of the individual, as a public body, by the huge scientifico-legal complexes of the modern mercantile, state-endorsed, and regulated economy, as exemplified, for example, in the coincidence of the rise of the factory and the prison emphasizing corrective detention rather than forced labour. The state develops a massive array of such repressive technologies of coercive power over the life of the individual, forming that individuality as the objectified individual subject from the undifferentiated masses of the population, a process marked by the bureaucratic control of each separated and numbered and filed unit. He traces the breakdown of autonomous and independent communities outside productive society by the application of disciplinary practices, ranging from the rise of psychiatry and the prisons to the growth of the 'objective' social sciences. The reverse side of the coin is the liberal discourse of reason and progress, which underlies and is underlain by the state and its concern with the economy. Foucault is concerned both with this dual process of the development of all-penetrating coercive power and the formation of the modern individual subject, and the relationship of rationalization to the abuses of the state's political power. He refers to this system of power/knowledge in our era as 'bio-power', a system of power/knowledge that has 'brought life and its mechanism into the realm of explicit calculation and made knowledge/power an agent of the transformation of human life'.[41] The application of the analysis of bio-power to religion has yet to be systematically undertaken.

In this last section I want to enter a plea for what might be called a 'genuine pluralism'. I have tried to show that the supposed universal notion of liberal rationality can and does have grave consequences for religious traditions in the context of the modern state. The question of rationality, as the universal reason, is central to this issue of religious pluralism. Noted above was the way in which the Jewish experience of universal and so-called neutral rationality was found to be shot through with Christianity, and this conviction has only been strengthened following the holocaust. It is interesting to note that recent studies drawing on Heidegger and others have provided a good case for arguing that the western tradition, from the Greeks via Christianity to the Enlightenment and beyond, does constitute a philosophical whole, a tradition informed by a shared core-set of issues and foundational structures. This supports the argument that there is an intimate connection between rationality and Christianity both conceptually and in the universality of its mission of application. If this argument has real foundations these are vital factors in any discussion of religious pluralism in states informed by this model of reason. For example, Derrida[42] has argued that the whole western tradition's presentation of reality, of 'presence', of what it means 'to be' – for him the very structure of sign-theory – is tied up with the Christian appropriation of Greek philosophy. He contends that Christian theology and western rationalism share the same implicit framework – for example, the distinctions between signifier and signified, the intelligible and the sensible, writing and speech; by deconstructing the discourses of reason in terms of these distinctions, as they are and have been made by philosophers, he asks if there are any grounds for the claim that the rational grounds for reason itself are rational. A second issue in this regard is the scrutiny of the universal claims of the Enlightenment by thinkers such as Foucault (above), J. L. Lyotard, and Richard Rorty,[43] who all (in very different ways) advocate that the limits of reason entail that we can no longer accept either the concept of an absolute perspective for knowledge or the rational extension of such a belief as manifest in the teleological belief in progress or universal emancipation. In this context Sartre's assertion, in the quotation at the beginning of the paper, becomes more plausible, in that a Jew utilizing the canons of reason uses a framework laden with past theological 'truths' that can serve to alienate him from his own tradition of thinking and doing. A second but related theme, found in the writings of Kuhn and Feyerband, is the recognition that reason has a history.[44] This historicism of reason leaves reason shorn of its universalism and yet still able to operate by consensus in a pragmatic fashion. It is not simply the case of 'which rationality?' (as Macintyre puts it in his latest book) but the formation of a rational consensus overlapping in the centre but not necessarily at the edges.[45]

Religious traditions have been restructured in the light of the public-private distinction and transformed into partial systems due to the coercive nature of the modern state. Western liberal rationality challenges the most basic assumptions of many of our religious traditions; what is true and what is false, what is prohibited and what is permitted are questions determined by reference to the logical canons of this rationality. A genuine pluralism would recognise that liberal rationality has no prior claim to truth, nor justification for being the yardstick by which all other traditions are to be evaluated, judged, and transformed. Given the above studies we must begin to recognize that in connection with our religious traditions European liberal rationality has no greater claim to universality than that of rabbinic Judaism, a world-view based on the Quran, or one based on the religious texts of other religions (although, of course, in a sense the very concept of 'universality' is part of that European discourse). It is an unequal contest between a liberal world-view and a 'private', 'subjective' religious tradition. When freed of the (super)imposition of liberal rationalism, these religious views can be recognized as world-views (with private and public, subjective and objective aspects, as total views of the world, as complete systems). It is only possible to subsume a partial view of the world by a total view; it is not possible to subsume a complete world-view under an alternative world-view. Western rationality is only one world-view amongst many different world-views. There is not one truth, that of liberal reason, by which all other 'truths' are to be tested, but many truths representing our diverse traditions. Our different religious traditions have different aims, utilize different methods, and conceive of and employ different resources in order to achieve their different ends.

A final note: Rousseau contended that the knowledge of what other men believe is an evil, in the absence of the knowledge of whether those beliefs are true or false. He argued that such knowledge was merely manipulative, a lever by which we can influence the other's behaviour, and that this leads, not to understanding but only to being manipulated in return.[46] Whilst I possess no vantage-point from which to judge the beliefs of others, and would not coerce or impose my own beliefs, nor subscribe to an intellectual apartheid, my experience of reality demands a response to the question of the truth or falsity of another's beliefs. I am aware of the logical difficulties of an unresolved relativism.[47] But we all live, more or less, within the worlds both of liberal rationality and of our own traditions; we have developed what we might call a 'pluralistic personality'. The perceptive reader will have noticed that the liberal autonomous 'I' has crept back into my argument in connection with the idea of 'consent'. It is not possible for us to return to the Middle Ages or the Persian or Turkish Empires, nor would we wish to do so. Jews have no desire to return to their ghettos, and the Enlightenment cannot be undone. Nor should we reject Kant's understanding of man's responsibilities to use his critical rationality, entailing a relentless examination of our most cherished and central beliefs, nor must the freedom of individual choice in all aspects of our lives be lost. What must change is the state, which must begin progressively to understand the possibilities of differential reason and legislation by consent – that is, a plurality of rationalities, overlapping in the realities of our daily lives. The religious traditions, too, must make concessions, such as shared codes, rules on missionary activities, and subscription to, and representation on, national bodies that can incorporate their legal structures and institutions into the public framework of the pluralistic state. In the longer term we must all address the task of rethinking the conceptions of 'individual' and 'state', 'public' and 'private', and the public rights of coercion. With the return to the 'right', discernible in many of our religious traditions, we can only hope that this genuine pluralism will begin *within* our traditions (intra-religious),[48] as the foundations for a genuine inter-religious pluralism. We must be careful not merely to replace liberal rationalism with another (super)imposed framework, but by freeing our traditions from the constraints of a 'universal' liberalism, to allow them to become dynamic total traditions.[49] The religious price we pay for liberal freedom may be too high. We are only at the very beginning of this task.

Notes

1 Translated by G. J. Becker, New York: Schocken (1948).

2 The use of the masculine possessive pronoun elsewhere in this chapter has been deliberate and reflects one aspect of the myth of the independence of this liberal 'individual', an individual generally supported by women (mothers, sisters, and wives) who allowed for this masculine independence.

3 For a recent collection of essays on the topic, see L. S. Rouner (ed.), *Religious Pluralism*, Boston University Studies, 5, University of Notre Dame Press (1984), and for a brief sketch of some of the issues, H. Coward's *Pluralism: Challenge to World Religions*, New York, Orbis: (1985), and for a different view see my review article, 'Trying trialogues: pluralism and prejudicial pluralism', *Religion Today*, 5:1/2 (1989), 18–20.

4 Cf. M. Novak's essay 'Pluralism in humanistic perspective', in W. Petersen and M. Novak (eds), *Concepts of Ethnicity*, Harvard University Press (1982).

5 Political pluralism refers to the belief that democratic values can best be preserved in a system of multiple, competing elites, in which voters can exercise meaningful choices in elections, and in which new elites can gain access to power. It is a criticism of the fact that in a complex urban industrial society, the individual has little or no real access to power, except through multinational corporations, trade unions, etc. The state in this model becomes the 'referee' between these competing elites, e.g. the Monopolies Commission. At a more local level is the issue of 'black sections', an issue at the last two British Labour Party conferences. On political pluralism see (for example) T. R. Dye and L. H. Zeigler, *The Irony of Democracy*, New York: Duxbury Press (1972); W. Connolly (ed.), *The Bias of Pluralism*, New York: Atherton (1969); and R. H. Dahl (ed.), *Pluralist Democracy in the United States*, Chicago: Rand McNally (1967).

6 See, for example, A. Arblaster, *The Rise and Decline of Western Liberalism*, Oxford: Blackwell (1984); L. Hobhouse, *Liberalism*, Oxford University Press (1911); S. Lukes, *Individualism*, Oxford: Blackwell (1973).

7 The two are intimately linked – for example, in the writings of Descartes, the individual's freedom on the one hand is coupled with the concept of scientific method on the other.

8 See *Discourse on Method and Meditations*, both translated by L. J. Lafleur, New York: Liberal Arts Press (1951). Cartesian dualism has been subjected to extensive philosophical criticism in the works of Hegel and Marx, and in this century by thinkers such as G. Ryle and L. Wittgenstein.

9 For Spinoza's views on the relationship of the individual to the state, see his *Political Treatise*, ch. 10, and on the question of the relationship of religion to politics, see the *Theologico-Political Treatise*, especially chs 19 and 20, both in the Dover ed. New York (1951), trans. R. H. Elwes.

10 See T. Hobbes, *Leviathan* (first publ. 1651), chs 22–3, 31–4, New York: Everyman (1951); Locke's *Letter on Toleration*, ed. R. Kilibansky, Oxford University Press (1968), 123–9, where Locke distinguishes between 'the *public* good in earthly or worldly matters' and 'the liberty left to the *private* man in matters concerning the life to come'; and J. S. Mill's essays, 'On Liberty' and 'Utilitarianism' in *Utilitarianism, Liberty and Representative Government*, New York: Everyman (1951).

11 For Hegel, of course, the private and the public are finally to be sublated in the public to form the explicitly actualized 'concrete freedom' of the state community, where public and private man are synthesized, and even in the private sphere of civil society he finds 'reason glinting through' in that the pursuit of private ends turns out to be 'government by the universal laws of political economy, even if their universality is still only implicit'. See *Hegel's Philosophy of Right*, trans. T. M. Knox, Oxford University Press (1952), sections 66 and 270. Further, it should be noted that the term 'Privatreligion' appears in *Hegels theologische Jugenscriften*, ed. H. Nohl, Tübingen: J. C. Mohr (1907), 27, where his attack on contemporary Protestantism was read back into Greek and Roman religion. He held that initially the private and the public were unified in terms of religion (*Early Theological Writings*, trans. T. M. Knox and R. Karner, Chicago University Press (1948), 154–7), and their subsequent split led to a concern with individuality. He attacked private religion – 'private religion is concerned with forming the morality of the one individual person' (*Hegels theologische Jugenscriften*, 27) – and he argued that religion should not be confined to the private person. For Marx, see *Contribution to the Critique of Hegel's 'Philosophy of Right'* (1843), ed. J. O'Malley, Cambridge University Press (1970); and *The Marx-Engels Reader*, ed. R. C. Tucker, second edn., New York: Norton (1978), 34.

12 Cited in J. Katz, *Exclusiveness and Tolerance*, Oxford University Press (1961), 192. For similar sentiments see *Hegel's Philosophy of Right*, section 209 – 'A man is a man in virtue of his manhood alone, not because he is a Jew, Catholic, Protestant, German or Italian, etc.'.

13 This was apparently a maxim at the time of the French Revolution: cited in *The Jew in the Modern World*, ed. P. R. Mendes-Flohr and J. Reinharz, Oxford University Press (1980), 312, from the poem by J. L. Gordon, 'Awake my people'.

14 It is interesting to note that Marx, in his introduction to his book on Hegel's *Philosophy of Right*, claims that the critique of religion is the beginning of the foundation of all criticism. See also E. Bramstead and

K. Melhuish (eds), *Western Liberalism*, London: Longman (1978), 512–35.

15 See the classical analyses of the separation of bourgeois society and the state and the resultant 'privatization' of religion and depoliticization of the churches in *Hegel's Philosophy of Right* and Marx's critique (above, n. 11).

16 Trans. B. Flower, *The French Constitution*, London (1792), 18.

17 F. N. Thorpe, *The Federal and State Constitution*, 7 vols, Washington, DC: Government Printing Office (1907–9), vol. 1 (1907), 19. The First Amendment was binding on all state legislatures following the Fourteenth Amendment. For a recent optimistic study of the ways in which the First Amendment has been interpreted by the Supreme Court, in relation to religious freedoms, see W. G. Katz and H. P. Southerland, 'Pluralism and the Supreme Court', *Daedalus*, 96 (winter 1967), 180–92, where the authors claim to discern a growing appreciation of the issues raised by religious pluralism, a development that they characterize as a move from 'toleration to equal freedom'.

18 *Hegel's Philosophy of Right*, section 270.

19 See n. 10 above.

20 Spinoza in his *Political Treatise* went so far as insisting that natural religion be determined by the state. He argued that a diversity of religious sects and modes of worship was a danger to the stability of the state. Man's obedience to the state had to be absolute in order to 'curb the passions' by legislation according to reason. Men were to obey, not out of fear, but out of reason: man's freedom consists in his obedience by reason. He writes: 'Men are to be so led that they think themselves not to be led but to live by their own mind and their own free opinion' (*Political Treatise*, 10, 7). This very distinction between private and public, with the state's total responsibility for the public realm had, of course, disastrous consequences for the Jews of Europe. D. Bonhoeffer in 1933 wrote 'without doubt the Jewish question is one of the historical problems which our state must deal with, and without doubt the state is justified in adopting new methods here . . . The church cannot in the first place exert direct political action, for the church does not pretend to have any knowledge of the necessary course of history. Thus even today, in the Jewish question it cannot address the state directly and demand of it some definite action of a different nature. It is not the church but the state which makes and changes the law.' Issues in the public realm are to be dealt with by one universal, rational solution – the final solution of the Jewish problem. Christian failure to resist the Nazis was to some measure due to the fact that their religion was reduced to the private sphere, while in the public sphere Christians were to be loyal to the state.

21 I. Kant, *On History*, ed. L. W. Beck, Indianapolis: Bobbs-Merrill (1963), 129–130, 143–8.

22 A point made by almost all liberals. It is only very recently that a tradition of dissent has been formulated – see for example J. Rawls,

A Theory of Justice, Oxford University Press (1972), but even he writes, 'The denial of equal liberty can be defended only if it is necessary to raise the level of civilization so that in due course these freedoms can be enjoyed' (152).

23 Liberalism also bars the real possibility of tolerance within a tradition, as we are unable to consider our own past except from this evolutionary and historicist perspective. The trivialization of the past – and particularly of the religious past – is endemic to liberalism.

24 Although there are earlier examples of legislation granting Jews some measure of civil rights, such as Emperor Joseph's 'edict of tolerance' (1782), which allows Jews a 'second-class' citizenship (followed two years later by the abolition of rabbinical juridicial autonomy), the French case marks a breakthrough. The American situation is different in that the state did not have to contend with an already existing system of Jewish autonomy.

25 Cited in *The Jew in the Modern World*, 104.

26 M. D. Tama, *Transactions of the Paris Sanhedrin*, trans. F. Kirwan, London (1807), 130–4.

27 Cited ibid., 105–8.

28 For Mendelssohn, see especially *Jerusalem*, trans. M. Samuels, London (1838), vol. 1 (in particular, on Jewish autonomy, pp. 108 ff); A. A. Cohen, *The Natural and the Supernatural Jew*, New York: Pantheon (1963), 29.

29 I. Kant, from *Theorie und Praxis*, in *Kant's Political Writings*, ed. H. B. Reiss, trans. H. B. Nisbet, Cambridge University Press (1971), 80.

30 I thus assume that Protestants have fewer problems with western rationality than do Catholics and certainly fewer than do Jews and Muslims. At most, liberal democracy is a direct development of Protestantism, or at least liberal democracy is inconceivable without the advent of Protestantism. It is important and interesting to note the intimate relationship between religion and liberal politics, particularly in Hobbes, Locke, and Mill. See, for example, J. E. Eisenach, *Two Worlds of Liberalism*, Chicago University Press (1981). It has been argued (for example, by W. T. Bluhm, in *Force or Freedom?* Yale University Press (1985)), that Descartes modelled his *Discourse on Method* on the biblical account of the six days of creation. Bluhm argues for the identification of force with freedom in liberalism. See also I. Kant, *Religion within the Bounds of Reason Alone*, trans. T. M. Greene and H. H. Hudson, New York: Harper & Row (1960), 116.

31 See N. Rotenstreich, *Jews and German Philosophy*, New York: Schocken (1984), and E. Fackenheim, *Encounters between Judaism and Modern Philosophy*, New York: Schocken (1980).

32 The Pittsburg Platform, in *Yearbook of the Central Conference of American Rabbis*, 45 (1935), 198–200, Article 8, reads 'In full accordance with the spirit of Mosaic legislation which strives to regulate the relation between rich and poor, we deem it our duty to participate in the great task of modern times, to solve on the basis of justice and

righteousness the problems presented by the constrasts and evils of the present organization of society.' The platform (1885) was a statement of the principles of American Reform Judaism.

33 'On the self-exposure of faith to modern-secular world', in *Daedalus* 96 (winter 1967), 195.

34 Although Jews have consistently struggled for the separation of church and state because of the consequences of the past identification of Christianity with the state, there is also a sizeable body of orthodox opinion in Israel which supports a total separation.

35 The multi-disciplinary approach of religious studies is an attempt to counter this distortion, although sometimes it does not seem very aware of the historical and political dimensions of this task: for example, in the sub-discipline of the philosophy of religion, after a century or perhaps even two of religion being consigned to the private sphere with rationality claimed exclusively by the public sphere, a paper entitled 'Gods', by J. Wisdom (in *Proceedings of the Aristotelian Society*, 45 (1945–6), 185–206), which argued that statements about 'god' are statements not about the world but about the believer's attitude towards the world, was hailed as a breakthrough.

36 The recent history of religions is replete with examples of the attempts to overcome the limitations of the 'private', e.g. the moral majority in the USA.

37 *Gillick* v. *Norfolk and Wisbech Area Health Authority* in *All England Law Reports*, Part 6 (8 November 1985), 402–37, London: Butterworth (1985).

38 Shops Act, section 53 (1950); Factories Act, section 109 (1961).

39 *Anarchy, State and Utopia*, New York: Basic Books (1974).

40 See M. Foucault, 'The Subject and Power' in *Michel Foucault: Beyond Structuralism and Hermeneutics*, ed. and trans. H. Dreyfus and P. Rabinow, Chicago University Press (1982), and the following books by Foucault: *Madness and Civilization*, trans. R. Howard, New York: Random House(1965); *The Order of Things*, New York: Random House (1970); *Power Knowledge*, ed. C. Gordon, New York: Pantheon (1980); and *The Foucault Reader*, ed. P. Rabinow, Harmondsworth: Penguin (1986).

41 M. Foucault, *The History of Sexuality*, vol. 1, New York: Pantheon (1978), 143.

42 J. Derrida, *Of Grammatology*, trans. G. Spivak, Johns Hopkins University Press (1976), 13 ff, 34–5 and *Glas*, Paris: Galilée (1974), 67–8, 92.

43 See R. Rorty, *Consequences of Pragmatism*, University of Minneapolis Press (1982); J.-F. Lyotard, *The Post-Modern Condition*, Manchester University Press (1983).

44 See, for example, T. Kuhn, *The Structure of Scientific Revolutions*, Chicago University Press (1962); P. Feyerband, *Against Method*, London: Derson (1978).

45 Perhaps, in terms of shared 'virtues'. See A. MacIntyre, *Whose*

Justice? Which Rationality?, London: Duckworth (1988), especially chs. 19 and 20.

46 One of the manifestations of this manipulation is, of course, inter-religious dialogue. Dialogue is often conceived of as a relationship between one individual and another. Often such dialogue rests upon a misunderstanding of Buber's *I and Thou*, Edinburgh: T. & T. Clark (1984), a careful reading of ch. 3 of which offers a more balanced approach.

47 A number of recent articles on conceptual and moral relativism are to be found in a collection (edited by J. Meiland and M. Krausz), *Relativism*, University of Notre Dame Press (1982); see also M. Hollis and S. Lukes (eds), *Rationality and Relativism*, MIT Press (1982).

48 All our traditions are beset with difficulties of intra-religious pluralism, and in a way these often seem more urgently pressing issues than broader concerns with liberalism, although I would argue that they almost always have the same basis.

49 For a recent attempt at the imposition of a supra-framework, see W. C. Smith, *Towards a World Theology*, Philadelphia: Westminster Press (1981); consider also the possibilities of changes within a tradition, particularly in relation to parochialism and moral issues, e.g. feminism.

IV
Institutional aspects of pluralism

13

Religious pluralism and the law in England and Africa

A case study

Antony Allott

Introduction

This chapter attempts to do two things: first, to consider what in general is the relationship between law and pluralism in the religious domain; second, to examine what expedients have been resorted to, what policies followed, and what problems presented, by experience in two different kinds of legal jurisdiction. The problems of legal + religious pluralism (we must use the + sign to indicate that the two exist in isolation, but may find themselves in association, in a given society, when it is the cumulation of the two that poses problems) are profoundly different in a modern country such as Britain and in one which has recently emerged via the colonial experience with typically pluralistic sets of political and social institutions.

Taking England first, we note to begin with the anomaly that, since the creation of the 'United Kingdom' by the union of England and Scotland, initially with a common sovereign, and eventually as a united realm, we have in Britain one country but already a plurality of legal systems, English law (applying to England and Wales) being distinct from that of Scotland. Accordingly, the exact correlation between a unique legal system and the country to which it appertains cannot be explored in the British context. This is the first of numerous paradoxes, since we commonly think of Britain as an exemplar of the uniform type of national legal system in contradistinction to countries (such as India or Nigeria) which have an avowedly plural one. It is uniform with a difference. By way of contrast, the independent successor states which have emerged from British overrule in the Commonwealth do not have all the one-country/one-law phenomenon.

In making this analysis and comparison, this chapter attempts to sketch a dimension of the phenomenon of religious pluralism which is largely absent from other chapters in this book – namely, the relationship of religion with state and law. So we move out of the world of theology and ethnographic observation into what we may term the 'real world', the world of prisons and Parliaments, law-courts and Bills of Rights. It is, in this real world, not just a question of what you think or how you pray, but of what the state legal system commands you to do, or punishes you for doing, or protects you while you are doing.

This aspect of the location of religion, and specifically of religious pluralism, in the real world poses policy choices, not just for those who have charge of the state machine and who thereby determine what rules will prevail governing the practice of or belief in a given religious system, but for us too, the citizens of a polity. As such, we must remind ourselves, we are endowed with law-making power through numerous mechanisms, formal and informal, including both formal rights to choose one's rulers (in some societies) and informal influences on the making and validity of law through expressions of opinion, conforming or rejecting behaviour, and so on.

A chapter touching on religious pluralism ought, in my opinion, to define two things: first, what meaning is attributed to the term 'religious pluralism', and second, what is the personal position of the writer from which he or she writes. 'Pluralism' as such is not confined to the religious domain, of course. One is familiar, as a comparative lawyer, with the concept of legal pluralism – the situation, common overseas, where in a given country more than one legal system coexists. In the former colonial territories this legal pluralism is one of the legacies of empire. But legal analysts are now beginning to discover that legal pluralism may also exist, officially or unofficially, in countries such as our own, whose legal systems are purportedly unitary. In such societies unofficial or informal legal systems may exist, legally or otherwise, alongside the formal or official law. Where such unofficial legal systems contradict the formal law (as with the 'law?' of the Mafia), this may pose problems, both for the analyst and for the administration. But we now recognize that private and unofficial legal systems may licitly exist, embedded within the permissive framework of the official legal system. This I discuss in greater detail in my Conclusion. My chapter is accordingly divided into two parts, which respectively explore and reflect this twofold locus of legal pluralism.

As for religious pluralism, this – to my mind – may conceal a certain ambiguity. On the one hand, it may connote a state of affairs, the coexistence in one society of more than one religion;

or it may refer to a philosophy or attitude of mind, which holds that one religion is as true as another, or (less strongly) that one religion is as good as another, or at least that every religion, whether true or good or not, is entitled to equal respect. In this chapter I take it that one is concerned with how governments, through the instrumentality of law, react to the factual state of affairs where more than one religion prevails within its jurisdiction. If the law accommodates itself to the privileged coexistence of more than one religion within the society, one may say that the governmental authority has adopted a policy of religious pluralism.

There are two partial lacunae in this chapter. First, a chapter on religious + legal pluralism could examine in greater detail the constitutional position of religion in different societies. One notes, for example, the official recognition of, say, Islam or a particular variety of Christianity as the sole recognized religion in the constitution of some modern states. Second, and often as a consequence of this privileged position accorded to one official religion, there is the question of how far the law permits missionary activity. In some Muslim countries Christian missionary activity is proscribed or restrained by law, as in the Sudan; in some countries a similar result is achieved by administrative means. This is to follow through the logical thought-process that, since only one religion is true and the others are to varying degrees false, then the state, if it intervenes in this matter, can as governing authority decide to prohibit the propagation of what it sees as error. Of course, if one adopts the position that all religions are equally true ways to enlightenment and right conduct, then one cannot logically justify missionary activity by oneself, while not leaving it open to others to propagate their views. Because of constraints of time and space, neither of these aspects of the topic is dealt with in this chapter.

The relationship between law and pluralism in the religious domain

Before one can explore this relationship, we must ask what is the nature of the relationship between law and religion. Both are normative systems, whose norms often compete with each other; both seek to shape behaviour; both purport to be issued by authority and to be reinforced by sanctions. If the reader will allow me to summarize the argument and analysis in my *Limits of Law* (1980), I observed that law might compete with and be excluded by other normative systems, each seeking to shape the behaviour of those subject or responsive to them:

Law is only one normative system among many which compete for the attention and the allegiance of those to whom they are addressed. Religion, morality, community *mores*, are three examples of such normative systems . . . Two main issues arise from this competition: the problem of detection or discrimination of the legal message; and the exclusion or enfeeblement of the legal prescription by other prescriptions which the subject takes to be of prior importance or to have prior claim on his allegiance. (p. 120)

And I went on to try to separate the diverse ways in which a law and religion might relate to each other. In a given society, the relationship may be one

1. of fusion, where law and religion are seen as part of the same cultural complex, and there is no structural separation between them; such is true of what one may call the 'integrated' societies;
2. of infusion, where – without there being such structural fusion between law and religion – a ruler or other promulgator of laws seeks to make them conform to his own religious perceptions;
3. of co-ordination, where the legal system and the religious system exist on equal and parallel lines;
4. of subordination, where religion is subordinated to law and controlled by it – one might call this the politicization of religion;
5. of toleration, where the law tolerates, without being either inspired by or seeking to reinforce, the dictates of religion;

and finally

6. of suppression, where the law is inimical to religion and purports to outlaw it.

As an instance of fusion, we may cite the pure Islamic state, since for Islam religion and law are effectively one; but we might also add traditional customary societies, of Africa and elsewhere, whose normative systems present a wholeness or integration.

Instances of infusion are to be found in pre-conquest England, and to a lesser extent in post-conquest England too, where the rulers conceived their duty to be to make and uphold such laws only as conformed to Christian teaching and discipline, and in the *siyasa* jurisdiction of Muslim rulers, when they legislate in the public or penal domain.

As for co-ordination, we find parallel jurisdictions of

ecclesiastical and secular courts in England under the Normans, and in Muslim states too.

The effect of the Reformation in England under Henry VIII was to subordinate the Christian religion and church law and courts to the general law of England.

An overtly secular society such as that of contemporary Britain can be taken as an instance of toleration of religion. The contemporary English law neither favours and protects, nor discourages or prevents, the practice of or belief in religion. The same would not have been asserted, say, 100 or more years ago, when it could still have been affirmed, though with less confidence than centuries earlier, that Christianity 'is parcel of the law of England.'

As for suppression, avowedly militant atheist states, of which Albania is an extreme example, outlaw all religious practices and institutions.

The question, put shortly by Humpty Dumpty in *Alice in Wonderland* is, 'who is to be the master?' Fusion and infusion of law and religion suggest the paramountcy of religion over law: subordination and toleration suggest that of law over religion. In such a context, one cannot talk (as in the case of the United Kingdom with a monolithic and uniform national legal system) of the recognition of other 'laws' directly. A non-pluralist legal system presumably has no room for recognition of other legal systems within its jurisdiction. But the picture can change, and elements of plurality are creeping into the English legal system, as we shall see.

Fusion and infusion of law and religion indicate a commitment by the rulers to protect and promote a particular religion, this protection and promotion being achieved by granting a privileged position to those who operate that religion (the priests or religious functionaries), and to the tenets of that religion, and by incorporating the values, and even the dogmas, of the religion in the secular legal system. On the other side of the coin, there will be corresponding discouragement, ignoring, or suppression of non-conforming religions.

Typically, modern secular states such as Britain have legal systems which allow for the toleration, but not for the state promotion, of religions. However, this policy of neutralism has to sit with the acceptance of the values of free speech, freedom of association, and the right to promote any philosophy or policy which is not clearly contrary to any law currently in force. Religion is not just a set of beliefs, but a set of institutions and of practices, even of culture. So it is not enough to ask whether a tolerant state allows freedom of propaganda; it must also be asked what are the limits it sets to freedom of behaviour. It is particularly in the field of family law that contradictions can arise – for example, between the still monogamously orientated, but no longer 'Christian', character of recognized marriage under English law and the potentially or actually polygamous character of some other marriage laws, inspired, in the Muslim case, by religious teachings; or between laws on cruelty to animals on the one hand, and methods of ritual killing of animals for food in accordance with the dictates of Islamic or Jewish religious 'laws' on the other. One can now discern a more protective and interventionist approach to the treatment of religions by the law in England – there is evidence which suggests a new and 'pluralist' approach in the framing and administration of the laws. Partly this is the work of Parliament, partly that of the judges, and partly that of those called on to administer under the law. Acts of administration help to shape the real meaning of laws – the bare text is not enough.

What is a 'religious law?'

Religious pluralism, so far as the legal system is concerned, involves the recognition of diverse religions; more importantly, it may involve the recognition of diverse 'religious laws'. This concept must now be examined. The label, for that is what it is, is too readily and loosely applied to describe various kinds of legal system. Without delving too far into ancient history, one might make a case for saying that pre-classical Roman law was a religious law in the sense that it sprang out of, supposed a background of, and in part was implemented by legal devices and institutions, the beliefs and practices of the old Roman religion. Jewish law is typically claimed as a 'religious' law. Of all the cases, Islamic law, springing from the commands of God as transmitted to Man through God's prophet, Muhammad, and to be found in the sacred text of the Quran, the teachings of the Prophet, practice, and the opinions of jurists, may be thought of as a religious law.

But in fact 'religious law' refers to a number of distinct types of legal system. What it means and whether a legal system is to be termed 'religious' or indeed 'law' depends on the point of view of the speaker. As Hart distinguished the internal and the external aspect of rules, so we may distinguish the internal and the external viewpoint as regards religious law. The internal viewpoint, that of the adherents of the religion in question, is how they see their own religion/law. To adherents of the religion its mandates are obligatory, whether they refer to what we may think of as religious practices or to what the outsider may treat as secular concerns.

So – to the pious Muslim – it is not a matter of choice whether or not to comply with the dictates of the Sharia. If the Muslims are in a minority and do not constitute the governing forces of the society, they will still expect that the secular or non-believing ruler should make no law, or administer no regulation, that will contradict the commands of Islam. Whether that expectation is satisfied depends on the position adopted by the ruler as regards variant systems of rule and belief. A ruler who accepts the postulates of pluralism may be prepared to accord some recognition to Islamic, or indeed to other laws; but this recognition will generally be as a *personal* law. This means that it applies to, and by reason of the religious affiliation of, adherents of the given religion. Further, the juridical basis of the application of such a religious law by a secular ruler will be entirely different from that which will apply to a religious law which is also the law of the ruler or the state. In the former case, the religious law will apply by virtue of concession by the ruler; the law has validity and effect only, and so far, as the ruler allows it. In the latter case, the religious law applies because it is the command of God or some other force or deity, and derives its validity and effect therefrom. The ruler then becomes merely the channel, rather than the source, of validity.

One may argue that the law of the Christian church in western Europe during the age of faith was a religious law in a different sense. It was a law providing for the internal regulation of the body of believers in their religious capacity. It was not, and did not purport to be, a comprehensive code regulating all aspects of life in society, even though there was what we may term 'leakage' into the secular world, where Christian injunctions in such matters as marriage and sexual morality were given the force of law, in the strict sense, by being incorporated in the general legal system.

Religious law takes on yet another meaning when it is descriptive of the law actually followed by adherents of a religion, without being or purporting to be religious in the sense of having otherworldly inspiration. Much of Hindu law, even though it is imbued with religious ideas (for example, in family relationships), might well be considered a kind of customary law applying to Hindus, and thus varying from locality to locality according to the custom locally followed.

Jewish law, as the law of the rabbis, while in part the command of God, is also in part a casuistic law developed by the jurists; and is perhaps no more and no less a religious law than the common law of England, developed on the same casuistic basis by persons who were convinced adherents of another faith.

Perhaps at the end of the day it is all a question of sources. Where does one go to find the rules of the law? If one goes to a sacred text, purporting to contain the instructions of a divine or para-divine lawmaker, then the law may be called religious; if one goes to non-divine sources, such as the decisions of courts or the opinions of jurists, or the customs of the people, then at most one is dealing with a 'religiously inspired' law. We shall henceforth take 'religious law' in the broader sense for the purposes of this chapter.

Religious pluralism and the law in England

English law in its relation with religion has gone through all the stages already mentioned, with the sole exception of suppression. Today the current law of England no longer seeks to recognize or enact any particular religious point of view; we are therefore currently in a phase of toleration or religious neutrality. But one cannot decouple the current English law, statutory or common, from its previous connections with religion, and that the religion of Christianity. The religious tide may have receded from the legal shore; but stranded on the beach is the detritus of former ages. We may mention a few exceptions:

The content of large sections of the law The law of crimes in particular includes many examples of offences whose genesis is to be explained by the religious past. Some of these offences are now under criticism for this very reason – the law of bigamy, springing from a semi-sacramental notion of marriage and the supreme virtue of monogamy (though now represented as either an offence against public record-keeping or a fraud on an innocent third party); or blasphemy (almost totally gone). But the very fabric of criminal liability traces back to a Christian analysis of guilt, with its notion that criminal liability is not created merely by a wrongful act but must be accompanied by a guilty mind (*mens rea*).

The notion of 'reason' and the 'reasonable man' The common law was founded on the law of reason, itself a derivation of Christian understanding of the moral and legal order. The reasonable man has been a central figure in the calculation of legal liability; the domain of the reasonable is now being extended by statute or judicial decision – frequently, the law now requires what is reasonable. We must pay our debts in a reasonable time; terms in a contract may not be enforced if they are unreasonable; on divorce the judge makes reasonable provision for the spouses and their children; and so on.

Equity   Equity took its origin in the semi-religious and definitely ethical jurisdiction of the Chancellor – always a senior cleric of the Christian church to begin with. He sought to do what was morally right in the circumstances of the case – religion and law here came together.

At the time when Christianity was held to be officially part of the law of England – a relationship cemented after the Reformation by the recognition of an 'Established Church' regulated by Parliament – the position could be reached where heresy or disregard of the religion as by law established could be construed as a form of treason, as under the Tudors. Religious emancipation proceeded slowly over the succeeding centuries. Both Catholics and Jews were for a long time under legal disabilities by virtue of their adherence; despite legislation, both in the nineteenth and twentieth centuries, complete equality before the law has not yet been attained (a Jew or Catholic is still disqualified for accession to the throne, whereas presumably an unconfessed agnostic or atheist would be eligible). We cannot recapitulate here the gradual process by which this emancipation has come about. Since the Second World War and the immigration and settlement of large numbers of non-European adherents of other religions – these religions – especially those of oriental origin such as Islam, Sikhism, and Hinduism – have gradually won a degree of recognition by the official legal system. So far this recognition has been largely (with interesting exceptions) passive; that is, the legal system does not discriminate against, but does not positively recognize, still less promote, these and other religions. But the scene may be changing: there are straws in the wind which may betoken a shift to legal pluralism which will mirror this religious pluralism. Some of the evidence for this conclusion is examined below.

We are thus in an era of shift of fundamental positions and conflict of currents. History has left us a legacy of christianized law; today's devotion to aggressive neutralism or indifference at the legal level cuts across this current from the past. The result is a whirlpool in which our institutions are now trapped, issue from which is problematical. In this conflict religions compete with what may be seen as new 'religions', though without God; one dominant strand in contemporary social thinking bases itself on the creed of equality and non-discrimination – all are entitled to equal treatment before the law – with an attachment to interventionist government to promote this equality. Both wings of this creed find expression in legal provision and legal action, through the enactment of anti-discrimination legislation and the undertaking of positive remedial action by public authorities in such fields as housing, jobs, and tax. It is suggested that the concept of religious pluralism must be broadened to include such rivals to religion, that is, to include new secular religions embodying a world-view and pragmatics to go with it.

Examples of the pluralist factor in English law today

Overt recognition of religious personal laws   As at the time of writing, English law does not give overt recognition domestically to religious personal laws. In other words, for those whose permanent home is in Britain, there is only one system of personal law (that which regulates personal relations) in force, and that – for England and Wales – is English law. This straightforward principle has already been breached in various direct and indirect ways (as reported below), but the principle remains.

The situation is quite different when we take account of Private International Law and its effect on law administered by English courts. Private International Law (otherwise, conflict of laws) is the body of rules recognized by English courts as determining whether, and to what extent, foreign systems of law will be recognized in those courts in cases involving a 'foreign element'. To take a simple illustration: will English courts recognize contracts made abroad under some other system of law? A more pertinent example lies in the field of marriage and divorce: will an English court recognize, and give effect to rights and duties under, foreign marriages and divorces celebrated under some other system of law, which might include a religious system of law, and one which, for instance, permits polygamy or extra-judicial divorce? The answer is that English courts have been prepared for some considerable time to concede such recognition, subject to major constraints imposed by public policy, which can vary from time to time in line with changing perceptions.

The most important of these constraints in the field of marriage law, where many such conflict situations arise, was that English courts were not prepared to exercise jurisdiction over foreign marriages which did not conform to the pattern set by English law itself. This pattern was that of the so-called 'Christian marriage', as defined and explained in a famous judgement of Lord Penzance in the celebrated Mormon case of *Hyde v. Hyde* (1866). There recognition was refused to a Mormon marriage celebrated abroad because it was potentially polygamous and thus failed to satisfy the test of a 'Christian marriage', which alone would be recognized by English courts as amenable to their remedial jurisdiction. As Lord Penzance said,

> it may well be doubted whether it would become the tribunals of this country to enforce the duties (even if we knew them) which belong to a system so utterly at variance with the Christian conception of marriage.

However, there was nothing categorically religious about the definition of Christian marriage for this purpose: 'a union of one man and one woman for life to the exclusion of all others'. But the conception was religiously derived.

One must interject here the startling paradox that what English courts in England could not bring themselves to do, according to Lord Penzance – namely to administer marriage laws which did not conform to 'marriage as understood in Christendom' – English courts overseas in the colonial empire were quite prepared to do with their recognition of non-English personal laws. There was nothing intrinsic therefore to the judge being British and wearing a wig which would prevent him from applying such foreign laws. All that mattered was where he sat.

Space prevents a detailed statement of how *Hyde v. Hyde* was qualified by the English courts subsequently; but Parliament stepped in in 1972 with the Matrimonial Proceedings (Polygamous Marriages) Act specifically to repeal this rule. Henceforth, English courts are competent to exercise matrimonial jurisdiction over marriages formed under a law permitting polygamy, and regularly do so.

Some statutory exceptions have now been introduced to the general principle that overt recognition is not given to religious personal laws in England. It still remains the case that a marriage celebrated in England, if it is to be recognized by English law, must conform to the local law so far as form is concerned. A religious ceremony receives no such recognition unless either conducted by a licensed minister or supported by a civil ceremony. So far as the status and effects of the marriage are concerned, English law restricts these to those appropriate to English law; and thus if two persons who are foreign nationals or with a foreign domicile whose own law permits polygamy marry each other in England, their marriage – so far as English law is concerned – is and must be monogamous.

Among the exceptions to be noted – all introduced in the recent past and reflecting the presence in Britain of large immigrant populations adhering to non-Christian religions – are the law on motor-cycle helmets; the law on ritual slaughter; and the law on racial discrimination. It is worth reminding ourselves however that the first non-Christian religion which attracted special attention from the law was that of Judaism. Exceptionally, 'persons professing the Jewish religion' did not, and do not, under Lord Hardwicke's Marriage Act of 1753, have to conform to the usual requirements of time, place, and minister required for the validity of a marriage celebrated in England, and so Jewish weddings may, provided they follow the usages of Judaism, be celebrated at any hour and in any place. However, a similar tolerance of extra-judicial Jewish divorces by *get* has been removed by the Domicile and Matrimonial Proceedings Act 1973.

Motor-cycle helmets   The requirement that those who ride motor cycles must wear helmets, and that failing to do so is a criminal offence, has only recently (since 1973) been introduced by legislation. Male Sikhs who claimed that their religion required them to wear turbans both objected to the new law applying to them, and began to disregard it. The government, as so often in these matters, took the softer option: instead of insisting on rigid and universal application of the law, they decided to adjust the law to suit the behaviour, rather than the other way round. Religiously inspired breach of a regulatory law led to modification of the law in 1976 by the Motor-Cycle Crash Helmets (Religious Exemption) Act, which provided that the law should not apply to any follower of the Sikh religion when wearing a turban.

Although an apparently minor matter, this question has implications of some importance. The equal application of the laws, enshrined as an overt constitutional principle in the United States and taken for granted in the law of England, was here overridden by concessions to followers of a particular religion. Religious pluralism translated into legal pluralism must imply inequality before the law.

Ritual slaughter   It is the policy of the law, expressing the settled commitment to avoiding causing unnecessary pain or suffering to animals, that animals for food consumption must be humanely slaughtered, which means that either they must be instantaneously killed, or at least instantaneously stunned before being killed. The Jewish ritual method of slaughter, *shechita*, and the Muslim method, *halal*, both involve cutting of the animal's throat without pre-stunning. Societies and persons committed to the protection of animals have often averred that this involves some unacceptable cruelty to slaughtered animals, an averment rejected by orthodox

Jews and Muslims. Since causing pain and suffering to animals during slaughtering is, under the Act, a criminal offence, the issue is of some importance.

Unlike some of the other religious legal concessions noted here, the special concession, now granted to Jews and Muslims by the Slaughterhouses Act 1974, repeats a concession originally granted by the Slaughter of Animals Act 1933, and this antedates the post-war wave of immigration. The 1974 Act specifically exempts slaughter by the Jewish method for the food of Jews and by a Jew duly licensed for the purpose, and similarly by the Muslim method for the food of Muslims when carried out by a Muslim, from the requirements of the Act regarding instantaneous killing or stunning. Feelings run high in contemporary Britain over cruelty to animals; and those who champion this cause run headlong into those who are equally concerned to protect religious beliefs, practices, and susceptibilities. A report from the Farm Animals Welfare Council to the Ministry of Agriculture, Fisheries and Food in 1985 faced up to this contradiction:

> We recognize the minefield to be crossed in trying to deal with such a combination of religious symbolism and ceremonial, ethnic and religious identity and practical issues concerning the humane treatment of animals. We believe, however, that members of the Jewish and Muslim faiths should once again be encouraged to adapt their methods of slaughter in ways which still meet the needs of dietary habit and religious identity, whilst accepting modern methods to ensure that the bird's or animal's welfare benefits from sound contemporary practice.

Racial discrimination   The current law on racial discrimination is contained in the Race Relations Act 1976. This outlaws various forms of direct and indirect discrimination on 'racial' grounds. Racial discrimination is expressly defined in the Act, section 3 (1), to mean discrimination on grounds of colour, race, nationality, or ethnic or national origins only, and categorically does not catch discrimination on religious grounds alone. It is therefore, unless prohibited by some other law, perfectly legal to discriminate against someone because he or she is of a particular religious persuasion. If however the discrimination can be tied into discrimination on grounds of colour, race, ethnic group, and so on, it will be caught by the Act, as the leading case on the subject, *Mandla v. Dowell Lee* (1983) shows. In this case a Sikh father wished to enter his son for a private school. The school was not prepared to admit the son if he insisted on wearing a turban. The father insisted that it was a required part of the Sikh religion for male Sikhs to wear turbans and that this refusal to permit it was racially discriminatory. This involved a consideration of what the Act meant by the word 'ethnic'. The Court of Appeal took a narrow view, that 'ethnic' basically involves a genetic rather than a cultural or religious tie between the members of a given ethnic group. The House of Lords in a landmark decision took the opposite point of view. To their Lordships 'ethnic' went beyond the biological; and an ethnic group might be constituted by a shared history; a shared cultural tradition, 'often but not necessarily associated with religious observance'; a common geographical origin or descent from common ancestors; a common language and literature; 'a common religion different from that of neighbouring groups or from the general community surrounding it'; being a 'minority or being an oppressed or a dominant group within a larger community'. With all respect to Lord Fraser who enunciated these criteria, which led the House of Lords to hold that the Sikhs, whom one would normally have thought of as a distinct religious group, were also an ethnic group for the purposes of the Act, these criteria can hardly be accepted *in toto*. Their Lordships, in their perhaps laudable, or perhaps dubious, attempt to find for the plaintiff Sikh in the case, can be criticised for so distorting and expanding the definition of racial discrimination as to comprehend what was intentionally omitted from the Act, namely discrimination on grounds of religion. It may be that religious discrimination should also be outlawed – indeed, the present writer shares this view; but it cannot be achieved by a misreading of the words of the Act and a revision by the judges of what Parliament has chosen to enact.

In the result, not only Sikhs but also probably Jews, and indeed the Christian community of Britain, might claim to be an ethnic group for the purposes of the Act. The implications of this reading for the recognition of religious laws in Britain need careful evaluation. Being forbidden to discriminate on 'ethnic' (for which now read 'religio-ethnic') grounds might imply a corresponding duty to accept what adherents of a given religion treat as part of their religious law but what the legal system of England would now treat as part of their culture – in other words, an acceptance of religio-legal pluralism by the back door.

An example of this approach at work is to be found in the handling of Rastafarians. Rastafarianism seems to be both a religion, a political creed associated with the back-to-Africa movement, and a cultural manifestation linked to membership of a particular, Caribbean, ethnic group. To adherents the various practices of the religion are commanded by it, and could be classified as a sort of religious code. Wearing the hair long, and wearing a covering cap, as well as the sacramental use of cannabis, are associated with membership. Each of these practices may conflict with the law of the land or with officially approved behaviour-patterns. Thus a Rastafarian charged in a court of law may refuse to remove his head-dress; one committed to prison may resist the cutting of his locks; and use of cannabis is of course itself contrary to law. Here the sociology of law comes in to complement the formal exposition of legal rules and requirements. What do we actually see in practice? We see the Nelsonian approach, turning the blind eye, in full force. By refusing to make an issue of these matters, those in authority are in practice granting an unofficial partial dispensation from the standard rules and regulations of society in favour of the practices of a given minority. This is the first stage, as the battles with Sikhs over the wearing of turbans show, towards a formal recognition of these practices by the official system. Pluralism has again entered by the back door.

Social customs, which outside Britain would be considered part of a religious personal law, may also be given indirect recognition by courts and authorities. For example, the demands of the Hindu joint-family system, or the pattern of marriage among Hindus and the relationship of brides with their mothers-in-law, may be accorded recognition, not overtly, but as part of the cultural background to be taken into account by a court in applying what on the surface are the uniform rules of English law. Wherever a law lays down that a party, or the court, shall do what is 'reasonable', subjective and personal factors such as these may enter into the definition of the applicable norms.

The policy implications and the future

Three important questions arising from the situation just described pose themselves in this transitional era which English law has now reached:

1. Can one discern a coherent policy towards religious pluralism and the law?
2. How does one square a partial recognition of religious/legal pluralism with the legal philosophy inherited from and enshrined in the common law of England?
3. What does diversity of patterned behaviour and non-compliance with the law do to its authority?

Present policy It would be too kind to those who direct affairs or make and administer our laws to say that there is a coherent and articulated policy which is now followed. Certainly, despite certain privileges accorded to certain religions (as with maintained schools, or the status of the Church of England in English law), the present legislative policy is neutralist or pluralist as regards religious observance or adherence. The difficulty comes when this adherence or observance impinges on the public law, or on the private-law rights and privileges of others, and is set to challenge the existing legal rules in some way. Non-complying behaviour in regard to motor-cycle helmets illustrates the challenge to public law; the claim to turban-wearing as a natural right, based on religion, claimed to be superior to the private-law claim of a school proprietor to determine who shall attend his school and on what terms, illustrates the private-law aspect.

We live now in a somewhat ill-defined 'liberal-egalitarian' consensus, expressed notably in relaxation on the one hand of laws against freedom of speech and action (cf. the obscenity law), and in tightening of laws on discrimination against gender or race minorities (cf. the race and sex discrimination laws). The one appears to contradict the other. Anti-discrimination laws now have an international, as well as a domestic, dimension. British adherence to the European Convention on Human Rights, and the possible enactment of this into domestic English law, complicates the matter. Article 9 of the European Convention guarantees freedom of thought, conscience, and religion; and this freedom manifests itself not just in belief or even in expression, but also in 'practice and observance'. It is with practice and observance – whether ritual slaughter, turbans, polygamy, extra-judicial divorce, property arrangements, and so on – that the religious law intersects with the general law. How far can a signatory state go in refusing to recognize such divergent practices? The Convention only allows such derogation in the interests of public safety, for the protection of public order, health, and morals, or for the protection of the rights and freedoms of others. It is difficult to fit many of the ordinances and practices of imported religious laws into any of these categories. There will undoubtedly come a time when the official legal system will have to face these issues.

Some of the religious communities now established in England are in no doubt about what policy changes they seek. In the vanguard (as always) are the Muslims, drawing on their experience in what we may call their motherlands of Pakistan, India, and Bangladesh particularly. Muslim bodies in each of these countries and spokesmen in England have already made known their ambitions in this regard. So far they have not been seriously considered by any law-reform body or government agency. But the door has already been opened by such decisions as the *Mandla* case. If the Muslims open the door, other communities, especially Hindus and Sikhs, will follow. Britain would then reach the state which is normal in overseas countries within the Commonwealth with plural legal systems involving recognition of religious personal laws.

It is important to note that Britain would not be the first major Commonwealth 'First World' country to reach this position. In Canada (with the recognition of Inuit and Indian law), in Australia (with the new status now being given to aboriginal law), and in New Zealand (with the long-standing recognition of Maori law), plural legal systems are already a reality. In none of these cases is the basis of the pluralism religious affiliation; but this does not matter, once the principle of pluralism has been accepted. If Britain now, in a fit of absence of mind or as a result of serious reflection and deliberation, moves to this new position, one must recognize a stunning paradox which cries out for comment. This is that the parent countries from which many of the immigrant communities come have generally moved in the opposite direction, to the reduction or abolition of legal pluralism and the creation of uniform national law. India and some of the African countries have been particularly conspicuous in moving in this direction. As so often, law in the First World seems to change places with law in the Third World.

The inherited philosophy of the common law   Two dominating characteristics of modern English law must be briefly referred to here. The first is expressed neatly in the very term, 'common law'. It was the achievement of the Anglo-Norman kings to replace local and customary laws with a single national common law applying to all persons everywhere. Eventually local and pluralist systems disappeared. After the Reformation the dichotomy between common-law courts and ecclesiastical courts was minimized, and eventually in its turn effectively disappeared. The second characteristic is that this common law was essentially of Christian inspiration and character. Both these salient characteristics are threatened by the conversion of English law to pluralism.

Non-compliance and the authority of law   Law can lead, or law can follow. In other words, law can shape behaviour; uniform law hopefully makes uniform behavioural responses. Or law can reflect society, and its rules and institutions may evolve as a result of social pressures and changes in personal or group behaviour.

Most law does both. Law in so far as it is behavioural shaping loses that authority which is essential to any legal system if behaviour does not correspond with rule. Law as reflector of social opinion and conduct has sociological rather than legal value: often, the modification of law is a result of non-compliance with its requirements by those subject to it.

It would be the final irony of the history of the United Kingdom and its relationship with the empire if the last act of the drama were entitled, 'The Empire Strikes Back'. What are and were the legal arrangements, characterized by legal pluralism and the recognition of religious personal laws, we must now briefly examine in the next section of this chapter.

Religious pluralism and the law in Africa

When Britain assumed administrative overrule of the African territories subjected to the British Crown, certain distinct policy choices were available as regards the legal system to be imposed or created. Given the contempt which had characterized earlier dealing with indigenous laws in Africa, a feasible option would have been to withhold recognition of these legal systems as laws in any serious sense, recognizing only law of the European type, the conquerors' law, as valid. This option was effectively that which commended itself to the Portuguese, the first colonizers of Africa. Alternatively, while conceding some effectiveness to indigenous laws, these could have been classified as mere 'customs', different in rank and quality from the true law, the law of the colonial power: this effectively is what the French, with their distinction between *droit moderne* and *droit coutumier*, achieved. A third choice was to have no frank policy at all, applying English law and recognizing indigenous law at the same time as the simplest option – a policy effectively pursued by the British during the period of first contact with Africa. Finally – the policy generally adopted in British colonial Africa – a sort of dualism might be installed, under which both the imported English law and the indigenous customary and religious laws had validity, though with the latter subjected to the former.

In the result, in countries such as Nigeria, Kenya, and Ghana, all formerly under British rule, English law as in force in England was officially extended to the territories in question; while at the same time customary and Islamic law in West Africa, and customary law and religious personal laws, notably Islamic and Hindu law, in East Africa were given official recognition, subject only to the overriding qualifications imposed by the 'repugnancy clause', that indigenous laws applied only if they did not offend the principles of justice, equity, and good conscience, or justice and morality (according to the territory). The justice and morality that was applied thus as a censor was British, and hence Christian, justice and morality; but this was moderated by a willingness to recognize non-Christian practices and belief systems.

While most of the customary laws could not be classified as 'religious' laws (even though predicated on traditional beliefs and practices), religious laws *stricto sensu* were recognized, notably Islamic law (even including Islamic public and criminal law in Northern Nigeria), Hindu law, and other systems of Asian personal law in East Africa. These personal laws were especially applicable in matters relating to personal status, marriage, the family, and succession. These laws as recognized were not only subject to the 'repugnancy' requirement, but could not run counter to the general law of the land. Obviously, though, their existence and recognition implied some derogation from the general application of English law. The problems of reconciliation between possibly conflicting systems of law were resolved by 'internal conflict' rules, which were to be found either in general legislation, or as an appendage to a particular provision.

This dualism, or more exactly pluralism, though expedient during the earlier days of colonial rule, was found something of an embarrassment by the colonial power as the territories developed, and western notions of the family, property, contracts, commercial dealings, and the like, took a firmer hold on the population. Accordingly, during the late colonial period (the 1950s and early 1960s) colonial administrations in Africa addressed the problem of plurality of laws, and determined that unification, or at least integration, of laws was desirable in a modern state system. Several territories accordingly set in train a process of review of pluralistic legal provision in such domains as the law of marriage and divorce, and of testate and intestate succession. Kenya was in the van in this movement, appointing two commissions, broadly constituted, to review these areas of law. They came down firmly in favour of an integrated law, in which not all elements of the variant legal systems were suppressed, but where broadly there were common requirements for validity, e.g. of marriage, and common legal consequences, whatever the procedure by which particular relationships were established.

In a decision of great interest for our theme of religious and legal pluralism, the Kenya commissions decided that they could not, in an integrated law, hope to incorporate and reflect all the divergent rules of different personal laws – a typical example being the contrast between monogamy and polygamy. While therefore refusing to attempt the incorporation of positive elements of these variant laws – Muslims who wished the formal incorporation of the rules of Islamic law were thus to be disappointed – the commissions held that their reports should contain nothing which was offensive to particular religious sentiments. No one, in other words, was to be commanded to do anything which contradicted his religion.

Many of the early ventures, especially in the 1960s in countries such as Uganda and Ghana, to achieve integration of laws and the building of a single national law met with failure because of particularist and local resistances to the imposition of a uniform law. A unique personal law was seen as an expression and a mark of cultural identity. It was just for this reason that many African governments, obsessed with the need to 'build the nation' in their newly created states, wished to eliminate diversities in law. Tanzania was in the forefront of this movement. Despite the power exerted by its president, Dr Nyerere, and its single-party government, it was deemed inexpedient to go the whole hog and wipe out the difference between Islamic and other personal laws; but a major programme of unification of customary personal laws, where the religious element did not obtrude, was undertaken with less retrospection and has enjoyed a degree of apparent success.

The search for national unity and the imperatives of nation-building contradict the demand for pluralist treatment of laws and religions. In this perspective, 'tribal' and particularist sentiments must give way to national demands for unity. Law, as a powerful expression of particularism and difference, is especially significant in this context. While progress measured in terms of laws both enacted and complied with (one thinks of Ethiopia and its desperate attempt to construct a single national law, which entirely ignored the fact that the majority of the population were Muslims devoted to their own Islamic personal law) has been disappointing, the will to unity, both politically and of laws, still exists in Africa. In this it corresponds to the factual coming together of diverse populations under the common influence of western economies, educational systems, social patterns and religions: a uniform law would best express this tendency to uniformity of social practice.

Conclusion

But let us not deceive ourselves. The myth of national unity is a myth, and no more than a myth. Even if we delete religious differences, the experiences of Africa show that new diversities develop. And in our own society and law in England the hope of a uniform law is no more than a mirage while society is fundamentally stratified and divided. The architects of any effective legal system must always admit that one code cannot cover all groups and all behaviour. The English way of coping with this demand is to allow the maximum freedom to subsidiary home-made legal systems, constituted by contract, by membership of a group with its own customs – we have done this in the commercial domain with the recognition of mercantile custom. Maybe we must do it also in the family domain with the recognition of diverse systems of personal law. The betting is that the law of England in the twenty-first century will differ dramatically from that which we now take for granted. The outlines of such a new system are just beginning to emerge from the contemporary mist.

14

Pluralism
The relationship of theology to religious studies

Adrian Hastings

Pluralism is, I believe, a matter of absolutely primary importance for theologians, philosophers, students of religion, human beings, because human and religious experience is irremediably pluralist. But pluralism has come to have so many forms and meanings which require to be distinguished rather carefully if their consideration is not to become hopelessly confused. My intention in this chapter is to consider one quite limited, almost methodological, aspect of the subject by focusing on two rather closely linked developments within the recent intellectual history of the Christian west: one, the transformation of university departments of 'Theology' into departments of 'Religious Studies, (either by change of name or effectively); the other, the proposed transformation of Christian theology itself, with its hitherto irreducible core of particularism, into a pluralist 'world theology' which gives no centrality or primacy to any specific religious tradition of revelation or salvation. The latter is, of course, particularly connected with names like John Hick and Wilfred Cantwell Smith. These two developments have gone very closely together, the one often appearing as the justification of the other. They might well be claimed to represent collectively the most characteristic contribution of the late 1960s and 1970s to the theological area of study.

I will begin with what might be called, a little simplistically, an attempt to delineate the *sitz im leben* of John Hick's *God and the Universe of Faiths*.[1] The establishment of a *sitz im leben*, as should be obvious (but often is not), in no way demonstrates the truth or falsity of an idea, but understanding is undoubtedly helped by the contextualization of its genesis. The book was published in 1973 and represents the most influential example in this country of the rewriting of Christian theology to accommodate the apparent requirements of a religiously pluralistic world. It is closely paralleled by the work of Wilfred Cantwell Smith[2] in America, among others. To understand this exercise, and the apparent need for it, it seems to me helpful to consider the cultural world which had finally broken up a few years previously. It was not, strange as it may seem in retrospect, a pluralistic world. It is true that from the seventeenth century at least, the west was laying the intellectual and religious foundations for pluralism. It is true also that for two hundred years the British Empire had straddled cultures and faiths with, on the whole, remarkable tolerance and aplomb: India could not have been ruled otherwise. But it was only, and very deliberately, tolerance up to a point. Indian culture and religion, it was officially agreed, were good enough for Indians, but they were not something open to an Englishman – however affectionate a Kipling or a Forster, at least, might be towards them. The underlying tragedy of *A Passage to India* lies precisely therein. Indian culture and society could be a tourist attraction, but it would be very dangerous for all concerned if they became more than that.

The Victorian model coupled a world-wide empire and commerce with the most emphatic commitment, explicit or implicit, to the mental, moral, and religious primacy of western man, conceived in a unitary and rather missionary way. Despite the growth of a multiplicity of denominations, a pluralism of public experience was not significantly reflected in a pluralism of world-view but rather in an unquestioning consciousness of superiority, guaranteed by printing press and gun, railroad and telegraph. Perhaps there was no other way in which Europe's political domination could have been appropriately justified or motivated. If a diversity of culture and religion was admitted, it was not on a fully pluralistic basis but on a strictly two-tier model: ours and theirs, and never the twain shall meet.

'Ours' was not as such necessarily Christian – or at least it did not remain so. Take that much-used nineteenth-century phrase 'civilization and Christianity'. For some people the one took primacy, for some the other. The missionary, expatiating upon the power and wealth of Queen Victoria's empire to a bemused petty African potentate might wave the Bible before him and declare impressively, 'Here is the explanation of Britain's greatness', but the late-Victorian mind was increasingly regarding the Christianity element in the package as expendable, and for some colonial officials it was just a nuisance. They remained no less firmly convinced of the inherent superiority of westernness.

Certainly the typical missionary, mini-theologian, or person in the pew rather easily equated the most particularist claims of Christianity, of Christ, of Bible, the '*solus*' of Reformation theology, with the inner principle of the west's primacy, the

227

conclusive reason why Britain was *super omnes*. England's providential role, declared Frederick Temple, at the time a young man, but later to be Archbishop of Canterbury, was 'the sublimest position ever occupied by any nation hitherto, that of the authoritative propagator of the Gospel over the world'.[3] The theological and religious particularism always inherent in the Christian gospel took on or coalesced with, in the context of the nineteenth century, this world-embracing western cultural particularism of political, even racial, domination – a domination which would not exterminate other breeds and faiths, but regulate them, study them conscientiously, hopefully perhaps in due course convert them. *Christus vincit* melted into 'Britannia rules the waves', and the more confident one was in the inherent superiority of Victoria's Britain, the more affected one might be both with a high sense of protectionist duty towards lesser breeds and by the call of the Student Christian's new watchword 'The evangelization of the world in this generation'.[4]

Of course I am simplifying, even perhaps caricaturing a little, the world-view of our ancestors – the world-view in which at least some of us were still brought up. But not too greatly. In the first half of the twentieth century it was expressed less crudely and less confidently, yet it survived and, indeed, a large working empire continued to require it as a sort of civil religion. The final collapse of this civil religion came only after the Second World War, and even then not too quickly. But the conditions which both needed and stimulated it were rapidly disappearing. The economic and political decline of Britain in particular was obvious. By the mid–1960s the Empire had virtually disappeared. The United Nations had generated a new ethos of egalitarian international relations. Japan, China, Indonesia, India, Pakistan were major powers. Christianity had lost such world-wide political significance as it possessed before the war. Even within Europe the ding-dong struggle between religion and secular humanism which had continued within the western tradition for many generations seemed to have reached a new phase in the ever-more-apparent triumph of the latter.

The 1960s were the decade in which the customary ideology of the west became manifestly unnecessary and hence patently absurd. It happened coincidentally, but perhaps not wholly coincidentally, with other, less easily to be anticipated, cultural revolutions: a general deriding of structure and tradition, a discovery of permissiveness, community, and experience: culture-free, gender-free, race-free.[5] The quintessential qualities of the sixties seemed all that the Victorian spirit was not. This transformation, partially but by no means wholly ephemeral, was made a great deal more complex for Britain by an extra but not unrelated development – the arrival of hundreds of thousands of Caribbean and Asian immigrants, the latter bringing their own non-Christian religions. Britain itself was becoming religiously a highly pluralist society in which Muslim, Sikh, Hindu, and Buddhist communities were important, just at the time when its Christian commit-ment was, at least in numerical terms, declining more rapidly than in any previous decade of the century, and just too as the old model of a two-tiered humanity was disappearing as absurd.

Western man had lived hitherto – even, paradoxically, if he lived in India or Malaysia – in an essentially unpluralistic society, and that society was motivated by an unpluralistic western religion, whether Christian or liberal-humanist, the two accommo-datingly interwoven. All that was now over. In the sixties our western world became stridently pluralist. The model was no longer Eton but California. Strangely enough, just as the tradition-ally unitary and missionary west turned in aspiration pluralist and undogmatic, much of the rest of the world began to move with almost equal suddenness and even cruelty towards unitary, anti-pluralist models. The late 1960s can be seen as a crucial moment for both developments. So much so that western society's rather hastily embraced pluralist ideals, intended especially to accommo-date the religions of Asia, could become for others new grounds for suspicion rather than any obvious bridge. It is within an almost world-wide anti-pluralist surge that the modern western concern for pluralism must be assessed.

In the late 1960s, however, that was not evident, and the newly perceived cultural pluralism of the west could well be seen as standing in need of a civil religion grounded in an appropriate theology. No faith should be established, yet each should be accorded appropriate respect and drawn into the functions that society asks of civil religion. There was an implicit need for an intellectual framework for the new religious order, even if that order could not fully be brought into being all at once. The inter-relationship of religions could, of course, be looked at in purely secular sociological or historical terms, even in Marxist ones, but to a religious sympathizer such terms would be reductionist and demeaning. Civil religion and the theology behind it must not be that. Parallel approaches to a number of different religious tra-ditions must inevitably generate institutions which are in principle religiously pluralist – that is to say, orientated sympathetically to religion in general but to no specific religious tradition in particu-lar. For such approaches and institutions to be genuinely attractive to believers themselves, it could then be argued that they ought to be justified not in merely secular terms but in those of an over-arching theology, an umbrella religious outlook, 'global or human theology' as Hick called it,[6] in terms of which all these various religions could intercommunicate and, in good Durkheimian manner, contribute religiously to the onward march and moral health of the contemporary city. That, I take it, forms a large part of the agenda behind Hick's *God and the Universe of Faith.* Of course he did not, and doubtless does not, see it quite like that. It would indeed be socially reductionist to see it merely like that. The point is that a consciously pluralist theology looked appropriate to the contemporary context, especially the context of Birmingham. Hick in all honesty stressed that the whole subject of the relation between Christianity and other religions was one he had 'largely ignored until coming to live . . . in the multi-cultural, multi-coloured, and multi-faith city of Birmingham and being drawn into some of the practical problems of religious pluralism' (p. xiv). Precisely. As a result of this experience he found it personally no longer possible to maintain a Christ-centred or 'one's own-religion-centred' theology. Instead, he made what he called his 'Copernican revolution' to a God-centred or, later, a 'reality-centred' theology. He tells us that 'for at least twenty-five years' he had believed that 'those who do not respond to God through Christ are not saved but, presumably, damned or lost' (p. 121).

> I believed by implication that the majority of human beings are eternally lost . . . this was the position in which I was for a number of years concerning the relation of Christianity to other religions . . . but as soon as one does meet and come to know people of other faiths a paradox of gigantic proportions becomes disturbingly obvious, (p. 122, cf. p. 100)

the paradox being that these people are far too good to be 'lost'. Hick,of course, went on to re-examine traditional Christian the-ology, criticize it, and develop his own 'human' or 'global' the-ology. But I do not think I am altogether mistaken in judging that for him the theological reanalysis was secondary and that it indeed looks rather weak in strictly theological terms. The 'Copernican Revolution', while claimed as a splendid clean fresh start, is too evidently committed to its conclusion in advance, yet too confused as to what those conclusions really are. The overwhelming impression I am left with is that for Hick the revolution was an experiential rather than a strictly theological one. He had pre-viously lived in a Christian world and taken for granted a fairly simple Protestant Christ-centred view of salvation, doubtless more devotional than theological in essence and hardly thought out at all. Entering into a professorial role in a genuinely pluralistic world, he felt quickly compelled to discard this over-simple and dubiously Christian evangelical view of salvation and damnation and create instead what he thought of as a new 'global' theology. As he himself stresses, theology derives from a particular cultural situation. So it is not unfair to point out how very closely his own does.

This was, similarly, the situation within which new university departments of Religious Studies suddenly flourished. The university department of Theology, supported in the past as an honoured part of a national university, itself maintained by public funds, was an appropriate – almost necessary – part of a religiously single world. It existed primarily to develop a coherent ongoing rationale for society's dominant faith or ideology – in the case of western Europe, some form of Christianity – and hence to service a major public profession, the Church's ministry. Theology was needed to relate Church to society, and it was needed by both sides. From the 1960s, however, such a department was increasingly anomalous. By 'theology' I mean what it has traditionally meant, a discipline which is not merely concerned comparatively or historically with sacred scriptures and religious doctrines, including an understanding of man, but which does so from a position of faith. I remain unable to see how without faith one can have theology – a history of theology, yes, but theology itself, no. A department of Christian theology implies in principle staff and students working together from and within a common faith, though doubtless a vigorous department could reasonably carry, and indeed benefit from, the questioning challenges of the odd deviant. It seems to me perfectly proper in principle to have such a department. In an Islamic country a national university can appropriately maintain a department of Islamic theology; in a Christian country a department of Christian theology. Indeed, the absence of such a department is socially dangerous, the existence of a vigorous academic theology being the best defence against the dominance of irrational and intolerant fundamentalisms.

In reality, however, the one nation/one religion model has long been an anachronism almost everywhere, and the pursuit of it as an ideal in the pluralist reality of society may be a highly dangerous one. In a pluralist society a department of pure theology can only exist appropriately at a more private level, yet withdrawal from the public arena of a genuine university is likely, all in all, to be disadvantageous for theology – though it may still be the right, even the only, option in some circumstances. There can be little doubt that from the 1960s the department of Christian theology became less and less appropriate as a university institution in Britain. Our society as such no longer retains that degree of coherent Christian faith to require and justify university departments of specifically Christian theology, at least on the scale that they had existed hitherto. Nevertheless, religion and churches (that is to say, communities of faith) remain an important reality of life, personally, nationally, internationally. It requires study, sympathetic yet scientific, critical yet constructive. Room is still needed for the construction of theologies – the rational critique of human life, material existence, political, religious and social structures on the basis of the faith of significant minority communities. Such a critique is needed by society as much as ever, but it can only be done on the basis of a faith of some sort. As there is no more a majority faith in society, it must be done on the basis of one or more minority faiths. Certainly Christianity in Britain today has the right (in terms of social significance) as well as the capacity to mount a critical theology. Such a theology has no right to a university monopoly, but it has a right to be present there – and as something more than the mere systematizing of an individual's belief. Indeed, society itself would be dangerously the loser if influential religions within it were denied the opportunity to theologize effectively at university level and thus encouraged to fall back upon fundamentalism and quietism. If the theology of Hick can be understood as a characteristic development of post-1960s Britain, albeit an over-hasty and only superficially attractive one, the appearance of a Department of Religious Studies such as I am describing here seems to me an absolutely true and necessary development from the same situation.

Departments of Theology, even where they retain the name, seem to be effectively transforming themselves into departments of Religious Studies. Most elements of a modern course of Theology are in point of fact tackled with absolutely no necessary sense of religious commitment. Indeed, the specifically theological element within a theology course in most English universities is now quite a small one – probably too small. This should not, however, mean that it is unimportant, nor that theology cannot exist, even flourish, within a department of Religious Studies, whether so-called or not. It can. But it does so on the basis of the work of individuals and groups, bringing their personal- or community-faith commitment creatively to enlighten one or another area of study. In much the same way it is not appropriate to have a department of Marxism, but many a Marxist works creatively within departments of history, sociology, philosophy, or, indeed, Religious Studies. We may note here that if Religious Studies is in its way very much wider than Theology, Theology also remains in its way very much wider than Religious Studies. Religious Studies is, inevitably, the study of religion – all religion, including the relationship between religion and anything else. But Theology is not, as such, necessarily about religion at all. It is about existence in its totality, seen in the light of a faith. In the same way an appropriate department of Religious Studies in Britain today will be in principle pluralist, open to and, hopefully, containing Christians, Muslims, Jews, Marxists, agnostics. They are united, not in faith – as they should be in a department of Theology – but in a serious concern with the phenomena and significance of religion in a wide sense and in recognized skill in studying and interpreting such phenomena from a variety of standpoints. What exactly do we mean by pluralism from the viewpoint of Religious Studies? First, a recognition that the diversity of religions is a substantial, not a marginal, element within our subject, and that for an understanding of religion, it is crucial to consider the evidence of different traditions (including, especially, those outside ones own). Second, by pluralism in our discipline, we must mean the principle that one religion is not to be systematically interpreted in terms of another, and that the department has no over-arching principle of interpretation other than that of liberal scholarship. This does not mean that the comparison of religions is excluded – nor even the criticism of one in terms of the theology of another religion or any other appropriate terms – only that the department is not committed as such to any single religious or critical viewpoint. I cannot see any other way our subject can or should survive within universities in a society such as ours, however much it may be the case that in any one department all or most of the staff are in point of fact representative of a relatively small spectrum of belief. It seems sensible that in different departments the spectrum should be different.

It was natural enough, in the late 1960s and 1970s, that, as the department of Theology turned effectively into a pluralist department of Religious Studies, and as its concerns with religious traditions other than the Christian grew considerably, there should have been a feeling, an expectation, that Theology itself had to respond pretty drastically. In some way, indeed, it had to. The absence of serious consideration in nearly all post-medieval theology – to go no further back – of other religions and their significance *viz-à-viz* God, man, and Christ is obvious enough. The question really was, in what way should it do so?

Hick presents his 'Copernican revolution' as the only appropriate intellectual development for a Christian theologian in the pluralist city. Is it? It would be dangerous to imagine that just because a particular intellectual development appears on the surface appropriate to a particular context, it is therefore the correct development, or that there may not be other perhaps less obvious but better grounded approaches. That Hick's was truly in its way extremely appropriate in terms of cultural and social context, I have already tried to show. Was it, however, theologically appropriate? It is, quite obviously, necessary for Christian thinking to change in response to cultural change. Yet it is equally true that Christian thinking can be inappropriately hijacked by the spirit of the age into sudden developments alien to its own proper self. A Copernican revolution in theology can certainly not be finally justified in terms other than theological. This, of course, Hick fully recognizes and his arguments relate to the confused state – as he sees it – of the earlier theology of the relationship of Christianity to other religions (the number of 'epicycles' it had, he argues, been forced to develop) in order to justify change.

The companion volume to *God and the Universe of Faiths* should undoubtedly be seen as the symposium *The Myth of God Incarnate*, edited by John Hick in 1977 after three years of preparation.[7] The aim of the book was to argue that the Incarnation, usually regarded as the centre-piece of specifically Christian belief and theology, the key component of Christianity's distinctiveness, was no more than a myth or a shibboleth and one which today, 'the new age of world ecumenism' (p. 168, Hick's phrase), could very well be dispensed with. This, the Preface indicated, would have 'increasingly important practical implications for our relationship to the peoples of the other great religions' (p. ix). No longer, Professor Wiles observed in the opening chapter, would Christians be able to believe in 'the superiority of one religion over another in advance of an informed knowledge of both faiths. Such a change can only be regarded as a gain' (p. 9). Jesus would no longer be claimed as in some way 'the way for all peoples and all cultures', but as one of a number of powerful spiritual figures in human history who have taught the world about God. 'We should never forget', Hick confidently declared, 'that if the Christian gospel had moved east into India instead of west into the Roman empire, Jesus' religious significance would probably have been expressed by hailing him within Hindu culture as a divine Avatar and within the Mahayana Buddhism which was then developing in India as a Bodhisattva' (p. 176). One wonders how he knows.

'A divine Avatar' or 'a Bodhisattva'. One among many: a guru within a pluralistic world. That was the intended message of the book and one suggested succinctly in the Epilogue by Dennis Nineham. Professor Nineham summed up the matter, clear-sightedly enough, not in terms of the Incarnation but of the uniqueness of Christ. The latter too, under any form of words, would have to go. Now it is obvious enough that an explicit Incarnation-type theology is only one of the ways in which the New Testament writers endeavour to expound the mystery of Christ, and various writers in *The Myth* correctly stressed this pluralism in New Testament theology as, of course, within subsequent Christian theology. Does the vocabulary of the Incarnation doctrine, either in its Johannine or its Chalcedonian form, speak to us today? Does it contain Christology *tout court*? Or is it just one way to talk about Christ among other ways? May we not use other ways? Of course, we may. But beneath such questions there is slipped in an essentially different one: do we need assert in any verbal form at all that Jesus is 'necessarily in principle unique' (p. 202)? The Hickian function of the book is to deny it (though not all its contributors might have gone along with that denial). Now the book's appeal is intrinsically to Christian theological scholarship – an examination, principally, of the coherence of the Christian tradition's internal thinking in regard to Christ. Yet what it actually had to admit – as sound New Testament scholarship must admit – is that while the terms and images chosen for the formulation of Christ's religious uniqueness vary, the affirmation of that uniqueness can be found with basically equal weight in every New Testament writing as in all subsequent Christian credal affirmation. That embarrassing claim to religious uniqueness on behalf of one man, Jesus of Nazareth, and to a consequent ultimate universality of significance, has remained the central characteristic of the Christian tradition, formulate it as you will. Deny the uniqueness and defend Christianity as the appropriate folk-religion for the European west, and you are, I would hold, denying Christianity intrinsically, however many bits and pieces of Christian wreckage you may still find serviceable. Maintain that uniqueness and universality, in whatever linguistic form, and you maintain the continuity and vitality of the Christian claim, however many bits and pieces you may discard as unserviceable.

That seems to me the heart of the matter. Christian theology can only function as such in accordance with Christianity's own central internal logic as a way of faith and of life. That logic is

certainly not provable: the sound scholar can tackle the evidence
with much good will and not find it adequately convincing, because
the claims of that logic seem so improbable. But that is not
theology, which remains and has to remain a discipline issuing
out of a faith. It is philosophy, one form of common sense,
religious studies, what have you. A theology operates according
to its own awkward logic, a logic which functions rationally in
judging probabilities, seeking coherence in systems, examining
seemingly contrary statements, but all within the context of some
great basic presupposition. All Christian theology, from the earliest Christian communities before the writing of the New
Testament – in so far as we can know them – has operated on the
basis of this great supposition, the qualitative uniqueness of
Christ. No evidence of a pluralism, internal and subordinate to
that unanimity, can possibly justify, in theological terms, an abandonment of that presupposition in favour of a quite different
religious or secular world-view. The attempt of Hick and of The
Myth of God Incarnate to justify a rejection of that presupposition
in favour of an ultimate religious pluralism within human history
should be in principle a theological non-starter. It must also,
existentially, be destructive of Christianity as a coherent religious
reality. It is a strange stipulation that, in order to enter the age
of pluralism appropriately, you must first cease in principle to be
what you have been for two thousand years. It is not one which
makes theological sense (or sociological sense, in relation to
Christianity's ongoing community identity) and, equally, it should
not be one required by the integrity of Religious Studies or a
genuinely ecumenical approach to the situation of pluralism. That
integrity requires, I would suggest, on the contrary, acceptance
of the logically non-compatible claims of different religions, rather
than the attempt to relate them all systemically within an imagined
'world theology', which would be recognized by the believers of
no tradition. I am arguing, then, for an explicit dualism: recognition of the quite different requirements of 'Religious Studies'
and 'Theology'. For the former the remark of Maurice Wiles is
eminently correct: here we must, of course, not assert 'the superiority of one religion over another'. A department of Religious
Studies could function on no other basis. But such a department
operates in terms of a pragmatic secular liberal commitment to
mutual respect in the pursuit of learning, not in terms of an
implicit or explicit theology of its own. This may seem to privatize
theology, but there can be no alternative other than the setting
up of a bogus 'global theology' as a sort of civil religion for the

department: bogus because it relates to no recognizable community of faith.

Essentially different are issues such as an adequate theological evaluation in Christian terms of the relationship of other religions, ideologies, and moral commitments to the uniqueness of Christ, or again the limits of credal and denominational pluralism within the large historic tradition of Christian belief. The trouble with the Hickian and *Myth of God Incarnate* approach was that it mixed them all up. Such questions cannot, of course, be other than immensely important and their conclusions may well be significantly corrective for the thought and practice of the Christian community. Thus it should in fact be painfully evident that the very simple model of salvation through explicit faith in Christ alone, taken for granted by the younger Hick, was really not the central traditional Christian one at all – though doubtless it had been taken for granted over many generations by countless Christians, Protestant and Catholic. It is too evidently false to the full data of the tradition – including especially the explicit and breath-taking insight of Romans 5 that the grace of Christ has abounded more widely than the sin of Adam. Basic to the tradition was a tension between the every-frontier-breaking-down universality of salvation and the particularity of its symbolic personal initiator and centre-piece. The abandonment of neither is acceptable. Again, basic to the tradition, was the relationship between old covenant and new, whereby the adherents of both were included within a single history of salvation 'ab Abel', whether or not they knew anything of Jesus of Nazareth. Any appropriate advance in the Christian theology of salvation or of the relationship of religions might best start at this point. The fact of that 'both' should, from the start, have ruled out a narrow 'Christians only are saved' doctrine. It should not be too hard to evolve a theology of other religions and other scriptures too drawn from the paradigm of Israel, much as most theologians have failed to do so. Earlier covenants are at least an under-analysed and under-used category in theological thought. But such a development would remain an evolution, not a Copernican revolution and not an epicycle either. This would not be a pluralist theology but it would be a Christian theology open to the full pluralism of human experience and able to build upon a wide rather than a narrow model of divine revelation and the way of salvation.

Different again, of course, is the question as to whether, philosophically, belief in Christ remains a very plausible belief; or whether Christianity is not now a dissolving reality without a future, because without a sufficiently coherent set of beliefs which a thoughtful twentieth-century person is able to identify. That, perhaps, was the true unwritten agenda for several of the *Myth of God* writers. A theologian can well come, theologically, to such a conclusion: he may come to decide that it is impossible to construct any more a credible and coherent system upon the basic Christian presupposition, and thus come finally to cease to be a Christian theologian, because no longer a Christian. If Christian theology is based upon a false premiss it should in due course wither, like many other dead ideologies and religious systems of the past. A theology, while grounded in faith, has still of its nature to establish an adequate and intellectually coherent and convincing system linking together a range of ideas relating to the basic aspects of contemporary human existence in the light of a central faith principle. This Christian theology has always tried to do and often effectively. If it can do so no more, it must crumble. But that is not a matter of pluralism, just one of the intellectual and spiritual senescence of a religious tradition.

It is manifest that an environment of radical pluralism must put an immensely greater strain upon the theologian, just as it does upon the ordinary believer, than an environment of shared belief. In the latter a scholar can easily tend to harmonize his conclusions with public faith without quite realizing he is doing so, in a way that simply ceases to happen when there is no longer a public faith of that sort. Such is the condition of modern Britain, and such is, accordingly, the condition of a modern department and the discipline of Religious Studies, within which the academic theologian has now very largely to work. It can certainly be a strain to be loyal to the exigencies at once of Religious Studies and of a theology. Each, of course, has a variety of possible approaches to pluralism. A department of Religious Studies will then have to carry along with it an internal pluralism, including a plurality of attitudes towards pluralism itself. Indeed, the tension of that plurality may be experienced within a single person. But such strains can be carried; indeed, they have to be. In fact, there is really no field of modern life and study in which a genuine loyalty at once to liberal and pluralist structures and to one's particular convictions, not shared with all one's colleagues, may not tax one's resources. It is really an unavoidable predicament. People who reject Christianity should not imagine that if they have principles and integrity they can escape it, though clearly some world-views may seem more awkward in their scholarly consequences than others.

Today's is certainly a much harsher environment in which to assert the Christian claim to an absolute religious particularity than was the privileged bondage of the European past. Maybe it will prove too harsh, and the battle will, quite quickly, be abandoned. But it should not, I think, be abandoned at the first moment that the new terms of service are read out, as the theologians recognize around them a pluralist world instead of Christendom. They should have been more on their guard, ready for the moment when the Christian claim would cease to be bolstered up by the claims of medieval or Victorian Christendom. After all, these did not start together. Christianity's non-pluralist commitment to the absolute particularity of Christ in relation to the ultimate meaning and purpose of mankind, God's will for the world, originated within a religiously pluralist world, and among its poor, and triumphed in that world. Faced with a multitude of cults, it was unyielding in relationship to them. The absolutist claims of Christianity were, one might suggest, masked rather than manifested in their true import by their subsequent connection with absolutist claims of western culture and political power. Now that the latter have so largely collapsed, as has the connection between the two (though not, of course, in much current American ideological warfare which unites a highly fundamentalistic Protestant Christianity extremely closely with American world-power and 'civilization', very much on a British Victorian model), it may well be an appropriate time precisely to speak forth the true scandal of Christian particularity in such a way that it can at least be heard for what it always claimed to be – the scandal of God's foolishness, not of British cleverness; of the weakness of the Cross, not of the power of the maxim-gun.

If the clever and the powerful of today's world have not time for such a message, seeking instead a more socially mellifluous new civic religion (inclusive or exclusive of God, 'reality-centredness', the tomb of the Unknown Soldier, Lenin's birthday, or whatever), it may be that the poor of the Third and Fourth World will think differently. Maybe they will be right to do so, finding in it indeed 'the way, the truth, and the life', or maybe they will simply be missing out on the most reliable intellectual advances of the twentieth century, in pursuance once more of an opium appropriate to their state of misery. In philosophical, historical, religious-studies terms, we cannot quite say which is the case. And a pluralistic department of Religious Studies must be open to all the possibilities. But a theologian, operating loyally within such a department and the pluralistic world it reflects, will still – if he is able to stick to his last, at once believer and scientist – maintain that the Christian faith has always had at its heart a paradoxical assertion of the improbable, never contemptuous of reason, scholarship, or other revelation, yet able again and again to outflank the broader ways of human wisdom and religion with the narrow particularity of a cross, a tomb, a tortured body, a resurrected hope – unique, yet everyman's experience. Such an assertion is in some way fulfilment of every aspiration of the most pluralistic of worlds, yet it remains no less committed to a singularly single salvific symbol, one no less improbable in the first century than in the twentieth, but which for both may still – just conceivably – contain the power and the wisdom of God.

Notes

1 John Hick, *God and the Universe of Faith*, London: Macmillan (1973); see also his later *God has Many Names* London: Macmillan (1980), *The Problems of Religious Pluralism*, London: Macmillan (1985), and 'Religious pluralism', 145–64 of F. Whaling (ed.), *The World's Religious Traditions*, Edinburgh: T. & T. Clark (1984)
2 Wilfred Cantwell Smith, *The Meaning and End of Religion*, London: Macmillan (1963), repr. London: SPCK 1978; *Towards a World Theology*, London: Macmillan (1981).
3 *Memoirs of Archbishop Temple*, ed., E. G. Sandford, London: Macmillan (1906), 54.
4 T. Tatlow, *The Story of the Student Christian Movement*, London: SCM (1933); H. Hans Hoekendijk, 'Evangelization of the world in this generation', *International Review of Mission* (January 1970), 23–31.
5 For an assessment of this see Part VI of Adrian Hastings, *A History of English Christianity 1920–1985*, London: Collins (1986).
6 *God and the Universe of Faiths*, 105 and 106.
7 John Hick (ed.), *The Myth of God Incarnate*, London: SCM Press (1977).

Religious pluralism and toleration

Reflections of an indologist

Richard Gombrich

Religious pluralism in Britain today means that we have to live with bodies of people who have decided opinions about what they claim are the most important issues in life, opinions which are incompatible and therefore cannot all be right – though of course it is still logically possible that they are all wrong. In this situation, how are we to conduct ourselves, and how, if at all, should we demand that other people conduct themselves?

At an academic level these are questions of moral and political philosophy, subjects in which I am unqualified. But philosophy can benefit from some factual input. India is a kind of laboratory of religious pluralism, and has been one throughout its recorded history. So the first half of this chapter will offer some observations about religion in general arising from my study of Hinduism and Buddhism, religions of Indian origin.

I begin with a long quotation which primarily concerns Buddhism in Sri Lanka, from a book simply entitled *Ceylon*, by Sir James Emerson Tennent, published in 1859, and I warn the reader in advance that I do not subscribe to the views it contains.

> Buddhism . . . is, properly speaking, less a form of religion than a school of philosophy; and its worship, according to the institutes of its founders, consists of an appeal to the reason, rather than an attempt on the imagination through the instrumentality of rites and parade . . . On comparing this system with other prevailing religions which divide with it the worship of the East, Buddhism at once vindicates its own superiority, not only by the purity of its code of morals, but by its freedom from the fanatical intolerance of the Mahometans and its abhorrent rejection of the revolting rites of the Brahmanical faith. But mild and benevolent as are its aspects and design, its theories have failed to realise in practice the reign of virtue which they proclaim. Beautiful as is the body of its doctrines, it wants

the vivifying energy and soul which are essential to ensure its ascendancy and power. Its cold philosophy and thin abstractions, however calculated to exercise the faculties of anchorets and ascetics, have proved insufficient of themselves to arrest man in his career of passion and pursuit; and the bold experiment of influencing the heart and regulating the conduct of mankind by the external decencies and the mutual dependencies of morality unsustained by higher hopes and a faith that penetrates eternity, has proved in this instance an unredeemed and hopeless failure . . .

No national system of religion, no pr´vailing superstition that has ever fallen under my observation presents so dull a level, and is so pre-eminently deficient in popular influences, as Buddhism amongst the Singhalese. It has its multitude of followers, but it is a misnomer to describe them as its *votaries*, for the term implies a warmth and fervour unknown to a native of Ceylon. He believes, or he thinks he believes, because he is of the same faith with his ancestors; but he looks on the religious doctrines of the various sects which surround him with a stolid indifference which is the surest indication of the little importance which he attaches to his own. The fervid earnestness of Christianity, even in its most degenerate forms, the fanatical enthusiasm of Islam, the proud exclusiveness of Brahma, and even the zealous warmth of other Northern faiths, are all emotions utterly foreign and unknown to the followers of Buddhism in Ceylon.

Yet, strange to tell, under all the icy coldness of this barren system, there burn below the unextinguished fires of another and a darker superstition, whose flames overtop the icy summits of the Buddhist philosophy, and excite a deeper and more reverential awe in the imagination of the Singhalese . . . DEMON WORSHIP prevailed amongst the Singhalese before the introduction of Buddhism . . . The ascendancy of these superstitions, and the anomaly of their association with the religion of Buddha, which has taken for its deity the perfection of wisdom and benevolence, present one of the most signal difficulties with which Christianity has had, at all times, to contend in the effort to extend its influences throughout Ceylon. The Portuguese priesthood discovered that, however the Singhalese might be induced to profess the worship of Christ, they adhered with timid tenacity to their ancient demonology . . .

As regards Buddhism itself, whilst there is that in the tenets and genius of Brahmanism which proclaims an active resistance to any other form of religion, Christianity in the southern expanse of Ceylon has to encounter an obstacle still more embarrassing in the habitual apathy and listless indifference of the Buddhists. Brahmanism in its constitution and spirit is essentially exclusive and fanatical, jealous of all conflicting faiths, and strongly disposed to persecution. Buddhism, on the other hand, in the strength of its self-righteousness, extends a latitudinarian liberality to every other belief, and exhibits a Laodicean indifference towards its own . . .

In the character of the Singhalese people there is to be traced much of the genius of their religion. The same passiveness and love of ease which restrain from active exertion in the labours of life, find a counterpart in the adjustment by which virtue is limited to abstinence, and worship to contemplation; with only so much of actual ceremonial as may render visible to the eye what would be otherwise inaccessible to the mind. The same love of repose which renders sleep and insensibility the richest blessings of this life, anticipates torpor, akin to extinction, as the supremest felicity of the next. In common with all other nations they deem some form of religious worship indispensable, but, contrary to the usage of most, they are singularly indifferent as to what that particular form is to be; leaving it passively to be determined by the conjunction of circumstances, the accident of locality, and the influence of friends or worldly prospects of gain. Still, in the hands of the Christian missionary, they are by no means the plastic substance which such a description would suggest – capable of being moulded into any form, or retaining permanently any casual impression – but rather a yielding fluid which adapts its shape to that of the vessel into which it may happen to be poured, without any change in its quality or any modification of its character . . .

If Christianity requires purity and truth, temperance, honesty and benevolence, these are already discovered to be enjoined with at least equal impressiveness in the precepts of Buddha. The Scripture commandment forbidding murder is supposed to be analogous to the Buddhist prohibition to kill; and where the law and the Gospel alike enforce the love of one's neighbour as the love of one's self, Buddhism insists upon charity as the basis of worship, and calls on its own followers 'to appease anger by gentleness, and overcome evil by good'.

Thus the outward concurrence of Christianity in those points on which it agrees with their own religion, has proved more embarrassing to the natives than their perplexity as to others in which it essentially differs; till at last, too timid to doubt and too feeble to inquire, they cling with helpless tenacity to their own superstition, and yet subscribe to the new faith simply by adding it on to the old.

Combined with this state of irresolution a serious obstacle to the acceptance of reformed Christianity by the Singhalese Buddhists has arisen from the differences and disagreements between the various churches by whose ministers it has been successively offered to them. In the persecution of the Roman Catholics by the Dutch, the subsequent supercession of the Church of Holland by that of England, the rivalries more or less apparent between the Episcopalians and Presbyterians, and the peculiarities which separate the Baptists from the Wesleyan Methodists – all of whom have their missions and representatives in Ceylon – the Singhalese can discover little more than that they are offered something still doubtful and unsettled, in exchange for which they are pressed to surrender their own ancient superstition. Conscious of their inability to decide on what has baffled the wisest of their European teachers to reconcile, they hesitate to exchange for an apparent uncertainty that which has been unhesitatingly believed by generations of their ancestors, and which comes recommended to them by all the authority of antiquity; and even when truth has been so far successful as to shake their confidence in their national faith, the choice of sects which has been offered to them leads to utter bewilderment as to the peculiar form of Christianity with which they may most confidingly replace it.[1]

Three things immediately strike us about this piece of writing. The first, I cannot help remarking, is that the Victorians certainly knew how to write English.

The second point we note is that religious pluralism is not at all new to British society; it is not a phenomenon of modern immigration, but has been with us since the Reformation, if not even longer (I am thinking of such proto-Protestant movements as the Lollards). People felt much more strongly about this older form of religious pluralism, the plurality of Christian denominations, than, by and large, they feel about religious pluralism today. And indeed the only religious conflict in Britain today which takes a violent form is that between Roman Catholics and Protestant nonconformists in Northern Ireland. We must remember that for a long time both Roman Catholics and Protestant nonconformists did not even enjoy equality before the law with Anglicans in this country, a disability which it would nowadays be unthinkable to impose on adherents of any religion, Christian or non-Christian. Tennent is certainly right to worry about this form of religious pluralism, for even today in most university departments of theology and religious studies a student is more likely to be taught something about Buddhism or Islam than about forms of Christianity which stand outside the Anglican tradition. What, to take but one example, do our teachers of Christianity know or say about the doctrines and activities of the Southern Baptist Convention of the United States, a denomination with nearly 14.5 million members, most of them active, whose convictions about the inevitability and even desirability of a nuclear holocaust threaten to make our deliberations reach a rather premature conclusion?

But above all, of course, we notice Tennent's arrogance. So the third thing to say about Tennent at this point is simply to note what a long way we have come in the relatively short time – about 130 years – since he wrote. British Roman Catholics had recently acquired the same civil rights as Protestants, a tolerance he reflects. He was an educated gentleman with wide experience of the world. However, the unquestioning assumption of his own cultural superiority and his contempt for other peoples and cultures now seem so remote from us, his cultural heirs, that they hardly even provoke an educated audience to indignation; they seem rather fit for mirth. But his attitude is typical – though already slightly better informed – of most of the past two thousand years of western history. We do then have some cause for self-congratulation: if we have lost the ability to write memorable prose, we have at least made rapid gains in tolerance and open-mindedness.

In the century before Tennent wrote, a few intellectuals of the Enlightenment, some of them weak in Christian faith, were sowing the seeds of an open-minded interest in other cultures which bore fruit in the scholarly study of the orient. In the field of Buddhist studies, this first reached maturity late in the nineteenth century. Let me quote from a book published less than a generation after Tennent's *Ceylon – Buddhism* by T. W. Rhys Davids. Rhys Davids later, in 1905, became the first Professor of Comparative Religion in the English-speaking world. (So new is the academic field of Religious Studies.) His *Buddhism* was the first English book on the subject which deserves to be called scholarly, and in fact it is still worth reading today. It was published in 1877 and went through many editions; it is noteworthy that the publishers were the Society for the Promotion of Christian Knowledge. How asymmetrical the study of religious pluralism turns out to be! History has determined that the debate is cast mainly in Christian terms. Aware of this, we also, Christians and non-Christians alike, tend to make Christianity the scapegoat. And yet – where in the world has a society for the promotion of Buddhist knowledge, or Hindu knowledge, or Muslim knowledge, been producing valuable scholarly expositions of Christianity?

Rhys Davids begins his book with these words:

> Several writers have commenced their remarks on Buddhism by reminding their readers of the enormous number of its adherents; and it is, indeed, a most striking fact, that the living Buddhists far outnumber the followers of the Roman Church, the Greek Church, and all other Christian Churches put together. From such summary statements, however, great misconceptions may possibly arise, quite apart from the fact that numbers are no test of truth, but rather the contrary.[2]

I shall return to that final remark, an echo of the Enlightenment reminiscent of Gibbon. Rhys Davids goes on to give figures showing that Buddhists account for 500 million, or about 40 per cent of the world's population, which in those happy days numbered only about one and a quarter billion. In presenting the figures, however, he reminds the reader that the Chinese simultaneously have three religions – Buddhism, Taoism, and Confucianism – and that it would

> be as impossible to express numerically the influence of Buddhism in India, as it would be to subtract from the Chinese numbers so as to show how much of the average Chinaman was Buddhist, and how much Taossean or Konfucian.[3]

Having alerted us to the problem, he goes on to say that the statistics

> are vitiated by the attempt to class each man's religion under one word. In point of fact, each item lies open to an objection similar to that made above against the Chinese figures: many of the Ceylonese so-called Buddhists, for instance, take their oaths in court as Christians, and most of them believe also in devil-worship, and in the power of the stars. Their whole belief is not Buddhist; many of their ideas run altogether outside of Buddhism; their minds do not run only on Buddhist lines.[4]

I have noted above that the debate on religious pluralism is cast mainly in Christian terms. Rhys Davids shows the first awareness of this. He is informing his readers, quite correctly, that Buddhism is not a religion on a par with Christianity, in that Buddhists may believe in other, non-Buddhist doctrines at the same time. Of course, in saying that the minds of Buddhists 'do not run only on Buddhist lines' Rhys Davids is confusing the ideal with the actual – as people so commonly do – and setting an impossible standard: one could say with equal justice that the minds of Christians do not run only on Christian lines. Nevertheless, Rhys Davids has an important point here, and so makes a great advance in understanding over Tennent. In almost all Buddhist traditions, Buddhism does coexist with systems of belief which the Buddhists themselves consider non-Buddhist. At the risk of some over-simplification, it can be said that Buddhists think of Buddhism as concerned with salvation and things of ultimate importance, and not with worldly welfare. While Christians, for example, have generally prayed for worldly as well as for spiritual blessings, considering that all come ultimately from God, Buddhists have a completely different view. Salvation can only come from within ourselves, as we follow the advice and example of the Buddha; but such things as health and prosperity, though they too are ultimately determined by our moral conduct, flow more immediately from what they consider natural causes. Of course, their ideas of what constitutes such a natural cause are very different from ours. One may petition a non-human being, a deity, to provide worldly goods, or ever coerce a demon; but such gods and demons are just a part of the cosmic power-structure. To petition a god is just to recognize where power lies and, for them, is no more 'Buddhist' than complying with a bureaucratic regulation or bribing a politician is part of a Christian's Christianity. At the least, then, a Buddhist tends to have one religion, Buddhism, for coping with spiritual problems and another for coping with this world; but for worldly purposes he may resort to several systems, just as we may go to our local GP, to a practitioner of 'alternative medicine', and to a faith-healer.

But Rhys Davids only began to tackle the problem of understanding how it is that a single group of people, and even a single individual, may well appear to us to have several religions at once. His Protestant origins (he was the son of a nonconformist minister) made him take too much for granted – and so far we have gone along with him. The mistake, as we now see it, was to equate a religion with a belief or set of beliefs.

This point, while obvious to anthropologists, is very far from obvious to most people in Britain. One of the most fundamental advances one could make in religious education – and it has barely begun – would be to explain to teachers of religious studies in schools that matters are not so simple. The subject of comparative religion, which has been the response of educational institutions to religious pluralism, has been founded on the idea that there is a certain, finite number of religions, each of which can be

249

characterized by holding certain beliefs. Certainly it is allowed that other religions too, like Christianity, may vary internally; a religion, it is thought, splits into 'denominations' or 'sects' which have slightly different beliefs from each other and/or from a parent body. But few people question this model of what a religion is, or realize that it is based on the Christian case. Belief is assumed to be the principle of organization, both for the whole and the parts. Belief so organizes the whole, it is thought, that a religion with a name, such as Hinduism or Buddhism, must correspond on the ground to a body of people who share certain fundamental beliefs. Belief so organizes the parts that named groups within the religion similarly share a creed, a variant of the creed of the larger unit, the whole religion.

To see the world like this is not merely to see it through Christian eyes: it is in origin distinctively Protestant. True, every Christian denomination has a Creed, a statement of the basic beliefs to which the member must formally subscribe. But in the Christian tradition, the Roman Catholic church has tended to lay as much stress on doing, on ritual and ethical action, as on believing. That, after all, was the central issue of the Protestant Reformation: the Protestants exalted faith above works. As Keith Thomas has put it, before the Reformation 'religion was a ritual method of living, not a set of dogmas'.[5] 'Medieval religion had laid its emphasis upon the regular performance of ritual duties, rather than on the memorising of the theological beliefs.'[6] The Protestant holds – indeed, assumes – that a religion is a faith, adherence to a belief which can be summed up in a few simple statements. Equating a religion with a faith has important corollaries: it means that ultimately religion is a matter for the individual and his or her conscience, and that all adherents, since they must believe the same, are equal in religious status when it comes to their chance of salvation.

This equation of religion with faith has had momentous consequences for the non-Christian religions. When Col. Olcott, the American Theosophist, arrived in Sri Lanka in 1880 as a kind of anti-missionary missionary, he was continually exasperated by the Buddhists' failure to get organized – scarcely less exasperated than Tennent had been by their failure to be good Buddhists. Tennent had complained of the Buddhists' 'stolid indifference' to religious doctrines. Now in the Buddhist case it is true that Buddhists hold certain fundamental beliefs, though like most people everywhere they have, as Tennant observes, inherited those beliefs and tend rather to take them for granted than to articulate them, let alone argue for them. But Buddhists, before Olcott reached them, were not Protestants; they considered that to study, pass on, and internalize the doctrines were the functions of religious professionals, the monks. Since the religious doctrines were thus the cultural heritage of a trained and specialized body of men, they were preserved in a certain sophisticated complexity, necessarily beyond the grasp of most uneducated people. This offended Olcott's sense of what a decent religion ought to be. He set about formulating and publishing a 'Buddhist Creed'. This 'Buddhist Creed' has been many times reprinted. It is Olcott's attempt to formulate what he considered every Buddhist believed or should believe. When the World Fellowship of Buddhists was formed, the only document which lay to hand which might explain what united them was Olcott's creed.

I am not sure that Olcott's misunderstanding has done much harm to Buddhism. As I said, Buddhists do in fact share certain beliefs, or at least define their allegiance at least partly in credal terms. The Protestant view of what a religion is has had vast effects on Buddhism; but these are by no means so startling as the parallel effects on Hinduism. When the Muslims invaded India, 'Hindu' was a term which covered all non-Muslims – but that negative fact was its only unity. The view that religions are so many doctrines, or 'isms', has gradually worked on bodies of men who follow different teachers and different customs so that some of them have tried to define themselves as having separate 'religions', and finally the rump is creating a 'Hinduism' which is currently building in Allahabad the first temple in history which will be simply 'Hindu' rather than Vaiṣṇava, Saiva, Sakta, or whatever.

The fate of Hinduism is however a complex topic which would divert me from my main theme. Let me return to Olcott, the American Protestant: in formulating a creed to unite Buddhism, he was only replicating on a smaller scale what Theosophy aimed to do for the whole world. Theosophy was a response to the new western concern with religious pluralism which began a generation before the founding of chairs of comparative religion. Like that academic subject, Theosophy saw religion in credal terms, and indeed it had not entirely dissimilar aspirations. Though the original inspiration of the movement, Mme Blavatsky, was a fraud, Theosophy tried to make sense of religious diversity by finding some underlying unity, a unity which settled the doubts of those who took the religious variety seriously and then concluded, 'But surely they cannot all be right?'

The Theosophist solution to the problem of religious diversity was essentially to deny it – and to deny it in a very Protestant way. Fundamentally, they said, all religions were in fact the same. If they looked different, that was because the purity of their original identity had been obscured by the corruptions introduced by interested parties – mostly priests. That it was priests who had corrupted the pristine message of Jesus was, of course, a traditional Protestant line. In their claim for the essential unity of all religions the Theosophists could take inspiration from the famous Sanskrit scripture, the *Bhagavadgita*, in which the god Vishnu, in his form as Krishna, says that he exists eternally but takes birth in the world in various forms in various ages. This ancient attempt by Vaishnava monotheists in ancient India to overcode and so claim hegemony over various religious sects was replicated by the Theosophists on a world-wide scale.

The Theosophists have dwindled into insignificance, but much of their influence survives. It is especially common in India, where the Theosophists made their headquarters and had great influence on the Hindu middle classes. But the view that 'All religions are the same really' is a very widespread response to religious pluralism, the well-intentioned easy-going attempt to get out of the difficulty by denying that it exists. And I herewith begin the second half of my contribution by repudiating this attitude. For it is, quite evidently not the case that all religions preach the same thing or that all religious people have a great deal in common, whether you define religion as belief, as practice, as emotions and experiences, or a varying mix of all those three dimensions.

Moreover, I agree with Rhys Davids that, 'Numbers are no test of truth.' Even if it could be shown that most people in the world do hold some religious belief in common, that in itself would not prove that the belief was true. And even if it could be shown that they all shared a certain value, a view of what ought to be done, that would be a very interesting fact to take into account, but would not show that that value was compelling or that it would be right for us to act in the same way.

Religious pluralism and its discontents have by now reached almost every part of the globe. Some have reacted by maintaining the usual traditional position: 'I and my group are right and the rest of you are wrong.' A few people, mostly intellectuals, have tried to maintain that everyone is right (which can also mean that no one is right). Over a large part of the globe, however, most people have tended to adopt an intermediate position. Let me consider these three reactions to pluralism.

The first reaction is represented in the long quotation from Sir James Emerson Tennent. It deserves serious treatment. The religions associated with the world's great civilizations are all soteriologies, systems for attaining salvation. Each tells its adherents what they must do to be saved. And as a corollary they explain the dire consequences of failing. Most of them in fact teach that failure to make a good showing in this life will lead to spending a very long time – perhaps an eternity – in a hell, a place of torture which will make this world's sufferings seem trivial by comparison. Now it might very well seem that anyone who takes one of these religions at all seriously – as many people claim to do – is simply bound to accept their rules and discipline, on even the most primitive hedonistic calculus. But it goes further than that. The primary thing we must do, the great monotheistic religions assert, is believe. Non-believers do not stand a chance. Hence the missionary imperative. It can be no more moral not to do your best to convert non-believers to your religion, and thus save them from damnation, than it would be to see a small child about to wander into the road in front of an oncoming bus and raise no finger to stop it. What could be of comparable urgency?

Many good people who do not share such beliefs habitually behave like ostriches before them: they try to pretend that they do not exist or will go away if ignored. The ostrich may have no other recourse; but we academics must do better. The missionary impulse seems to me to be as noble, and to present those who do not share it with a problem for which I shall suggest a palliative but to which there is really no solution satisfactory to all parties.

Clifford Geertz has characterized the religious way of looking at the world as 'the conviction that the values one holds are grounded in the inherent structure of reality, that between the way one ought to live and the way things really are there is an unbreakable inner connection'. For such people, their 'image of the world's construction' and their 'program for human conduct' are 'mere reflexes of one another'.

> The world view is believable because the ethos, which grows out of it, is felt to be authoritative; the ethos is justifiable because the world view, upon which it rests, is held to be true. Seen from outside the religious perspective, this sort of hanging a picture from a nail driven into its frame appears as a kind of sleight of hand. Seen from inside, it appears as a simple fact.[7]

A few examples will make this clearer. A traditional Hindu will believe that it is the nature of men born into the warrior caste to make war; therefore it is clearly their duty to make war when opportunity arises. Similarly, the Hindu, like many other people, considers it the duty of women to stay home and serve their husbands – because it is their nature to do so. The programme for women is derived from the image of women, and the image from the programme. Another example: a Marxist may hold that it is the inevitable propensity of the capitalist to exploit the worker and therefore not merely pointless to tell him to stop doing so, but even worse, because for the capitalist to change his nature would upset the predetermined march of history. Or a Calvinist may hold that since God has made him God-fearing and thrifty, that is what he has to be.

Underlying all these examples is some concept like the traditional view of 'nature', a view we have all but lost. But there is still a trace of it: when we say that baby-bashing is not natural, we mean that it goes against our understanding of the nature of parents: parents should not beat their defenceless children because that is just not what parents do. The image and the programme are reflexes of one another.

What is the relevance of all this? If one believes that God has so made the world that those who fail to believe in Him are denied the chance of Heaven, surely a moral imperative does flow from that. In burning heretics to save their souls, the Inquisition was in principle behaving quite logically, as well as quite morally.

Modern Christian theology has virtually abolished hell, reinterpreting it rather as the absence of heaven; but if heaven is to be taken seriously, given the length of the soul's prospective sojourn there, this would not seem to make an essential difference: the lack of it must still be an ill to outweigh mere earthly considerations. Religious pluralism, moreover, has created a whole modern theology of how the good Christian is to view other religions, some of which I do not understand. Some theologians have suggested that rather than the sole repository of the truth, the church should be viewed as a body of pilgrims set on earth to do their best under trying circumstances. But not only do these subtleties presumably reach few believers and convince even fewer. The real problem is that such playing with metaphors is mere prevarication: either you believe in God's commandment to Moses to have no other gods before Him, or you do not, and either you believe in the Christian afterlife or you do not. I have more respect for the intellectual and moral consistency of the inquisition and the missionary.

Whatever liberal theologians may say, there are always plenty of Protestants around to remind us of the famous passage in Matthew 10: 34–9:

34 Think not that I am come to send peace on earth: I came not to send peace, but a sword.
35 For I am come to set a man at variance against his father, and the daughter against her mother, and the daughter in law against her mother in law.

36   And a man's foes *shall* be they of his own household.
37   He that loveth father or mother more than me is not worthy
of me: and he that loveth son or daughter more than me is not
worthy of me.
38   And he that taketh not his cross, and followeth after me,
is not worthy of me.
39   He that findeth his life shall lose it: and he that loseth his
life for my sake shall find it.

This gives clear and specific guidance to the Christian who wants
to know how to put into practice the great commandment: 'Thou
shalt love they neighbour as thyself' (Mark 12: 31). Liberal theologians may claim that Christianity is about living agapistically
and about reconciliation, but others still carry on a harsher tradition. In Mojtabai's book about religion in Amarillo, Texas, a
leading Baptist minister declares:

> The basis of our fellowship is not the love of Jesus – that's a
> *characteristic* of it – but the Word of God. The very standard
> [of fellowship] is doctrinal unity, the plenary inspiration of the
> Word of God. We can't just have love feasts.[8]

I now turn to the second kind of reaction to religious pluralism,
the view that since exclusive claims are to be rejected, all are
equally true or equally false. This is a strong form of what is
known as cultural relativism.

Cultural relativism begins by taking account of the fact that
people in different parts of the world (and people *from* different
parts of the world) have different values, different ethical systems,
and says that we gain insight into those values by taking account
of the cultural context in which they are embedded. By studying
their history, religious, economic, and social, we can understand
why Americans tend to value private enterprise and individual
initiative more than do, say, Russians or Turks. That seems
uncontroversial. But in its strong form cultural relativism goes on
to say that values can only be judged within their cultural context;
in other words, that what people in a culture value is right for
them: rightness is conformity.

Probably no one actually holds so extreme a view. Just as few
Christians nowadays are prepared to go the whole hog and defend
the Inquisition, so cultural relativists tend to stop short of saying
that people who were good at gassing Jews were fine under the
Nazis, though they would not be admissible in societies with more
usual norms. If that is an outrageous example, cases like head-
hunting or widow-burning could be offered instead. A cultural

relativist who did not want anyone to gas Jews might say that German culture under the Nazis was not a true culture in the anthropological sense, but simply an aberrant corner of some larger cultural unit, such as the culture of north-west Europe. Whether or not my imaginary cultural relativist were to seek this way out, the example does point to a difficulty in cultural relativism: the problem of boundaries. Where exactly does one culture stop and another start? From the picture which Clifford Geertz draws, one can too easily derive a picture of cultures as self-contained and immutable wholes. If a world-view and an ethos are mutually supportive, they could crash together, but seem impervious to gradual change – for where could it begin? To be fair to Geertz, he says that this is what characterizes 'the religious way of looking at the world', not whole cultures; but not all relativists have been so careful. To see cultures as sealed within their own value-systems is to ignore the way they interpenetrate in space and change over time. Ideas and values do meet and compete in people's heads, and somehow they judge between them.

The strong cultural relativist, then, claims that your values are right for you. Seen from the outside, of course, there is no ground on which to make a value judgement, so there is no 'right' in a wider sense. Or is there? The cultural relativist does usually go on to make the claim that since people differ they should be allowed to differ. In other words he preaches tolerance, but he does so not because tolerance happens to be a value of his own culture, but because he thinks it universally applicable. I agree with him – but he has sacrificed consistency.

With this I turn to some intermediate positions: I shall sketch three of them, which may be called the Hindu, the Sinhala Buddhist, and the contemporary Japanese. These terms are strictly labels of convenience; they do not fully and precisely describe the cultures to which they refer, but seem useful as approximate characterizations.

Despite that caveat, it is fair to say that what I am calling the Hindu position has indeed characterized most (though not all) of the traditional Indian non-Muslim culture. It combines our first two positions and might be summed up as 'different strokes for different folks'. It is profoundly non-Protestant and non-egalitarian. The view is that you are born what you are, and that is right for you. Your behaviour, your belief-system, even perhaps your range of feeling is prescribed for you by your station in life: your gender, your caste, even, in some instances, your stage in the life-cycle. This is a wonderful way to keep the peace in a diverse society, but at a tremendous cost to personal freedom. As

Richard Burghart has pointed out,[9] Hindus often claim that their
religion represents a model of tolerance, but it is quite unlike
what is meant by tolerance in the modern west. Everyone does
their own thing, it is true, but 'their own thing' is not what they
have chosen to do, but on the contrary what is prescribed by the
category into which society puts them. The religious programme
laid down for each person is a reflex of society's image of who he
or she is.

Although this Hindu position originated within Hindu society,
Hindus have also tried to impose it on non-Hindus. The only
Hindu kingdom, the only legally Hindu state in the world today,
is Nepal. There, even Muslim and Christian are accepted
categories, but since their image is their programme they may not
change, any more than a cow may change into a horse. Until
recently, it was actually illegal in Nepal to change one's religion.
That is no longer the case: individual conversion is accepted, but
it is still illegal to try to convert other people – in theory, even to
Hinduism.

What I am calling the Sinhala Buddhist position is that
described by Tennent in the diatribe I quoted. It is to say: 'I am
not giving up my own religion but I am prepared to take to yours
as well.'

Enough has been said to show how this position, which seems
bizarre to the Victorian monotheist, comes about. For Tennent,
as for most Westerners, a set of beliefs about supernatural beings
is a religion. Sinhalese belief in devils is therefore a religion –
incidentally, one which he equates with Satanism – while he is
not even sure whether Buddhism is a religion at all: since its ideas
do not centre on God he prefers to call it a philosophy – though
in this he is not consistent. For the Buddhist, accretion seems
normal – Buddhism proper is concerned only with things beyond
this world, and one must surely have some views about how this
world operates and may best be coped with. The Buddhist reaction to a new system is therefore to try to fit it in. Tennent writes:
'They in fact admit Christ to have been a teacher, second only to
Ruddha, but inferior, inasmuch as the latter, who was perfect in
:sdom, has attained the bliss of Nirwana.' To this he adds the
ollowing footnote:

A curious illustration of the prevalence of this disposition to
conform to two religions was related to me in Ceylon. A
Singhalese chief came a short time since to the principal of a
government seminary at Colombo, desirous to place his son
as a pupil of the institution, and agreed, without an instant's

hesitation, that the boy should conform to the discipline of the school, which requires the reading of the Scriptures and attendance at the hours of worship and prayer; accounting for his ready acquiescence by an assurance that he entertained an equal respect for the doctrines of Buddhism and Christianity. 'But how can you,' said the principal, 'with your superior education and intelligence, reconcile yourself thus to halt between two opinions, and submit to the inconsistency of professing an equal belief in two conflicting religions?' 'Do you see,' replied the subtle chief, laying his hand on the arm of the other, and directing his attention to a canoe, with a large spar as an outrigger lashed alongside, in which a fisherman was just pushing off upon the lake, 'do you see the style of these boats, in which our fishermen always put to sea, and that that spar is almost equivalent to a second canoe, which keeps the first from upsetting? It is precisely so with myself: I add on *your* religion to steady my *own, because I consider Christianity a very safe outrigger to Buddhism.*'[10]

While many will agree in finding the Sinhala Buddhist more sympathetic than Tennent, ultimately his position will not do either. Logically it will not do, because at one level the Buddhist shares Tennent's misunderstanding: he has been taught that Christianity is all about God, so he thinks that it can be slipped in under the umbrella of 'Buddhist philosophy'. But in fact Christianity, unlike the systems of belief about God he is used to, is about salvation (among other things), and is therefore a direct rival to Buddhism, giving opposed answers to the same questions. Pragmatically, moreover, the Buddhist position will not do, for it fails to satisfy either Tennent or the headmaster in his story. A dispute cannot be settled if only one party is willing to give it up. From the monotheist's point of view, the Buddhist is simply failing to take him seriously.

The essence of the Sinhala Buddhist position is to claim that two (or even more) apparently incompatible religions are in fact compatible because they are not of the same kind and so not directly competitive. A version of this position is held by some modern Protestant theologians, under the influence, I believe, of Karl Barth. For them, 'religions' are historical phenomena – Buddhism, Islam, even forms of Christianity other than their own – but their own faith is not a religion, but superordinate to religions, on a different plane. Since it is a faith in what are in fact Christian dogmas, this seems to outsiders like myself to be an exercise in self-deception.

Before I come to my conclusion, I wish to avoid a possible misunderstanding. If I have tended to cast Christianity as the whipping boy, that is because I am contributing to a discussion centred on Christianity, and in a society which is still legally and officially Christian. Though a Christian church is established in this country, it is a liberal state, wholly unlike the intolerant theocracies which have emerged in the Middle East since the Second World War. But neither Christianity nor monotheism has held a monopoly of intolerance and religious aggression. It is of course important to distinguish between the prescriptions of a religion and the behaviour of its adherents: if Christians get drunk, that cannot be laid at the door of Christianity. Similarly, if Muslims, Buddhists, or members of any other religious community are intolerant, even to the point of murder, that cannot of itself justify criticism of that religion. Nevertheless, it is in practice not always easy to distinguish the religion, an abstraction, from its empirical manifestations.

Thus, Hindu kings have been known to conduct religious persecutions, for example against Jains. Even modern Nepal is not as even-handed as it appears superficially to be, since the state defines local Buddhists as Hindus, a fact with far-reaching practical consequences. As Tennent pointed out, Buddhism shares the New Testament view that hatred should be met by love, and in the modern world Buddhism is widely associated with pacifism, a cause in which some Buddhists have displayed great heroism. Yet Buddhist monks constituted a part of the traditional Tibetan army, and it is a commonplace of Japanese history that in the medieval period monks frequently sacked each others' monasteries. It is no doubt correct to claim that these deplorable acts of aggression generally lacked any religious justification or even pretext. But one famous Japanese Buddhist, Nichiren (1222–82), violently denounced all other Buddhist sects, and some of his followers in modern times have been martyred for their intolerance. Nichiren was able to point to a Chinese Buddhist text which says that to defend the Dharma (that is, Buddhism) one can and should stock arms and resort to violence.[11]

So I come finally to the contemporary Japanese position. The Hindu position, we have seen, copes with the socio-political problem raised by pluralism, but at a high cost to the liberty of the subject. The Sinhala Buddhist position allows for personal freedom and hopes for a pragmatic solution, but fails because it misunderstands the problem; as a result, the Sinhala Buddhists who actually held that position, when brought face to face with reality, have tended to abandon it and become more or less intolerant. It seems to me that the present Japanese position has the advantages of the other two while avoiding their defects.

The Hindu legal principle that people should keep to their own religions must be kept distinct from the theological principle that underlies it: that God, the ultimate, or whatever one calls it, is beyond the grasp of human thought and that all figurations and concepts under which it is worshipped are necessarily partial. (Not all Hindus believe this, but some do.) To that extent all symbols of the divine are worthy of respect – though that is not to say that all are equally attractive. This willingness to respect the religions of others carried over into many forms of Buddhism as it moved eastwards, and has tended to dominate Japanese religious history, despite the important exceptions just cited. Not only have Shintoism, Confucianism, and Buddhism coexisted, but within Buddhism the most astonishing variety of sects has survived for many centuries. The state has been hard on any religious leader or group who opposed its political interest, but strictly as a matter of politics, not in the interests of religious orthodoxy. The government has persecuted religious groups which it regarded as acquiring too much temporal power or which made absolutist claims which compromised the political loyalties of their followers. Of the latter, Nichiren was an example; but the most important instance of such governmental intolerance was its suppression of Christianity. At first, the Portuguese were allowed to make converts to Roman Catholicism; but after half a century, at the end of the sixteenth century, this policy was reversed. This was not only because the loyalties of Roman Catholics were divided, at least potentially, between Japan and Rome. The further problem, new to Japanese experience, was that the converts began to convert others by force and even to kill those who refused conversion. This led the Japanese government to proscribe Christianity and to seal the country off from foreigners for more than two hundred years.

I am not, of course, defending xenophobia, and I know that the anti-Christian policy was enforced with considerable cruelty; nor do I defend state absolutism. But in their treatment of Christians the Tokugawa government had correctly perceived what has been called the paradox of tolerance – though it is not really a paradox: one cannot tolerate the intolerant. Just as everyone must be free in general, but not free to deprive others of freedom, our demand for tolerance entails the further demand that intolerance be banned. It may even have to be banned pre-emptively, because if you wait for the intolerant to become powerful before you ban them, it may be too late.

What this means in practice will vary from country to country.

In contemporary Nepal there is a legal ban on missionary activity. (This is also true of many other countries, but usually with an exemption in favour of the state religion.) In contemporary Japan, no such ban is necessary. The Japanese constitution guarantees full religious freedom, and there are Japanese Christians, both Catholic and Protestant. Individual Buddhists, like the Sinhala Buddhists of Tennent's day, often go to worship in Christian churches. But unlike in Sri Lanka, the Christians in Japan do not object to this. They are restrained not merely by their minority position and the Tokugawa experience, but by the whole tenor of Japanese society today. There are now very many Japanese who consider themselves adherents of no religion. On a recent visit, I asked several Japanese Buddhist priests whether the traditional Buddhist sects were not making any propaganda effort. No, I was told, by and large they were not; and my question seemed slightly to amuse my Buddhist friends. On further questioning, I found out that recently laymen have indeed initiated a few organized attempts to spread Buddhism, mainly by the dissemination of literature. My clerical friends seemed to view these efforts with indifference or even a mild distaste. Such attempts to influence others are considered rather uncivilized, since they may disturb social harmony. The Buddha's injunction to monks not to preach unless asked three times to do so is still respected.

I hope and trust that the Japanese solution will work in our own civilized society. If it does not, we must not be passive, but remember that, as eternal vigilance is the price of liberty, intolerance is a danger that cannot be overlooked or tolerated.

Notes

1 Sir James Emerson Tennent, *Ceylon*, London (1859), 535–46.
2 T. W. Rhys Davids, *Buddhism*, London (1877), 3.
3 *ibid.*, 4.
4 *ibid.*, 7.
5 Keith Thomas, *Religion and the Decline of Magic*, London: Weidenfeld & Nicolson (1971), 76.
6 *ibid.*, 165.
7 Clifford Geertz, *Islam Observed*, Chicago and London: University of Chicago Press (1971), 97.
8 A. G. Mojtabai, *Blessed Assurance: At home with the Bomb in Amarillo, Texas*, Boston: Houghton Mifflin (1986), 121.
9 In a talk to Dr Bryan Wilson's seminar, All Souls' College, Oxford, 1985.
10 Tennent, *Ceylon*, 530.
11 I am grateful to Dr Paul Williams for this information.

Select bibliography

Adorno, T. W. (1973) *Negative Dialectics*, trans. E. B. Ashton, London: Routledge & Kegan Paul.

Allott, A. N. (1980) *The Limits of Law*, London: Butterworth.

Arbib, M. A. and Hesse, M. B. (1987) *The Construction of Reality*, Cambridge: Cambridge University Press.

Archer, A. (1986) *The Two Catholic Churches: A Study in Oppression*, London: SCM Press.

Asvaghosa (attributed) (1967) *The Awakening of Faith*, trans. Y. S. Hakeda, New York: Columbia University Press.

Bakvis, H. (1981) *Catholic Power in the Netherlands*, Kingston/Montreal: McGill-Queen's University Press.

Barker, E. (1982) *New Religious Movements: A Perspective for Understanding Society*, New York: Edwin Mellen.

—(1983) *New Religious Movements and Political Orders*, Canterbury: Centre for Study of Religion and Society, University of Kent.

—(1986) *The Making of a Moonie*, Oxford: Blackwell.

—(1989) *New Religious Movements: A Practical Introduction*, London: HMSO.

Barnes, M. (1989) *Religions in Conversation: Christian Identity and Religious Pluralism*, London: SPCK.

Beckford, J. (1985) *Cult Controversies*, London: Tavistock.

Benjamin, W. (1977) *The Origins of German Tragic Drama*, trans. John Osborne, London: Verso, 1977.

Berger, I. (1981) *Religion and Resistance: East African kingdoms*, Tervuren: Musée Royale de l'Afrique Centrale.

Berger, P. L. (1969) *The Social Reality of Religion*, London: Faber and Faber. (First published in U.S. in 1967 under the title *The Sacred Canopy*. New York: Doubleday).

—(1970) *A Rumour of Angels*, London: Allen Lane, The Penguin Press.

—(1980) *The Heretical Imperative*, London: Collins.

Chupungco, A. J. (1982) *Cultural Adaptation of the Liturgy*, New York: Paulist Press.

Coleman, J. A. (1978) *The Evolution of Dutch Catholicism 1958–1974*, Berkeley/Los Angeles: California University Press.

Coward, H. (1985) *Pluralism: Challenge to World Religions*, New York: Orbis.

Crollius, A. A. R. (ed.) (1987) *Cultural Change and Liberation in a Christian Perspective*, Rome: Pontifical Gregorian University.

Davis, W. (1980) *Dojo: Magic and Exorcism in Modern Japan*, Stanford: Stanford University Press.

D'Costa, G. (1986) *Theology and Religious Pluralism*, Oxford/New York: Basil Blackwell.

—(1987) *John Hick's Theology of Religions: A Critical Evaluation*, London/New York: University Press of America.

de Ste. Croix, G. E. M. (1963–4) 'Why were the early Christians persecuted?' *Past and Present*, vol. 26, 6–38 and vol. 27, 28–33.

Durkheim, E. (1915) *The Elementary Forms of the Religious Life*, tr. J. W. Swain, London: George Allen and Unwin.

Eisenach, J. E. (1981) *Two Worlds of Liberalism*, Chicago: Chicago University Press.

Eliade, M. (ed.) (1987) *Encyclopedia of Religion*, New York: Macmillan (16 vols).

Flanagan, K. (1986a) 'To be a Sociologist and a Catholic: a reflection', *New Blackfriars*, vol. 67, 256–70.

—(1986b) 'Ritual form: liturgy's sociological dimension', *Modern Theology*, vol. 2, 341–61.

—(1988) 'Liturgy as play: a hermeneutic of ritual representation', *Modern Theology*, vol. 4, 345–72.

Fogarty, M. P. (1957) *Christian Democracy in Western Europe 1820–1953*, London: Routledge & Kegan Paul.

Frend, W. H. C. (1965) *Martyrdom and Persecution in the Early Church*, Oxford: Blackwell.

Frye, N. (1982) *The Great Code: the Bible and Literature*, London: Routledge & Kegan Paul.

Garnsey, P. (1984) 'Religious toleration in classical antiquity', in: W. J. Sheils (ed.), *Persecution and Toleration* (Studies in Church History 21) (Ecclesiastical History Society), Oxford: Blackwell.

Geertz, C. (1971) *Islam Observed*, Chicago: University of Chicago Press.

Gibb, H. A. R. (1947) *Modern Trends in Islam*, Chicago: University of Chicago Press.

Gombrich, R. (1988) *Theravada Buddhism: a Social History from Ancient Benares to Modern Colombo*, London: Routledge.

Guardini, R. (1930) *Sacred Signs*, London: Sheed and Ward.

Habermas, J. (1972) *Knowledge and Human Interest*, tr. J. J. Shapiro, London: Heinemann.

Hacker, P. (1980) *Theological Foundations of Evangelization*, St. Augustin: Franz Steiner Verlag.

Hamnett, I. (1973) 'Sociology of religion and sociology of error', *Religion*, vol. 3, 1–12.

—(1986) 'A mistake about error', *New Blackfriars*, vol. 67, 69–78.

Hesse, M. B. (1980) *Revolutions and Reconstructions in the Philosophy of Science*, Brighton: Harvester Press.
—(1988) 'The cognitive claims of metaphor', *Journal of Speculative Philosophy*, vol. 2, 1–16.
Hick, J. (ed.) (1977) *The Myth of God Incarnate*, London: SCM Press.
—(1980) *God Has Many Names*, London: Macmillan.
Hiebert, P. (1987) 'Folk religion in Andhra Pradesh', in: Samuel, V. and Sugden C. (eds), *Evangelism and the Poor*, Oxford: Regnum.
Hinnells, J. R. (ed.) (1984) *The Penguin Dictionary of Religions*, Harmondsworth: Penguin Books.
Hooker, M. B. (1975) *Legal Pluralism*, London: Oxford University Press.
Kapferer, B. *A Celebration of Demons*, Bloomington: Indiana University Press.
Katz, W. G. and Sutherland, H. P. (1967) 'Pluralism in the Supreme Court', *Daedalus*, Winter.
Kedourie, E. (1980) *Islam in the Modern World*, London: Mansell.
Knitter, P. (1985) *No Other Name?*, London: SCM.
Kossman, E. H. (1978) *The Low Countries 1780–1940*, Oxford: The Clarendon Press.
Lane Fox, R. (1986) *Pagans and Christians*, London: Viking.
Lewis, B. (1986) *Muslim Discovery of Europe*, London: Wiedenfeld and Nicolson.
Lewis, I. M. (1989) *Ecstatic Religion* (revised edn), London: Routledge.
Lijphart, A. (1975) *The Politics of Accommodation* (2nd edn), Berkeley/Los Angeles: California University Press.
Meiland, J. and M. Krausz (eds), (1982) *Relativism*, University of Notre Dame Press.
Melton, J. G. (1986) *Encylopedic Handbook of Cults in America*, New York/London: Garland.
Mojtabai, A. G. (1986) *Blessed Assurance: At Home with the Bomb in Amarillo, Texas*, Albuquerque: University of New Mexico Press.
Nazir-Ali, M. (1987) *Frontiers in Muslim-Christian Encounter*, Oxford: Regnum.
—(1989) *Martyrs and Magistrates: Toleration and Trial*, Nottingham: Grove Books.
Neuner, J. (ed.) (1973) *God's Word among Men*, Delhi: Vidya Jyoti.
Novak, M. (1982) 'Pluralism in humanistic perspective', in: *Concepts of Ethnicity*, Harvard University Press.
Piscatori, J. (1986) *Islam in a World of Nation-states*, Cambridge: Cambridge University Press.
Poulter, S. (1986) *English Law and Ethnic Minority Customs*, London: Butterworth.
Rahner, K. (1963) 'Membership of the church according to the teaching of Pius XII's encyclical "Mystici Corporis Christi" ', *Theological Investigations*, vol. 2, London: Darton, Longman and Todd.
Rhys Davids, T. W. (1877) *Buddhism*, London.

Richards, G. (1989) *Towards a Theology of Religions*, London: Routledge.

Roebroek, E. J. M. G. (1979) 'A problem for sociology: contemporary developments in the Roman Catholic church', in P. H. Vrijhof and J. Waardenburg (eds), *Official and Popular Religion*, The Hague: Mouton.

Rouner, L. S. (ed.) (1984) *Religious Pluralism* (Boston University Series no. 5), University of Notre Dame Press.

Said, E. (1985) *Orientalism*, Harmondsworth: Penguin.

Saldanha, C. (1984) *Divine Pedagogy: A Patristic View of Non-Christian Religions*, Rome: LAS.

Samuel, V. and Sugden, C. (1983) *The Gospel among our Hindu Neighbours*, Bangalore: Partnership in Mission.

—(1984) 'Dialogue with other religions – an evangelical view', in: *Sharing Jesus in the Two Thirds World*, Grand Rapids: Eerdmans.

Schreiter, R. J. (1985) *Constructing Local Theologies*, London: SCM Press.

Simon, M. (1986) *Verus Israel: A Study of the Relations Between Christians and Jews in the Roman Empire 135–425 AD*, trans. H. McKeating, London: Oxford University Press.

Skultans, V. (1987) 'The management of mental illness among Maharashtrian families', *Man*, 22, pp. 661–79.

Smith, W. Cantwell (1978) *The Meaning and End of Religion: a Revolutionary Approach to the Great Religious Traditions*, London: SPCK.

—(1981) *Towards a World Theology: Faith and the Comparative History of Religion*, London: Macmillan, 1981.

Sordi, M. (1986) *The Christians and the Roman Empire*, Beckenham: Croom Helm.

Spiro, M. (1978) *Burmese Supernaturalism* (revised edn), New York: Prentice Hall.

Sugden, C. (1985) *Christ's Exclusive Claims and Inter-faith Dialogue*, Nottingham: Grove Books.

Tennent, Sir James Emerson (1859) *Ceylon*, London.

Thomas, Keith (1971) *Religion and the Decline of Magic*, London: Weidenfeld and Nicholson.

Von Balthasar, Hans Urs (1985) *A Short Primer for Unsettled Laymen*, San Francisco: Ignatius Press.

Wallis, R. (1984) *Elementary Forms of the New Religious Life*, London: Routledge & Kegan Paul.

Ward, Keith (1987) *Images of Eternity*, London: Darton, Longman and Todd.

Whaung, F. (ed.) (1984) *The World's Religious Traditions: Essays in Honour of Wilfred Cantwell Smith*, Edinburgh: T. & T. Clark.

Whyte, J. H. (1981) *Catholics in Western Democracies*, Dublin: Gill and Macmillan, 1981.

Wiedemann, T. (1981) *Greek and Roman Slavery*, London: Croom Helm.

—(1989) *Adults and Children in the Roman Empire*, London: Routledge.

Wilken, R. L. (1984) *The Christians as the Romans Saw them*, New Haven: Yale University Press.

Williams, P. (1989) *Mahayana Buddhism: The Doctrinal Foundations*, London: Routledge.

Worsley, P. (1984) *The Three Worlds: Culture and Development*, London: Weidenfeld and Nicholson.

Index

Abeyasingha, N., 144
Abraham, 66, 68, 71, 77, 150, 156
academic religion *see* religious studies
accommodation and exorcism, 44–9
accreditation and discounting, 61–2
Adam, 149, 156, 237
Adorno, T. W., 120, 124–5
Advaitan, 16
affliction, cults of *see* gender and religious pluralism
Africa: Christianity, 70, 74, 154–7, 161; independent churches, 32; Islam, 47–8; law, 205, 221, 222–4; new religions, 40; theological pluralism, 95, 102; traditional religions, 155–6
'aggiornamento', 53
agnosticism, 17, 25; and theological pluralism, 90, 100
AIDS, 33
Albigensians, 146
Alexander VIII, Pope, 144
Alexander Severus, emperor, 66–7, 77
Ali, Bishop M. N., 150, 164
Allot, A., vii; on law, 4–5, 10, 11, 205–25
Almond, P., 127
alternative religions *see* gender and religous pluralism
Alternative Service Book, 105
Amalricians, 146
Ambrose, 67, 77, 135
Ambrosiaster, 146
Amon-Ra, 69
analogy, principle of, 20
Ananda Marga, 32, 33
Anatolia, 72

Anderson, Sir N., 160–1
Anglicanism *see* Church of England
Anthony, D., 40
anthropology, 98; *see also* ethnographic
anthropomorphism, 92
anti-discrimination laws, 216, 217–19, 220
Apollo, 71, 72
Apollonius of Tyana, 66, 67
Aquinas, Thomas, 17, 135, 146, 167, 177
Arbib, M. A., 178
Arblaster, A., 196
Archer, A., 104–5
aristocracy in Roman Empire, 65–6, 68, 70–1
Aristotle, 8, 167, 168, 172–3, 177
Arles, Council of (314 AD), 135
Armenians, 139
Artemidorus, 77
asceticism, 18, 75
Asia, 118, 220, 228–9; Christianity, 151, 154, 158–61, 164; Islam, 44–6; law, 205, 221; Orientalism, 118–19, 122; theological pluralism, 95, 99, 102; *see also* Buddhism; India; Islam; Japan; Sikkhism; Sri Lanka
atonement, 122, 142, 160; absence of, 22
Augustine, St, 67, 72, 77, 132–3, 135–8, 141, 145–6
Augustus, emperor, 65, 69–70
Australia: law, 221; new religions, 40
authority of law, 221–2
Avatar, divine, 234–5
awe and wonder, 37, 93

Index

Hestia, 70
Heusch, L. de, 46
Hick, J., 10–11, 27, 226; on 'Copernican theology', 16, 22–3, 114–29 *passim*, 230–4, 237; criticism of *extra ecclesiam* axiom 131, 133, 136–41 *passim*; God defined by, 15; on incarnation, 81–2, 234–7
Hinduism, 229, 234, 251–3, 256, 259; and *extra ecclesiam* axiom, 132; karma, 17; law, 211, 213, 219, 221–3, 259; lower castes and Christianity, 158–9; ridiculed, 154; *see also* Vedanta
history, 153; historical method, 20–1, 23, 26, 27; historical perspectives *see* ethnographic and historical perspectives; historicism, 123–4, 194
Hobbes, T., 181, 183, 197
Holden, P., 43
Hollis, M., 201
holy, openness to, 81, 86
'homeless mind', 91
honour, 70
Hopkins, G. M., 90
Houghton, G., 154
House Church movement, 33
Hubner, J., 42
'Human Potential Movement', 32, 34
humanism, 22, 37
Hungary, 187

'Ideal Types', 37
ideology, religious, 6–7, 8, 10; co-existence and imperialism in, 4–5, 8, 10, 13–28; and theological pluralism, 82–5, 87, 89, 95
illness, curing *see* gender and religious pluralism
immigrants, 31, 35, 229–30; and law, 215–19
imperialism, political, 118, 150, 227–8
imperialism, religious: and co-existence in religious ideology, 4–5, 8, 10, 13–28; reconciliation without, 157–61
impersonal God, 15, 16–17
'implicit faith', doctrine of, 132, 140–1

Incarnation, 22, 84, 108
incommensurability of meaning, 85
inculturation 96, 99–109 *passim*: *see also* culture; society
India, 18, 220, 227, 228, 243; Buddhism, 243, 248; Christianity, 154, 158–61, 164; Islam, 251, 256; law, 205, 221; new religions, 31, 32; theological pluralism, 99; *see also* Buddhism, Hinduism; Vedanta
indigenization of ritual *see* inculturation
individualism, 180–1, 186, 193; *see also* liberalism; personal
Indonesia, 228; Christianity, 151, 161, 164
infant baptism and circumcision, 8
infusion of law and religion, 208, 209
initiation, 44
institutional aspects of religious pluralism *see* law; theology and religious studies
Intelligence, God as, 15
'intelligibility', 117
internal and external aspects of law, 210–11
internal pluralism, 36–8, 93–4; of Catholicism in Netherlands, 55–6, 57
International Society for Krishna Consciousness, 32, 33, 34, 38
Ireland, 6, 246; potato harvest as Lugnaisa festival, 69; theological pluralism, 82
Irenaeus, 117, 134, 135, 146
ISKCON *see* International Society for Krishna Consciousness
Islam, 4, 14, 18, 75, 188, 194, 229, 233, 258; adorcism and, 47–8; Africa, 47–8; circumcision, 8; and Crusades, 140; exorcism, 44–6; fundamentalist sects, 42, 91; India, 251, 256; law, 207–13 *passim*, 216–17, 220–4; in Middle Ages, 6; restructured, 183; ritual slaughter, 190, 216–17; theology and religious studies, 231; and Zar-cult, 49
Israel, 190–1
Isvara, 16

Jacob Baradaeus, Bishop, 139

Index

Pittsburgh Platform, 186, 199–200
Pius IX, Pope, 132, 145
Pius V, Pope, 144
Plato/Platonists, 124; Neoplatonists, 75, 78
plausibility-structures, 92–3
Plotinus, 75
pluralism *see* religious pluralism
Plutarch, 77
policy implications of law, 219–22
politics, 87; and Catholicism in Netherlands, 54, 55, 57; definition, 180–1; political pluralism, 179, 196; in Roman Empire, 65, 70, 73; *see also* state
polygamy, 96, 210, 214, 215
polytheism: in Roman Empire, 5, 6, 10, 64–78; *see also* Hinduism; paganism
Porphyry, 75
Portuguese, 221, 244, 260
possession *see* gender and religious pluralism
principle, God as, 37
Private International Law, 214
private sphere *see* public and private spheres
Procrustes, 122
Protestantism, 197, 199, 246–7, 253–5; and Hinduism, 251; and new religions, 31; rise of, 180; in United States, 247, 255; *see also* Calvinism; Church of England; Evangelicals; Reformation
'Ptolemaic theologies', 121–2, 131–3, 138, 140
public and private spheres, 180–2; and Judaism, 184–91 *passim*, 194, 197

Quakers, 61
Quine, W., 168
Quran, 194

Race, A., 101
race: barriers of 150, 151, 152, 154; discrimination and law, 217–19
Rajneeshee sannyasins, 32–3
Rajneeshpuram, 38, 42
Rajshekar, V. T., 159
Rastafarianism, 32, 34; and law, 218–19
rationality/rationalism, 14, 26, 76, 77, 115, 186, 193–4, 199; limits of,

107; and theological pluralism, 83, 107–8
Ratzinger, J. C., 95, 102, 107, 109
Rawls, J., 198–9
realism *see* naturalism
reality-centredness, 121
'reason' and 'reasonable man', 194, 212–13
rebirth *see* 'born again'
Rebirthing, 32
reconciliation and Evangelicals: in Christ without religious imperialism, 157–61; gospel of, 149–52, 153–4
reductionism, 86, 188
Reformation, 61, 209, 228, 246, 250; *see also* Protestantism
rejection: of Gospel by non-Christians, 135–6, 139–40; of non-Christians *see* extra ecclesiam
relativism, 8–9, 91, 195, 201
religion: definitions of 18; *see also* major religions
'religious freedom' and Judaism, 5, 8, 9, 11, 179–201
religious pluralism, 3–12; *see also* ethnographic and historical perspectives; imperialism; institutional aspects; theoretical perspectives
religious studies, 3–4, 23, 59, 200; identification of scholars with pagan writers, 67–8; and theology, 4, 5, 27, 226–40; *see also* theological pluralism
'repugnancy clause' and law, 222–3
Restorationist movement, 33
Resurrection, 82, 153
Rhys Davids, T. W., 247–9, 252
rigour, theological, 134–5
Rissho Kosei Kai, 32
rite/ritual, 86, 97–109; slaughter, 190, 216–17, 220
Riviere, J., 146
Robbins, T., 40
Robinson, J., Bishop of Woolwich, 37, 42
Rochford, B., 41
Roman Catholics *see* Catholicism
Roman Empire, 197, 234; religious co-existence in, 5, 6, 10, 64–78
Roof, W. Clark, 41
Rorty, R., 194

Index

184–96 *passim*, 198, 200; *see also* politics
status in society, 151–2
Ste. Croix, G. E. M. de, 78
Stephen, Pope, 135
Stoics, 66, 76
studies, religious *see* religious studies
Stuttgart Consultation on Evangelism, 161–3
Suarez, 147
Sudan, 207
Sugden, C., viii, 164; on Evangelicals, 5, 8, 9, 11, 27, 148–65
Sunday trading, 189–90
suppression of law and religion, 208, 209
Surin, K., viii; on 'materialist critique', 4–5, 7–8, 9, 10, 27, 114–29
symbolism *see under* science
Syme, R., 76, 78
Symmachus, Quintis Aurelius, 64–8 *passim*, 71–2, 76, 77
syncretism, pagan, 68–72
Syrians, 139

Tanzania, 224
Taoism, 248
technology *see* science
teleological explanations of change in Netherlands Catholicism, 60
Temple, F., Archbishop of Canterbury, 228
Tennent, Sir J. E., 243–7, 249, 250, 252, 257–9
Tertullian, 74, 77, 78, 117
Thatcher, M., 108
theocracies, 258
Theodosius, emperor, 76; Theodosian Code, 78
theology: pluralism, sociological critique of, 4–5, 7–8, 10, 81–113; and religious studies, 4, 5, 27, 226–40; *see also* 'materialist critique'
theoretical perspectives *see* evangelicals: *extra ecclesiam*; Judaism; 'materialist' critique; science; theological pluralism
theory, scientific, 168–72
Theosophy, 31, 251–2

Theravadin calm, 19
Thérèse of Lisieux, 94
Third World: and Christianity, 118–20; theological pluralism in, 95–7, 99, 101–2; *see also* Africa; Asia; Latin America
Thomas, M. M., 159
Thomism, 16
Thorpe, F. N., 198
Thurlings, J. M. G., 57, 63
Tibet, 32, 259
Tierney, B., 146
tolerance, 67, 260; demand for, 83; of law and religion, 208, 209; *see also* indologist
Torah, 19, 191
totalitarianism in new religions, 58–9
Towler, R., 37, 42
Tracy, D., 114
'traditionalism' in Church of England, 37
transcendence, 84, 92–3, 108
Transcendental Meditation, 40
Tridentine rite, 98–9
Troeltsch, E., 20–1, 116
truth/truth-claims, 13–15, 24–5, 82, 124, 125, 128, 194–5; of new religions, 36; and science, 167, 173–4, 175–6, 177
Tucker, R. C., 197
Turkey, 191
Turner, B. S., 119
Turner, H. W., 156
Turner, V., 98

Uganda: law, 224
Unam Sanctam (Bull), 138
Unification Church, 32, 33
United Kingdom, 227–8; Anglicanism *see* Church of England; Catholicism, 104, 189, 191, 247; Christianity, 54 (*see also* Catholicism *above*); immigrants, 229; Judaism, 9, 186, 188; law, 205, 208–9, 211, 212–22, 224–5; law in Africa, 222–3; new religions in, 31; political pluralism, 196; Protestantism in, 151; theological pluralism in, 88, 98, 104–5, 107–8; Theology and Religious Studies, 232–3
United Nations, 228
United States: Catholicism, 103;

278